NEW FOUNDATIONS

IRELAND 1660–1800

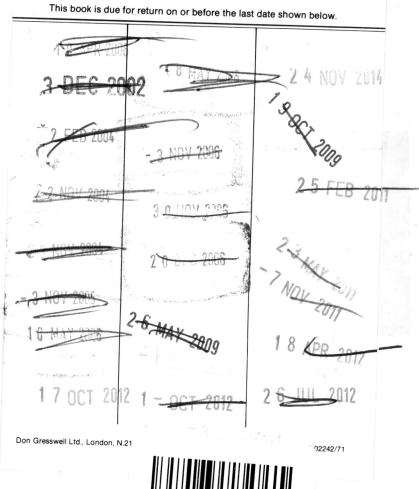

NEW FOUNDATIONS
IRELAND 1660–1800

DAVID DICKSON

Second revised and enlarged edition

IRISH ACADEMIC PRESS
DUBLIN • PORTLAND, OR

First edition published in 1987 by
Helicon Books, Dublin, Ireland

Second edition, revised and enlarged

First published in 2000 by
IRISH ACADEMIC PRESS
44, Northumberland Road,
Dublin 4, Ireland

and in the United States of America by
IRISH ACADEMIC PRESS
c/o ISBS, 5804 NE Hassalo Street,
Portland, OR 97213-3644

Website: www.iap.ie

British Library Cataloguing in Publication Data

Dickson, David
New Foundations : Ireland 1660–1800. – 2nd ed.
1. Ireland – History – 17th century 2. Ireland – History – 18th century
I. Title
941.5'07

ISBN 0-7165-2632-8 (hardback)
ISBN 0-7165-2637-9 (paperback)

Library of Congress Cataloging-in-Publication Data

Dickson, David
New Foundations : Ireland, 1660–1800 / by David Dickson.
p. cm.
Originally published: Dublin : Helicon, 1987.
Includes bibliographical references (p.) and index.
ISBN 0-7165-2632-8 (hc.). – ISBN 0-7165-2637-9 (pbk.)
1. Ireland–History–1660–1690. 2. Ireland–History–18th century. I. Title.
DA940.D54 1999
941.507–dc21 99-36787
CIP

Typeset by Vitaset, Paddock Wood, Kent
Printed by
Creative Print and Design (Wales) Ltd, Ebbw Vale

For Katie and Robert

Contents

List of Illustrations

List of Maps

Preface to the Second edition

THE FIRST edition of this book appeared as part of the nine-volume Helicon History of Ireland, and was written to complement Patrick Corish's *The Catholic community in the seventeenth and eighteenth centuries*. It was deliberately constructed as a study of the victors of 1660 and their political world.

In the dozen years since the first appearance of this work the output of articles, monographs, collections of essays and works of reference on Ireland 1660–1800 has been remarkable, both in quantity and in the unevenness of its coverage. New work has tended to be clustered around two periods of crisis, Jacobite Ireland and its aftermath, and the hydra-headed 1790s, a historiographical tendency not unconnected with the business of commemoration. Restoration Ireland has remained strangely neglected, and the study of the first half of the eighteenth century is still overly influenced by the magnetic field of Swiftian studies.

In the last decade or so, there have been a small number of highly important works of scholarship which have illuminated dark corners and in several cases colonised entirely new areas of study (for example, crime and the legal system, duelling, popular religion, family and gender, the book trade, political patronage, and the Irish house of lords), but their wider impact has yet to be felt. Several major political biographies have also opened up the subject (notably on Ormond, Burke, Flood, Fitzgibbon, Gandon and Tone), and there have been a handful of synoptic monographs of great interpretative sweep that have immediately attracted critical notice: Connolly on Ireland as a confessional *ancien regime*; Bartlett on the politics of the Catholic question; O Buachalla on popular and literary Jacobitism; Leerssen on cultural identities; Smyth on popular politicisation in the late eighteenth century; and Curtin on the United Irishmen. Religious history in all its many facets from the evangelical awakening to the decline of the Catholic religious orders has rapidly developed to become a central concern of new scholarship, but much of this work is so far only available in composite volumes of essays and articles. Some of the most exciting new research on the period has been regional or local (notably by Hill on Dublin politics, Agnew on Belfast merchants, and Power on the Tipperary land ownership), while Barnard's many probes into the social history of the gentry, regionally and nationally, are cumulatively a remarkable *tour de force*.

To have done justice to this renaissance of interest in the period would have required a major reconstruction of the present text. Such has not been attempted. This work remains an essentially chronological study of the history of public affairs, a narrative introduction to the period and to the interpretative problems that vex those who are seeking to understand it. Its emphasis on the material and economic foundations of political life may reflect a little on the time it was written, but this perhaps unfashionable perspective may be a useful corrective to some current historiographical tendencies.

Errors of fact and judgment have I hope been corrected from the first edition, but in most respects the integrity of the original text remains. I have however incorporated some recent findings, particularly those of a quantitative nature, where this has been possible. My thanks to Linda Longmore and the editorial team in the Irish Academic Press for encouraging me to bring this work back into circulation, and for helping me to refine it.

I am grateful to the Trustees of the National Gallery of Ireland for permission to reproduce the drawing on p. xvi, the painting on p. 142, and the engraving on p. 220; and to the British Museum Dept. of Prints and Drawings for permission to reproduce the engraving on p. 108.

David Dickson
August 1999

Preface to the First edition

THE STUDY of the history of Ireland between the collapse of the Cromwellian regime and the Anglo-Irish parliamentary union has evolved in the shadow of the great surveys of the period by Froude, Lecky and Bagwell, all now more than three-quarters of a century old. Fresh works of synthesis to displace these classics have not appeared until recently, and indeed have not totally replaced them. Meanwhile various networks of specialists have laboured long in their respective fields of interest – Anglo-Irish literature, architecture, the economy, fine art, Gaelic literature, parliament, philosophy, printing, religious organisation – but too often there has been a total failure to examine the wider context of the subject. Even within these fields the distribution of intellectual effort has been very uneven, and there are fundamental elements of Irish society and its workings during this period which remain almost totally unexplored. New methodologies have so far made little impact; computerised databases are almost unknown. Techniques associated with demography, social anthropology and semiotics are only beginning to be used.

Some of the most impressive research on the period still languishes in unpublished dissertations, since many aspects of the later seventeenth and eighteenth centuries have been deemed to be unfashionable in the literary market-place. 'Swiftiana' and 'Georgiana' have never suffered this problem, but there has been a remarkable dearth of published monographs on either high politics or rural life in the century after 1660. This historiographical weakness has led to an unbalanced presentation of Irish history by generations of teachers: the period between the 1650s and 1790s has been perceived as a slow-moving cycle during which 'Catholic Ireland' was ground down and then began, haltingly, to recover strength. Political developments not directly related to this process have often been presented in general surveys as irrelevant, when the criterion of relevance has been the influence of a particular process on the formation of Irish nationalism or on modern Irish society. Even among the confraternity of Irish historians, there used to be an unspoken assumption that as the eighteenth century was an era of Protestant domination, only scholars with a Protestant background would find it an intellectually stimulating age to investigate. However, the late Maureen Wall, perhaps more than anyone, helped to end that. It is now no longer possible to see 'the long eighteenth century' as a Cinderella period in Irish history, and the very successful launch in 1986 of the Eighteenth-Century Ireland Society, complete with its own journal, reflects the mushrooming of interest in the period and the sense that fundamental reinterpretations are under way.

My concern here has been to bring together much of the recent work, published and unpublished, within an essentially chronological framework – the time for a reflective, synoptic work is not yet. But there is a unifying issue running through the narrative – how far did the new foundations, laid in the 1650s, the new structures of power, determine the political evolution of the following one and a half centuries, culminating in the crisis of the 1790s, and how far was the seventeenth-century redistribution of control over wealth responsible for the eighteenth-century economic and social transformation of the country?

I am grateful for permission to quote from manuscripts held by the following archives and libraries: American Philosophical Society (Philadelphia), Bodleian Library (Oxford), British Library (London), Friends' Historical Library (Swarthmore, PA), Gilbert Library (Dublin City Libraries), National Library of Ireland, Public Record Office (London), Public Record Office of Northern Ireland (Belfast), University of London, Trinity College Dublin; and to Anthony Farmar and James Villiers-Stuart.

I am also very grateful to the archivists, librarians and fellow historians who have helped, knowingly and unknowingly, in the preparation of this book, and my thanks particularly to the staffs of the National Library of Ireland, the Public Record Office of Northern Ireland, the Royal Irish Academy and, not least, Trinity College Library. I carry a profound debt to my colleagues and former teachers, Louis Cullen and R. B. McDowell, who first stirred my enthusiasm for the period, and who have continued to stimulate me ever since, and I am deeply indebted to my fellow-researchers without whose intellectual generosity this book could not have been written – Anthony Malcomson, Tom Bartlett, Sean Connolly, Bill Crawford, Jim Donnelly, James McGuire and Bill McCormack. My thanks also to Pam Isaacson, Margaret Allister and Muriel Sadlier for their painstaking typing, and to the editors and publishers for their tolerance, good temper and sound advice in the face of a difficult author. Finally, I am aware how much my long-suffering family has had to put up with my absences – of body and of mind: my thanks above all to them.

Trinity College
Dublin

David Dickson

Kilkenny Castle, ancestral home of James Butler, first duke of Ormond and lord lieutenant of Ireland 1644–49, 1662–69 and 1677–85. It was, appropriately, the greatest house of Restoration Ireland. Elizabeth, first duchess of Ormond, was apparently the driving force behind its conversion into a great baroque palace.
(detail from Francis Place, View of Kilkenny, *c.* 1699: N.G.I.)

1

Restoration and Uncertainty, 1660–88

WHOSE RESTORATION?

THE WESTERN periphery of Europe was no exception to the general pattern of the seventeenth century; for most European societies it was a 'time of troubles', an era of religious repression, civil war, and diplomatic breakdown. Ireland was, however, unusual in experiencing the displacement of a whole property-owning class (Bohemia offering the nearest analogy), and was unique in seventeenth-century Europe in witnessing an immigration of many tens of thousands of settlers. This great migration from the neighbouring island began in the late sixteenth century and had almost spent itself by 1700. All inherited social institutions and conventions from the family unit to formal religious practice, all economic structures, were affected, some profoundly so, by this new cycle of anglicisation. The process was reversed in the 1640s when the Catholic 'Old English' gentry and the Gaelic lineage families formed an unstable military alliance and tried to take local advantage of the collapse of royal authority in England. Their challenge ended in comprehensive defeat by Oliver Cromwell in 1650–51. However for the next half a century a question-mark remained against that victory because of the uncertainties of British dynastic politics.

In contrast to the political and economic transformations, there was a continuity of legal form and constitutional practice in seventeenth-century Ireland, inherited from the medieval Hiberno-English colony. Except for the twelve years when there was no semblance of royal authority in the country (1649–60), the ancient institutions of crown government functioned: the *lord lieutenant* (or in his absence from the country, the *lords justices*) commanded the Irish army and headed the civilian government; he was advised by the Irish privy council, composed of local notables. A panel of eleven judges oversaw the three common law courts and the court of chancery. Local administration of justice was handled by the judges on their twice-yearly assize circuits, assisted in each county by the panel of gentlemen who made up the grand jury; local law enforcement was vested in justices of the peace (i.e. magistrates) appointed by the government. For most of the seventeenth century the old palatinate jurisdiction held by the Ormond family in Kilkenny and Tipperary, and the presidency courts of Munster and Connaught, survived outside direct control from Dublin but, in general, justice and administration were vested exclusively in crown officials answerable to London.

The counterpoint to royal government was the Irish parliament, a legislative institution more than three centuries old, which had evolved along lines similar to those of Westminster. Its upper house consisted of the bishops of the established anglican church and of the Irish lay peerage, a motley collection of Old English lords and of new Protestant families whose ennoblement was a measure of their wealth, influence and, less frequently, royal service. The house of commons, with 276 members in 1661, was elected by the freeholders of the 32 counties, by the university in Dublin, and by the freemen and burgesses of the 105 incorporated cities, towns and vestigial plantation villages, each constituency returning two members. In reality the landowning class controlled the votes in every county and in nearly every borough – making contested elections in the seventeenth century the exception – and they monopolised the membership of the house of commons itself. Because of the so-called Poynings's law of 1494 the formal powers of the Irish parliament to initiate and amend legislation were severely restricted, and although this gave lords lieutenants a vital lever of control, the Irish parliament gradually developed means of circumventing such restrictions. Parliament by the end of the seventeenth century became both the symbol of the pre-eminence of the new landed class in Irish society, and the mechanism by which they could influence, and at times even control, the government of Ireland.

* * *

The sprawling site of Dublin Castle was the nerve-centre of royal government in Ireland. The abortive attempt to seize it on 23 October 1641 had formed a dramatic prologue to the tidal wave of rebellion in Ulster. Eighteen years later and after the interminable confederate war, the Cromwellian reconquest of Ireland and the nine-year commonwealth regime, Dublin Castle was successfully seized on 13 December 1659, in itself an unspectacular and bloodless affair. The strong men behind this coup were drawn from leading second and third generation immigrant families from England, 'Old Protestant' landowners who had survived the decade of war and the radicalism of the first Cromwellian administration. Holding key commands in the huge army of occupation, they had been in a position to recover their political power during the relatively conservative governorship of Henry Cromwell (1655–59). However, the re-emergence of army radicalism in London in the spring of 1659 and Henry Cromwell's recall threatened the Old Protestants, and the 13 December coup was the result; it was successful because there was by then a political vacuum in England.

After the coup, a group of army officers and Old Protestant gentry issued a call for a general convention, and nearly 140 'old' and 'new' Protestants assembled in Dublin in February 1660. They agreed a declaration asserting the legislative independence of Ireland and denouncing the late king's execution. A restoration of the Stuart monarchy in Britain and Ireland was now highly likely – but on what terms? The convention leaders were divided: some sought to extract concessions from the young Charles Stuart in exile before giving a declaration of loyalty, others were more anxious to win favour by plunging with a tide they knew to be turning in his favour in England. In the event, whatever leverage the Irish convention briefly exerted on Charles was undermined by the surge of royalist support in England that spring. Charles was proclaimed king during May, and the Irish convention now became supplicant. A delegation was sent to London to petition for the calling of an Irish parliament, the re-establishment of pre-commonwealth judicial institutions and the legitimising of the momentous land transfers of 1653–59. The architects of the restoration in Ireland did not, in other words, seek a total return to the situation prior to 1641.

The implications for Ireland of Charles's return were not at all clear. Old Protestants hoped for an early resolution of uncertainties in regard to property, the church, and finance. The New Protestants, those who had arrived since 1641, became less audible politically as their sponsoring regime crumbled. They feared for their land, their religious rights, even, in the case of the regicides, for their lives. Catholic prospects were even less clear: their hopes were pinned on the king honouring the terms of the 1649 peace, in which the duke of Ormond in the king's name had guaranteed the confederate Catholics religious freedom, a general pardon vis-à-vis 1641, Catholic access to public office, and the cancellation of the government's pre-war confiscations. If Charles were to accept *these* terms the effect would necessarily be to undermine all the post-1649 confiscations of Catholic land.

Too much had changed. On the eve of the 1641 rising, Catholic landlords of Gaelic and Old English background had still owned three-fifths of the profitable land surface; in 1660 nearly all non-corporate property outside Connacht was possessed by Cromwellian grantees or by Old Protestants who together formed a powerful vested interest. Catholic ex-proprietors from Leinster, Munster and Ulster had in the years after 1649 chosen between three bleak options: escape into exile, which for many meant military service under Charles; transplantation to Connacht or Clare and the acceptance of token estates there; or continued residence on or near their old properties as tenants of the new grantees. Catholic estates in 1660, including the Connacht grants, can hardly have exceeded 10 per cent of the total profitable acreage of Ireland. In addition to this rural eclipse, Catholic merchant communities, which before 1641 had controlled the trade of most of the southern ports, were between 1644 and 1652 completely uprooted and dispersed. And some 35,000 confederate soldiers, survivors of the Cromwellian nemesis, had been sent out between 1652 and 1654 to other theatres of European war; most presumably did not return.

The Catholic church was in 1660 doubly weakened – by the decimation of lay patrons of the church and by the attempted suppression of all Catholic religious practice after 1649. When priests and bishops began to function again in 1658 they discovered a disturbing number of recent conversions to the Protestant sects. Given the depth of religious commitment of some Cromwellian administrators and the material prosperity of all classes of tenant after 1652, a period of puritan zeal lasting several decades might have had profound consequences for Catholicism in Ireland.

Relations between the denominations were irreversibly affected by the tensions of the previous quarter-century, in particular by the now unwavering Protestant belief that the 1641 rising had been a religiously motivated massacre, an attempted genocide of non-Catholics. As a belief, this convenient half-truth about the Catholic 'rebels' provided justification in perpetuity for the drastic Cromwellian confiscations of Catholic land. Changes in religious demography during the interregnum reinforced the Protestant position: an absolute fall in Catholic numbers since 1649, and a more than proportionate replenishment of Protestant numbers in the 1650s, was the common perception. Henry Cromwell's secretary, William Petty, was later to estimate that three-elevenths of the population of Restoration Ireland was Protestant, compared to two-elevenths in 1641; there is no evidence to challenge this.[1]

However the character of conventional Protestantism had also been shaken during the commonwealth. Before 1641, the doctrinally undemanding Church of Ireland had held the loyalty of nearly all Protestants. Then in the 1640s Presbyterian church organisation and a narrower Calvinist theology took firm root in those parts of Ulster where strong Scottish settlements survived, nurtured by the presence of a Scottish army after 1642. Cromwell's English soldiers introduced further versions of the truth, and by the late 1650s there were large numbers of Anabaptists, Quakers and 'independents', not just within army society but throughout the Protestant community, especially in the towns. The anglican bishops and liturgy were banned; members of the former Church of Ireland either stayed covertly loyal to the *Book of Common Prayer* and the spiritual authority of the bishops, or were ministered to by ex-anglican clergy who had accepted the state's *Directory of Worship* with little enthusiasm.

The 1660 convention and indeed the commissioners who made up the first Restoration Irish government were divided as to what sort of state church should now be established. Many favoured a 'broad' church that would unite at least anglican and Presbyterian. But the decision in London by the end of 1660 was unequivocally in favour of a revived anglican episcopacy. Ormond's views were critical in this; he had spent most of the 1650s in France and the Low Countries with Charles, where he had been treated as the Irish lord lieutenant in exile. His commitment to an episcopal structure was bound up with his intense royalism, and he was supported by several Old Protestant leaders, notably the leader of the Boyle family, Lord Broghill, now earl of Orrery and a government commissioner, who was particularly anxious to isolate the religious radicals. Thus a narrow anglican Church of Ireland emerged, led by a bench of bishops many of whom had suffered for their beliefs in the previous decade. Several promptly began a Presbyterian purge: some sixty parish clergy in Ulster who refused to conform to the anglican rite were ejected from their livings in the early 1660s. Yet anglicanism remained weak: in William Petty's calculation of 1672 one-third of the Protestant population was reckoned to be then Presbyterian, and the best part of another third belonged to the smaller non-conforming sects.[2]

For Catholics, the Restoration brought mixed fortune. Promises of general toleration throughout the kingdoms, made by Charles while still in exile, augured well. But throughout the twenty-five years of Charles's reign, Catholic policy would always be dependent on the tidal flows of

English politics. At the time of the Restoration, there was no uniformity among the Irish government commissioners, some anxious to appoint Catholics as magistrates and to adopt a lenient policy towards religious conformity, but most of them, led by Orrery, extremely hostile towards Catholicism. And a majority in the new all-Protestant Irish commons which met in 1661 tried to secure legislation outlawing the Catholic hierarchy. However, toleration of Catholic worship continued at the government's discretion.

Catholics were to find that prospects of religious security lay in royal favour rather than Irish parliamentary concession, at Whitehall rather than Dublin. Within weeks of the proposal to outlaw the Catholic bishops, 98 peers and gentry of the old religion drafted a statement or 'remonstrance' of Catholic grievances, asserting their total loyalty to the king (God's lieutenant) in all matters temporal, a loyalty not compromised by their recognition of the spiritual authority of the papacy. This was hardly revolutionary, given developments in church-state relations in France, and the intention was to neutralise the standard Protestant arguments for Catholic civil disabilities. Peter Walsh, a Franciscan and Ormond's ally back in the 1640s, sought clerical support for the remonstrance. In this he was only modestly successful, and indeed the document was firmly condemned by the papal internuncio in 1662; the almost complete absence of old Irish names on the Remonstrance was indicative of the political camp which had drafted it. Four years later, some hundred Catholic bishops and clergy were called to Dublin by the then viceroy, Ormond, who hoped to isolate the more intractable clergy; however, he was to reject their compromise formula, a concordat on the French model – much to the Vatican's later relief. Underlying these efforts to define Catholic loyalism was more than Catholic opportunism; there was a profound and unifying sense among all Irish Catholics who voiced an opinion that the house of Stuart in general, and Charles II in particular, were the legitimate, rightful monarchs of the kingdom, whatever the unwisdom of advisers, courtiers and servants. Not that this registered in Whitehall. For the rest of Charles's reign, religious policy towards Catholics was determined by volatile external factors – international diplomatic shifts and the king's tense relationship with his English parliament.

The Catholic elements most anxious for a religious compromise with the state were also those who sought a major reversal of the Cromwellian land grants. Again the new parliament would be no ally; it was preoccupied with the confirmation, and not the overturning, of the Cromwellian settlement. Admittedly, of the Irish parliament's 276 MPs, only about one quarter were 'adventurers' or former Cromwellian soldiers. But a firm majority in the commons supported the propertied *status quo*, first because wholesale restoration of Catholic ex-landowners would upset the political ascendancy that older established Protestants were now enjoying, secondly because many pre-1641 families had materially benefited from the confiscations, either directly or through purchases from new grantees, especially from soldiers.

In the political struggle between new proprietors and the almost exclusively Catholic dispossessed, Charles's advisers and the Dublin government sought a solution satisfying some in each affected group. Hard bargaining in London produced a royal edict at the end of 1660 establishing a series of ambiguous principles which, by a crucial legal judgment, required an act of the Irish parliament before their implementation: most Cromwellian grants were confirmed in the royal declaration, but where a grant was made of land owned by a Catholic deemed innocent of rebellion, the former owner was to be reinstalled and the Cromwellian grantee assigned other land from the stock of property still unallocated in 1659. In addition, all royalist army officers who were owed arrears from 1649 were to receive settlement in land carved from Cromwellian grants. Close supporters of the king received individual grants, and the Protestant royalists of 1649 were given special treatment. The wider implications of the 1660 edict were not immediately obvious. It seemed to the Irish MPs who supported a land settlement bill along these lines that Catholic prospects of establishing their innocence and thereby retrieving their estates were remote, and that all existing landholders' titles would be confirmed. Yet the Act of Settlement (1662) did nothing of the sort, and Ormond, now lord lieutenant, had no wish to validate the Cromwellian settlement. The act established a court of claims to hear the petitions of 'innocent papists', but left the definition of innocence unclear. As soon as it became apparent that the (mainly English) commissioners were favourably disposed towards Catholic grievances, something close to panic spread through the whole settler community. Anger in the Irish commons was such that parliament was prorogued in April 1663, and in May Ormond uncovered a major plot to seize Dublin Castle, a plot including disaffected officers and a number of Old Protestants. The intended coup, with at least eight MPs implicated, gave the viceroy powerful political ammunition to demonstrate to Whitehall the strength of Protestant feeling against the court of claims and the dangers of excessive concessions to the Catholic party.

The volume of claims – five to six thousand – would have kept the court busy for years. In the event, English parliamentary pressure and the furore in Ireland led to the proceedings ending in the late summer of 1663, by which time 86 per cent of the first 820 claims arbitrated on had succeeded, four-fifths of the victors being Catholic. Within its short active life, the court more than doubled the share of Catholic-owned land, with Catholic ownership in Leinster counties such as Meath and Dublin recovering sharply. Families of Old English background, related to or friendly with Ormond and other Protestant royalists, regained most. Thousands of petitioners, small ex-freeholders and pre-transplantation Connacht gentry, were given no hearing. Some Cromwellians and 'Old Protestants' successfully used legal counter-measures to prevent their being evicted.

To meet a modest Catholic restoration and the claims of the 'officers of '49', a drastic attenuation of most Cromwellian land grants became necessary. A formula was eventually worked out in 1664 by the Irish government and the court of claims: one-third of the estates of all but a few Cromwellian families was to be 'resumed' by the crown under an Act of Explanation, and this land used to compensate Cromwellians displaced by 'innocent' Catholics. Ormond lobbied energetically for this compromise, but the proposal was only carried in October 1665 by ninety-three votes to seventy-four, which 'shows sufficiently how impracticable it would have been to have got a bill passed with further advantages to the Irish'.[3] The imminence of war with Holland and France played its part in gaining a majority of MPs for Ormond and Orrery. A second court of claims was established to implement the Act of Explanation, and this lingered on for several years of intricate arbitration.

This haphazard pattern and the inequity of Restoration property adjustments kept the issue alive. When circumstances favoured Catholic lobbyists at court, as in 1671, the settlement was reopened and a commission appointed to examine the two key acts and their implementation. By contrast, in 1673 the king's submission to his English parliamentary opponents resulted *inter alia* in the Irish land question falling dormant once more. Religious policy and land title were intertwined. The competing Irish vested interests were pawns in a larger game, and this engendered deep feelings of insecurity, in turn affecting political behaviour.

The problem with the army was almost as intractable. It was impossible to disband the Cromwellian force – mostly English-born recruits of the 1640s – for all Protestants wanted a standing army deployed across the country under the lord lieutenant's command. Nearly 35,000 at its peak, it had been financed up to 1656 in roughly equal measure by English subventions and Irish taxation of various novel kinds. The size of the army decreased under Henry Cromwell, but complaints of the unprecedented taxation levied to pay for it and the arbitrary mode of tax collection were aired by the Irish MPs attending the protectorate parliaments in Westminster. English lack of sympathy towards these grievances helps explain the Dublin convention's call in 1660 for an Irish parliament and, by implication, Irish control over Irish taxation. Doubts about the army's loyalty to the crown led to the establishment in 1661 of an elite regiment of guards newly recruited in England and quartered permanently in Dublin. There had been much talk of fanatic cells and disaffected officers (particularly in Ulster), but Orrery, Mountrath and other midwives of the Restoration were competent military leaders who could carry their subordinates along with them.

As it turned out, the army was remarkably passive; there was only one serious mutiny – over arrears – during the whole of Charles's reign. It accepted a massive reduction in scale, maladministration and financial incompetence, and endured the dispersal of its personnel across the country in some 134 locations, billeted in small forts, private castles and even inns. For most of the Restoration the army remained largely unregimented, at times more like a militia than a centralised professional force. Gentry officers maintained quarters on their estates, recruiting among their tenants, with the private soldiery often enjoying a quasi-civilian life. The army's primary task was to police the country, forestalling any political threat from Presbyterians or independents opposed to the monarchy, and pursuing any former Irish Catholic gentry who turned tory, i.e. resorted to brigandage or sabotage against their successors. There were of course the predominantly Irish regiments officered by Catholics which had served Charles in exile. No Protestant parliament could accept them for home service; the north African fortress-town of Tangiers became their suitably remote posting until the place was abandoned to the Moors in 1684.

In connection with the domestic army, the Dublin government was more concerned with pay than discipline. In the face of huge arrears on pay, the king's English advisers sought drastic reductions in troop numbers, but these plans were answered in Dublin with dark talk of plots, tories and invasions. Ormond, however, accepted from the outset that the army would have to be scaled down: its payroll accounted for some 85 per cent of current government expenditure. From an English perspective, the need for major financial retrenchment was the most compelling reason for summoning an Irish parliament in 1661. Temporary financial expedients were approved in that session (a poll-tax), and negotiations between the lord justices, the king's advisers and leading Irish MPs continued for months in Whitehall. Early in 1662 the commons' Speaker, Audley Mervyn, agreed to a political trade-off in which the crown would be granted in perpetuity income from the new 'excise' duties and from a tax on every private hearth, in return for the continued suppression of the hated Court of Wards and, more crucially, for crown approval of the Bill of Settlement.[4]

Once the volume of foreign trade began to grow and collection procedures improved, government finances – thanks to this trade-off – became much healthier and no further Irish parliament was called in Charles's reign after 1666. Yet in the years immediately after the fiscal settlement, the government experienced severe budgetary problems. Projections made before the trade-off proved very unreliable, and further subventions from England were necessary in the short term. By pre-war standards the tax burden on the still brittle Irish economy was high, the machinery for collecting it very inefficient. In the first three years of the reign roughly one-third of all customs and port excise receipts were lost in administration. In 1665 the government had to revert to farming out the collection of customs and excise to Irish merchants and public officials.

The budget deficit grew in 1665–67 despite the return to tax-farming. External factors were mainly to blame; maritime war with the Dutch depressed prices and foreign trade, and consequently government revenue. The army shouldered even greater arrears and accepted (under duress) various forms of credit notes linked to future tax revenue. Having succeeded in reducing the army to 7,000 demoralised and ill-armed men, the Irish government began to fear a French invasion. At Orrery's prompting in 1666, Ormond authorised the raising of a county militia and, in all, 16,000 men were temporarily mustered under the local gentry. In most areas its composition seems to have been largely Protestant but in Tipperary, for instance, Catholic gentry received warrants. In Cork, the paranoiac Orrery was reporting that leading Catholic families were in league with the French. He managed to win approval for the extensive refortification of the main south-coast deep-water refuge and victualling station at Kinsale between 1667 and 1669.

From 1662 until his dismissal in 1669, Ormond as viceroy and commander-in-chief took seriously his responsibility to set the army on a firm royalist basis, confront the land question, and improve state finances (and thus army pay also). Outside the military sphere, he carried the Act of Explanation through a reluctant parliament and completed the restoration of the Church of Ireland with the Act of Uniformity

(1666). Yet such political achievements understate his impact on the country. His return to Dublin had been expected from 1660, despite the conflicting wishes of Albemarle, Clarendon and Orrery. When he arrived in 1662 he had already played a central role in shaping Irish policy in Whitehall. His loyal reputation and intimacy with both Charles and his father, together with new honours bestowed on him in England, enhanced his prestige even before his arrival.

His presence for most of the next seven years allowed him to repossess the huge Ormond estates, mainly in Kilkenny and Tipperary. These, together with his official fees and perquisites, gave him an income far ahead of any Irish landlord and, despite the evident mismanagement of his properties, made him one of the king's richest subjects. In 1681 his gross rental stood at about £25,000 p.a.,[5] while his income from offices, fees and sinecures exceeded £20,000. He was in fact the most powerful lord lieutenant of the century – with the exception, as we shall see, of Tyrconnell. Not extravagant by Restoration standards, he nevertheless set the tone for a Dublin enlivened by his conspicuous consumption in the form of private entertainment, public ceremony and architectural enterprise. His most important initiative was the laying-out of a 2,000-acre deer park abreast the viceregal Phoenix House, which became a semi-public amenity for the expanding capital. He also helped to revitalise the country's two largest inland towns, Kilkenny and Clonmel, by funding public buildings, reconstructing his family's mansions, and settling foreign textile workers as tenants.

Though he was no political philosopher, Ormond as viceroy pursued a gently authoritarian path. His instincts were conservative, and these were to prove his undoing. Remaining a firm opponent of all but the most accommodating Catholics, he was generous in the patronage of his kin, nearly all of whom still professed the old faith. He managed to provide a real counterweight to the New English and Cromwellian Protestant interests which dominated the Irish commons.

After initial harmony, mutual suspicions grew up between Ormond and the parliament, with interpretation of the Act of Settlement the visible point in contention. In 1663 and 1665 the opposition was led by Richard Jones: having a former archbishop of Dublin and the first earl of Cork as grandparents, Jones found his age – he was in his mid-twenties – no impediment to prominence. Though Jones assiduously fanned Protestant resentment of court and viceroy, Ormond avoided any public trial of strength with an assembly still hesitant to assert itself. He eventually won over Jones, who in 1668 became chancellor of the exchequer. By then, Ormond's critics had a new if discreet leader in Orrery.

In the 1660s Ormond's failure was not as a politician but as an administrator; he made no direct attempt to adapt the structures of government to the particular problems of the Restoration. Admittedly he did authorise a council of trade to advise the Irish privy council, but there was nothing fundamentally innovative, even in Ireland, in the state concerning itself with the protection and promotion of economic activity. Given the sensitivity of exchequer income to the commercial climate, such a move was only logical. But the whole Irish treasury needed urgent reform, yet its lax administration was not disturbed by Ormond.

By 1665, when the Act of Explanation was signed, two developments were working to weaken Ormond's government – economic trouble at home, and court intrigues in England against his ally, Clarendon. Initially, post-war reconstruction in the 1650s had been built around the expansion of the cross-channel trade in live cattle, but after 1660 stock (and cereal) prices were falling. The general depression in farm prices stirred rival cattle producers in England to agitate for a restriction of Irish cattle shipments. Despite strong Irish government objections, the first English Cattle Act directed against Irish imports came into force in 1664, but it turned out to be more irritant than obstacle for Irish producers. The second Anglo-Dutch war of the following year brought greater disruption, with trade lines breached by privateers and most Irish commodity prices tumbling. To compound this, cattle disease greatly thinned stocks. Persistently depressed conditions in England led to a fresh parliamentary campaign to ban all Irish cattle and sheep imports. Clarendon's enemies at court used the issue to force a confrontation. With the war going badly, Charles was forced to accept Westminster's demands for a 'temporary' total exclusion of Irish cattle in return for fresh taxes. In February 1667 the English market for Irish cattle, sheep and pork was formally closed; the Scottish government followed suit a month later.

Resentment in Ireland, directed towards the English parliament, was bitter, though the measure was not entirely without precedent. The limits of Ormond's power were now only too clear, and those who hoped that the king could save his loyal Irish subjects from an overmighty English parliament were to be disappointed. In practice, the prohibition did not have the apocalyptic consequences he and other Irish lobbyists predicted, and Irish customs receipts actually rose (from a mid-war trough) in each of the two years following. The diversification of Irish pastoral exports was an established trend, and this continued with the return of peace in 1668 and 1669. Increased wool exports to England formed one response to the Cattle Acts, but more striking in the medium term was the relative decline of England, and the growth of France, as a market for Irish exports. The real hardship undeniably caused by the acts was felt in the poorer and more remote counties of the Irish north and west.

The recovery in revenues at the end of the decade came too late for Ormond. The disastrous Dutch war led to Clarendon's dismissal in England and Charles's surrender to an angry English parliament. Old cavaliers like Ormond were left vulnerable. Orrery's opportunistic realignment in 1667 had indeed been an omen. An English treasury commission was set up in 1668 to investigate Irish financial administration, and widespread criticisms of Ormond's government were a major precipitating factor in his dismissal in 1669. The 'cabal' of new and aggressive politicians in the ascendant in London was out of sympathy with Ormond's approach and was anxious to bolster the king's financial independence. But the duke's loss of Irish office did not deprive him either of royal favour or immense residual influence in Ireland – as his successors quickly discovered.

AFTER ORMOND

Ormond's first viceroyalty was followed by a period of weak, at times directionless government in Ireland. Three lords lieutenant with little knowledge of the country arrived in as many years – Lord Robartes (1669–70), Lord Berkeley (1670–72) and the earl of Essex (1672–77). Until Essex established his authority the exact focus of policy remained unusually obscure. The cause of this lay not in Ireland but in London. Clarendon's fall in 1668 and the rise of the 'cabal' ministers brought no end to the jockeying for power at Whitehall. The king's brother and heir James, duke of York, decided at about this time to switch religious allegiance and become a practising Catholic. Once this became public *c.* 1672, English politics became even more unsettled. Meanwhile the king's diplomatic liaisons with Louis XIV and his search for financial independence from parliament had culminated in the secret Treaty of Dover (May 1670) by which Charles agreed to become a Catholic and, by implication, to advance the old faith throughout his kingdoms. The ensuing alliance with France against the Protestant Dutch created tensions in England the likes of which had not been seen since the civil war. Louis' victories in the southern Netherlands in 1672–74 further inflamed popular feelings against popery, absolutist government and the overmighty French.

James's new religious zeal, Charles's perpetual embarrassments over money, and the English court's commitment to *détente* with France and revenge against the Dutch, rebounded on Ireland. Robartes and Berkeley failed to make any impression on Irish affairs as a result of confusing signals from court. Ormond's associates on the Irish privy council and in the army remained powerful, and they refused to co-operate where reforms threatened their interests. Neither the touchy Robartes nor the tactless and indulgent Berkeley was an intuitive leader as Ormond, for all his faults, had been. Both failed to take account of the power play at Whitehall, and loss of influence in London quickly reduced a viceroy's standing in Dublin.

The most distinctive shift in policy during the years 1669–73 was in religion. Attempts to obstruct the religious freedoms of non-anglicans had continued throughout Ormond's viceroyalty in the 1660s, with Ulster Presbyterians and Munster Catholics the most often disturbed. But all recusants were vulnerable if bishops and anglican magistrates chose to enforce the powers they derived from the new Act of Uniformity (1666). Robartes as a Presbyterian, and Berkeley as husband to a Catholic and the close friend of the duke of York, were not committed to its enforcement. Under Berkeley, the readmission of Catholic merchants into borough corporations was officially encouraged, and some 150 Catholic gentlemen were added to the magistracy. George Hamilton, one of Ormond's Catholic nephews, was allowed to recruit his co-religionists to the French flag, and a large Jesuit school opened at Drogheda. Thanks to adroit lobbying by Richard Talbot, James's attendant and the new agent for the Irish Catholics at court, an English privy council commission was created to investigate the workings of the Acts of Settlement and Explanation. In Munster the atmospheric change was dramatic: since the Restoration, the interpretation of the criminal law had been heavily influenced by Orrery's presidency court, based at his new town of Charleville, and the earl became a scourge of religious independents and a foe to all Catholic ecclesiastics. Having misread the drift of Charles's policy, Orrery prohibited Catholic worship throughout Munster in 1670 and ordered the demolition of several churches. So unsuited to Whitehall diplomacy was persecution at this stage that the following year saw the Munster presidency court abolished and Orrery humiliated.[6]

For Presbyterians also, religious freedoms fluctuated. The strengthened Act of Uniformity had given anglican bishops increased powers of interference (particularly in education), and several in Ulster used them. But political instability in lowland Scotland, arising from an even more unpopular Restoration settlement there, aided Ulster non-conformists. They did not disguise the possible influence in Ireland of Scottish events which only practical toleration could check. The intervention of Sir

Arthur Forbes, marshall of the Irish army from 1670 and a Presbyterian of Scottish extraction, contained tensions in east Ulster. In 1672 a small royal contribution to Presbyterian ministers' salaries (£600 p.a. *in toto*) inaugurated what became known as the *regium donum*, for long after to be an ambiguous symbol of the legitimacy of Presbyterianism in Ireland. It did nothing to reduce the animosity of meeting house towards parish church.

None of these *de facto* modifications in policy was directly a Dublin decision. Their culmination was Charles's new Declaration of Indulgence in March 1672 in which he announced his intention to suspend all legislation restricting dissenters and Catholics. The declaration was at least partly tactical, aimed at maximising domestic support for the Anglo-French coalition. In effect, however, it strengthened anti-Catholic sentiment in England, and the English commons next year challenged the royal prerogative and declared the indulgence illegal. The king's need for war finance was by then so pressing that he was obliged to comply and to sign a Test Act to exclude all but anglicans from public office in England.

Irish government policy followed these twists. Before taking office in mid-1672, Essex had received private instructions to allow full liberty of conscience to all the king's Irish subjects, and he maintained Berkeley's discreet friendship with Archbishop Plunkett, the Catholic primate. Fifteen months later, he was signing proclamations against Catholic bishops, regulars, and schools. The commission raking over the land settlement was dissolved, and the Talbot brothers forced into exile. In 1674, Orrery was once again able to insist on the letter of the religious law in Munster when he became major-general of all troops in the province, a position which gave him supra-magisterial powers. However, in general, persecution during Essex's regime remained no more than a threat; priests were not harassed and no rewards were offered for the capture of bishops.

The direct relation between Charles's money problems and Irish government behaviour was highlighted by 'the Ranelagh undertaking'. In 1671, Richard Jones (now earl of Ranelagh) suggested to the king that the Irish exchequer should be, in effect, privatised. He offered to head a small consortium to receive all payments due to the crown from the revenue farmers and to pay out all charges on the Irish treasury – to handle all government expenditure – during the life of the farm. By this highly irregular proposal the king would be relieved of worries that Ireland might need further emergency subventions. The consortium would also collect the huge arrears and from 1675 pay the king a fixed sum (£80,000 in all) for the right to hold on to them. Ranelagh's proposal in relation to arrears was less risky than it seemed, not least because of a secret codicil in which he promised covert payments during the agreement in return for a private indemnity from Charles, should the public commitments of the partnership not be honoured.[7] The king accepted the offer, and by the autumn of 1671 Ranelagh had completely undermined the lord lieutenant as overseer of Irish revenue collection and disbursement. The ruthless way in which he ensured optimal financial and political returns from the revenue flow under his control angered Berkeley and infuriated his more formidable successor, Essex. One move that Charles particularly appreciated was Ranelagh's success in having an Irish regiment transferred to England to serve under the duke of York at a time when no funds were available to enlarge the small English army; these troops continued during their stay in England to be paid from Irish revenue.

The inner workings of Ranelagh's undertaking remain obscure, but it now appears that the king covertly received nearly £50,000 in 1671–72 by way of private payments, but little thereafter.[8] Ireland had become financially self-sufficient, and this was quite an achievement, given royal bankruptcy at the end of the war. Self-sufficiency was at least in part the result of Ranelagh's drastic methods, his hounding of revenue farmers and their agents by means of his own more efficient network of collectors, and by delaying official payments to those who were politically useless to him. When the great reaction came in the winter of 1673, Ranelagh's enemies had no difficulty in linking him with the 'Dover' policy, but he retained powerful court support and continued to draw unfathomed profit from the undertaking, even after its formal close in 1675. He prevented Essex from inquiring into Irish army finances, and even when the viceroy recovered control over payments to the army, Ranelagh defeated him on specific issues, most notably concerning the place where the advance payments promised by the third consortium of revenue farmers in 1675 should be paid – Dublin or London, to the Irish government for public uses or direct to the king for private needs. Essex sought to hold Irish revenue within the state, but Ranelagh won.

Essex did succeed in strengthening Castle control over the boroughs. Restoration governments had become interested in municipal affairs in order to control the denominational balance in the towns, and to influence the composition of the urban magistracy, that is, the principal officers who determined the outcome of borough elections to parliament. In 1661, the king had instructed the Irish government to ensure that Catholics once again enjoyed trading privileges in the towns, but this did not guarantee them civic freedom. Throughout the 1660s the position was confused, but town councils almost everywhere stayed in the Protestant hands that had grasped them in the 1640s, or after Cromwell's victories. All the larger towns except Galway, Wexford, Limerick and possibly Cork had by now a predominantly Protestant citizenry. The rights of Catholics to own urban property was obscured by the Acts of Settlement and Explanation, but were reaffirmed early in 1672 as part of the Dover policy. A few days before the Declaration of Indulgence, it was proclaimed that Catholics were to be restored to all municipal privileges they had enjoyed under Charles I, without reference to any religious oath.

The Act of Explanation had vested in the government certain powers to renegotiate town charters; these largely neglected provisions were due to lapse in 1672. Essex set aside the previous policy of toleration, responding, it seems, to Protestant merchant fears of a Catholic fifth column. From September 1672, the Oath of Supremacy was to be required of all elected municipal officers except those exempted by the lord lieutenant, in effect to secure an exclusively Protestant civic leadership. These 'new rules' were to have the secondary effect of giving government a veto over all senior city nominations. The rules differed from city to city; in Dublin, for instance, they defined clearly the exclusive character of the corporation and specified the near total control of aldermen over nominations to the mayoralty and other offices. Whether this reduced the rights of guilds and freemen, or merely blocked the future development of more open municipal government, is unclear. Essex faced considerable opposition within the Irish privy council before he was able to put these new arrangements into operation and Dublin, in particular, remained bitterly polarised between those prepared to co-operate with him and those who continued 'to promote ... seditious designs'.[9]

Government concern to influence municipal elections was related to the recurring expectation that a new parliament would be summoned. For twenty years after the dissolution of 1666, no parliament met, though Essex claimed in 1675 that if a viceroy was popular 'he may, with care, make the house of commons what he will'.[10] He and his successor urged London to approve the calling of a new Irish parliament, but a variety of powerful interests feared the political consequences of its recall. Orrery resisted in 1668–69 when he was scheming for Ormond's dismissal, and again in 1678 because of the threat of legislation that would confirm all the decrees of the court of claims. Ranelagh, with his arcane accountancy and intense unpopularity in Anglo-Ireland, worked privately against a recall in the mid- and late-1670s. Revenue farmers opposed a new parliament which might increase excise taxes and so reduce trade to the detriment of their income. Catholic lobbyists in London were equally opposed on the rather different grounds that a new parliament might well consider concrete legislation to restrict Catholic freedoms.[11] More fundamentally, no parliament was called because the gradually improving state of commerce had led – thanks to the trade-off of 1662 – to improving state revenues. Despite the fiscal distortions of the customs farms and Ranelagh's undertaking, net receipts were rising, particularly in the late 1670s, so that the political risks of recalling parliament often seemed to outweigh the financial benefits. In due course, the long silence in the parliament house made MPs of the next generation, in 1688 and in 1692, all the more careful in asserting their rights. A regular parliamentary assembly throughout the period might have subjected Castle government after 1666 to a closer scrutiny.

During Essex's regime, the viceroyalty was increasingly compromised by the new involvement of English agencies in Irish affairs. The English privy council's committee on Irish affairs, which had determined policy at the height of the 'cabal' ministry, continued to function. In addition, the English treasury was becoming more competent to supervise Irish financial affairs, having been deeply immersed in negotiations concerning the second and third Irish revenue farms. Indeed, the tendency to appoint English financiers, many of them already involved in English tax farms, reinforced the pattern. Ranelagh's alliance with Danby, the first treasury lord, gave the English treasury a critical role in their contest with Essex. The extent of this penetration of the Irish administration only became apparent during the next Irish government, after Essex's recall in 1677.

WHIGS AND TORIES

The new viceroy turned out to be the ageing duke of Ormond once again, who had secured his appointment despite Ranelagh's vigorous canvass for the king's natural son, the duke of Monmouth. However, Ormond's control over financial matters was now to be very limited. The early years of his new term were dominated by the strange turns of international diplomacy. War in the Low Countries between France and the Dutch dragged on after English disengagement from the French alliance in 1674. Continuing French gains sharpened English fears of Louis's long-term intentions. By 1677, even Charles's court was growing hostile and the diplomatic shift was symbolised by the marriage of James's Protestant daughter Mary to the Dutch military leader, Prince William.

In September 1678, as a general European peace was being concluded, the English privy council was informed by one Titus Oates of a far-reaching Jesuit conspiracy to assassinate the king and the duke of Ormond. Though many leading English Catholics were implicated, Archbishop Talbot was the only Irishman named. The duke of York would be the obvious beneficiary of such a wild scheme, and indeed his secretary was implicated. Of course Oates's gothic tale was a fabrication, but its impact was enormous. English public opinion was already suspicious of Catholic fifth-columnists and French machinations. Moreover, privy council inspection of the correspondence held by James's secretary revealed highly compromising information on the bribery of MPs, and the expectations of England's reconversion when James became king. Moves began at Westminster to exclude James by statute from the succession to the throne, to raise a Protestant militia, and to disband the new additions to the army. During two years (1679–81) and three parliaments, English politics became drastically polarised between exclusionists or 'Whigs', led by the duke of Shaftesbury, and 'Tories' who, in reaction to Whig excesses and the fear of a new civil war, rallied to crown and court. No exclusion act was passed, but Charles paid a high price for this victory: three bitter elections in England and Wales (fought for the first time on a national issue and using novel electioneering techniques) led to the parliamentary supremacy of the English Whigs.

Even in remote Kerry it was reported that news of a Catholic plot 'startles and amazes' the English in Ireland.[12] Within a month, the aged Archbishop Talbot, who had just returned from France, was imprisoned in Dublin Castle, and a week later a new proclamation banished Catholic bishops and regulars, this reinforced some months later by the offer of cash rewards for their apprehension. For the second time since 1660, the bishops went into hiding, and though parish priests were not directly affected, local harassment of all clerics resumed in some places. At first Ireland was scarcely implicated in the plot, but under pressure from London Ormond issued proclamations against Catholics bearing arms without licence and against further Catholic migration into the major towns. This moderate reaction reflected his confidence that Ireland need not be affected by the rumpus. However, the hysteria in England convinced Orrery that the viceroy was blind to the danger about him; up to his death in October 1679 Orrery sent a series of damaging reports of Ormond's laxness to Westminster, encouraging the Whigs to dig deeper for an Irish plot. The search for informers, genuine or otherwise, was on. Independent of this English initiative, bills of indictment were presented in 1679 at county assizes in Limerick and Waterford, accusing several Catholic and conforming gentry of implication in French invasionary plans and of conspiracy to murder their Protestant neighbours. All were thrown out by the grand juries. But gradually the lineaments of an Irish plot were discernible in London and its existence was formally affirmed by a resolution of the English house of lords in January 1681.

Before the fabrication of an Irish plot to strengthen the exclusionist case had been completed, the energetic Catholic primate Oliver Plunkett was arrested in Dublin. At first, he seemed destined for banishment to the continent. But a motley of Franciscans, several parish clergy and some Catholic laymen with Gaelic patronymics and hailing from south Ulster were encouraged to present evidence showing him as the principal in organising 70,000 Catholics for a rising, and as implicated in a planned French landing at Carlingford. No Ulster equivalent of Orrery lay behind this story, and most Irish Protestants respected the urbane Palesman or at least accepted that, unlike the Talbots, he was not one for 'engaging into intrigues of state'.[13] Most of the hostile witnesses had fallen foul either of canon or statute law, had private grudges against the primate, or else saw prospects of personal pardon from the London government. Unconvinced by the charges, Ormond had the indictment presented at Dundalk in Plunkett's own diocese; when the chief prosecution witness failed to appear in July 1680, the case was adjourned. But Plunkett was transferred to London where an indictment for high treason succeeded. Tried before hostile judges in the King's Bench and failing to obtain witnesses from Ireland in time to challenge the prosecution, he was found guilty in June 1681 and executed at Tyburn shortly afterwards. If anything, the anti-popery crusade was now discredited by Plunkett's trial and execution. Charles had not doubted his moral integrity and innocence, but the king's primary concern had been James's succession rights. The king was reported to have admitted to Essex in relation to Plunkett, 'I cannot pardon him because I dare not'.[14] Nor had Charles defended Ormond in 1679–80 when the viceroy's moderation was bitterly assailed. Many expected Ormond's dismissal then, but he rode out the storm and regained explicit royal support in 1681. Cowardice and machiavellianism were indeed well mixed in Charles.

Ormond had weathered other crises. During the south-west Scottish rising of 1679, he sent reinforcements to prevent trouble in east Ulster. Defeat of the Covenanters at Bothwell Brig in June concluded this episode, but it increased the influx of non-conforming Presbyterians from Scotland into Ulster. A substantial part of the 7,000-strong Irish army stayed in the north-east, and the pattern of its deployment – despite Redmond O'Hanlon and other tories in the interior – was coastal: in 1680 only about one-sixth of the army was quartered in the thirteen inland counties. And concern for the army was Ormond's first priority now that financial and religious policy was directed from London. Reorganisation into regiments was completed in 1683, and morale was improved by greater regularity of payment. Symbolic of this enhanced management were the massive new fortifications at Kinsale and the Royal Hospital buildings at Kilmainham outside Dublin. The latter project, a refuge for maimed and pensioned soldiers, had been initiated by Forbes during Essex's viceroyalty – to be modelled on the new *Invalides* in Paris. Ormond endorsed the plan for what became in 1687 Ireland's largest civil building, erected at a cost of £23,000.

Ormond's second viceroyalty lasted seven years, until 1684. Apart from his role in tempering the Irish consequences of the popish plot and his support for a more effective army, he remained something of a spectator – and even at the end of Charles's reign the Irish army was still an under-trained, under-equipped force with no active service experience. In the financial and economic spheres he had even less influence. Ranelagh was now extricating himself from Irish affairs, having made a personal profit between 1671 and 1682 of *c.* £210,000 (less backhanders), according to Egan's estimate.[15] Lawrence Hyde, younger son of the old duke of Clarendon and since 1680 the new power in the English treasury, had no time for Ranelagh. With Sir James Shaen, Hyde planned a total reshaping of the Irish tax farms, but when the scheme collapsed in 1682 the English treasury had to devise emergency arrangements to collect Ireland's revenue. Five commissioners, the earl of Longford and four Englishmen of experience, were quickly appointed by London. This inauspicious arrangement marked the beginning of the revenue commissioners in Ireland. Their well-regulated and aggressive management turned a temporary expedient into a permanent institution. Gross customs and import excise receipts rose by 11 per cent between the six years of Shaen's farm (Dec. 1676–Dec. 1682) and the first three years of direct management, and net receipts (deducting collection costs, fees, etc.) rose by 22 per cent; gross and net inland excise returns rose even more impressively.[16] The revenue commissioners remained accountable to London, not to the lord lieutenant, and this allowed them to ignore local sensibilities in appointing officers and to enforce an increasingly complex code of navigation law on Irish merchant communities without consideration of local political patronage. The earl of Arran, while running Dublin Castle during his father's absence in 1683–84, observed that 'the lords of the treasury intend to make this kingdom no better than a province'.[17]

The new commissioners were helped by the buoyancy of Irish overseas trade after the mid-1670s and by the consequent growth of the inland economy. The last ten years of Charles's reign brought real economic advance, assisted by indigenous population growth and, more spectacularly, by immigration from Scotland and England. International peace also contributed, and harvests were in general good; the only real subsistence crisis during the Restoration period had occurred in 1673–74 when war prevented emergency grain imports. Three decades after the Cromwellian land settlement, many rural landscapes were changing through land reclamation, field enclosure and new building. Change occurred most clearly on estates where at least part of the tenantry was of immigrant stock. But the most distinctive rural innovation related to the landowning class. The first large unfortified country mansions, incorporating classical and Dutch influences and set in their own demesnes, were constructed in the generation after 1660; some of these admittedly compromised between civility and security with corner turrets or large curtain walls. Political power was in the vanguard of this rebuilding – Ormond's family in Kilkenny, Forbes in Longford, Orrery and Perceval in Cork, Lord Chancellor Boyle in Wicklow, Coote in east Galway. A few of the wealthier Catholic proprietors abandoned castle and tower-house to build in the mannerist style also, notably the Talbots in Kildare and the Cotters in Cork. Some waited for quieter times; Petty, the great Cromwellian venturer and father of political economy, contented himself 'by contriving many noble palaces on paper', including a project for the reconstruction of Dublin Castle after the major fire there in 1684.[18] By contrast, the housing of the small partnership farming class remained to outside eyes almost barbaric, 'the creats made of sallow or other wood like great wicker baskets turned topsy turvey ... covered with turf and sedge'.[19] Brittle prosperity had brought disproportionate benefits to those who owned or controlled land, were engaged in wholesale trade, or held public office.

During Charles's last years, a 'court' government under Rochester and Sunderland resumed the political initiative in England, with the Whigs deeply embarrassed by the Rye House plot of 1683. James felt strong enough to return to court, becoming in effect his brother's regent. His immediate interest lay in building up the separate armies of the three kingdoms, and the Irish army received almost as much of his attention as the English. Where Charles (and Ranelagh) had sought to use Irish revenue surpluses to support private income, the more ascetic James aimed to use them to strengthen the Irish army and – indirectly royal power in England. Thus, recurring English anxieties over Irish commercial prosperity were more than mercantilist calculations; Whig opponents of a stronger crown were certainly on firm ground in the 1680s in seeing a link between buoyant Irish trade receipts and a politically more autonomous king.

In practice, this improved Irish performance was used to extend coastal fortification, to enlarge the army (by about 600 men) and, more sinisterly, to support a Scottish Catholic regiment, first in Tangiers and then in England. On the surface, the court's policy coincided with Ormond's. However the old viceroy's conception of an exclusively anglican army, officered by the gentry, gave rise to difficulties. Close to James was the veteran spokesman for the Irish Catholic cause in London, Richard Talbot, whose enmity towards Ormond had been hardened by the long imprisonment and ultimate death of his brother, the archbishop, in Dublin Castle. Talbot sought to show that Ormond's personal policy had copperfastened old Cromwellians and other extreme Protestants in the army, men that would not peaceably accept James's imminent accession. Control over army commissions was thus to be withdrawn from the lord lieutenant and given solely to the king. Ormond's opposition was assumed and so the enfeebled king was persuaded to recall him a second time, in November 1684. But before Ormond could hand over, the king was dead.

CATHOLIC ASCENDANCY

For four of the years between James II's accession in February 1685 and the Treaty of Limerick in September 1691, Ireland was at peace. Yet over the two years prior to the first skirmishes of December 1688 the country was transformed from Protestant-dominated stability to a dangerously rumour-ridden condition in which Protestants were universally scared and Catholics at all social levels touched by euphoric expectation and political excitement. All of this, with attendant consequences for religious policy, army recruitment, and the land settlement, stemmed from a single event: the smooth accession of a Catholic monarch and his effective retention of control over the three kingdoms until November 1688.

In the first months of James's reign, the planned changes in Irish army appointments were implemented, and Ormond left Ireland for the last time. Granard and Chancellor Boyle were made lords justices, retaining executive power until a new viceroy should arrive. Court politics and James's caution delayed the choice; the appointment of the second duke of Clarendon, Rochester's elder brother, disappointed Catholics and came as some reassurance to the anglican interest, for long before Clarendon arrived in January 1686, Protestants had become alarmed. On the eve of Charles's death, the Catholic Justin MacCarthy had been given command of an infantry regiment. MacCarthy, Ormond's nephew, had distinguished himself fighting alongside the French in the 1670s, but his appointment to a command in the Irish army 'raised by Protestant parliaments to secure the Protestant interest'[20] marked a new departure. The new king confirmed MacCarthy's appointment, and a few other Catholic officers were given commissions.

By far the most significant of these appointments was the grant of a regiment to Richard Talbot, who was intent on a 'remodelled' Irish army to be achieved through a massive increase of Catholics within its ranks. Despite his remarkable adventures forty years earlier in the confederate wars, Talbot was more courtier than colonel. His interest in the army was primarily political – a transformation of its denominational composition was a means of altering the balance of power in Ireland. Prominence in James's entourage for three decades, together with an extraordinary personality, made him an easy man for Protestants to hate. But, 'behind the explosions of rage and dyspeptic inconsistency lay an acute political brain'.[21] He was moved by strong loyalties; in ascending order, to James, to Catholic Ireland, to the Old English families of Leinster, and to the Talbot connection.

In May 1685 Talbot was created earl of Tyrconnell and was further strengthened by a royal order that the lords justices were to consult him on all matters concerning the army. Though Granard was still commander, Tyrconnell, a mere colonel, determined policy. The number of Catholics drafted into the ranks that year was actually quite small – little more than 10 per cent of privates were Catholic at the year's end – but the Monmouth and Argyll rebellions across the water led to a more significant diminution of Protestant strength in that Tyrconnell pressed for confiscation of all militia arms. These risings in Britain embarrassed the many Irish Protestants who were still keen to demonstrate their loyalty to James. Their lack of resistance, then or later, to the gradual catholicisation of the Irish state is striking. One factor may have been feeble leadership: Orrery and Conway were dead, Ormond dying, Chancellor Boyle an octogenarian, Granard strangely supine, and none of these but Granard was to be succeeded by vigorous heirs. A generation gap of crucial importance divided Restoration Ireland from the new men who were to be moulded in the coming crisis.

Clarendon arrived early in 1686 to implement James's policy – as he understood it:

> [the king] would support the English … [and] though he would have the Irish see that they had a king of their own religion and that they should enjoy all the freedom thereof, yet he looked upon them as a conquered people, and that he would support the [acts of] settlement inviolably, but I must endeavour to find out some way to help him relieve some of the Irish, who had deserved well of him …[22]

Neither king nor viceroy had any immediate knowledge of Ireland or a clear-cut policy for the country. Clarendon was very much the patrician, his restricted sympathy for Catholic aspirations tempered by a deepening solidarity with the anglican interest and by his family's traditional royalism. King James himself recognised that the existing structures guaranteed Ireland's dependent status commercially and constitutionally, and that any pro-Catholic policy risked an upset of colossal proportions in England;[23] less frequently, but no less deeply, he acknowledged Irish Catholic suffering in the past, and knew that his brief reign might offer a historic moment of recovery before the accession of his Protestant daughter Mary.

Tyrconnell manoeuvred against Clarendon from the start. His first success came with the appointment of three Irish Catholic lawyers to the judiciary, and the addition of eleven Catholics to the privy council, changing the latter from an all-Protestant body to one in which Catholics formed a substantial minority. Clarendon, who played no part in these appointments, was privately appalled. His position was further marginalised when Tyrconnell returned from England in June 1686 with full military authority as lieutenant-general, and proceeded during an eighty-day sojourn to purge the army. At nearly every regimental muster, Protestant soldiery were dismissed wholesale under Tyrconnell's gaze, and in their place were recruited raw youths and 'poor silly cow-keepers and wretched creatures',[24] as one of his critics described it. In the three months ending 30 September, nearly 3,500 such enlistments occurred, so that by that date two-thirds of the ordinary soldiery were Catholic. Clarendon relayed Protestant protests to London and pointed out both the inequity of Tyrconnell's behaviour and its impact on discipline. Sunderland ignored the viceroy; the king evidently neglected to read his despatches.

Beyond the central institutions of state, three areas of change were visible in Ireland by the end of 1686: Catholics and the magistracy,

Catholic admission to the corporations, and the freedom of Catholic religious practice. The brief religious toleration of 1670–73 had been permissive and oblique, but the new policy was overt, even in some respects coercive. Protestant magistrates were now dismissed (ostensibly because of their politics), corporations which delayed Catholic admissions were threatened, and arrangements commenced for a royal payment to all Irish twelve Catholic bishops.

These shifts in religious policy began to affect public order during 1686. Turmoil in the army caused riots in Dublin between Protestants who had been summarily dismissed and Catholics flocking to the city in the hope of conscription. In the autumn reports of 'great meetings in the night of armed men' spread through Cork, Waterford, Longford and Westmeath, causing 'great fears amongst the poor people inasmuch that many of them left their houses and lay in the fields'.[25] The legacy of intense intra-communal suspicion was being revealed; such behaviour was triggered not by any upsurge of collective violence but by the perception that it was imminent. There was, for example, much talk of growing 'tory' attacks on the wealthy but no dramatic rise in rural crime. By September 1685 Catholics in Cork were said to be

> so confident to be restored to their estates forfeited by their rebellion … that they do not spare openly to call the detention of them by wicked names, and to magnify themselves and their ancestors for the only brave subjects, and term the English Protestants Cromwellians.[26]

The same merchant-observer nine months later recorded the first celebration of mass within the walled city since the early 1640s, at the same time noting a slump in investment confidence: 'it makes my heart ache to consider how things are changed'.[27] While reports of Protestants departing the country were to swell by 1688, survivors of the old Gaelic poetic order, such as Daithí O Bruadair, were beginning to celebrate in verse the unexpected transformation of their and their patrons' prospects, and the triumph of the Catholic 'high king'. The world was not yet turned upside down, however. Rents continued to be paid normally until 1688 when cattle mortality, bad harvests and an acute scarcity of coin first diminished proprietors' incomes. Nor was commerce initially depressed, for Irish exchequer receipts reached record levels in 1686, with a marked decline only setting in during 1688. For many Irish Protestants, particularly dissenters who had felt discrimination, the new regime held out momentary promise.

With a new Catholic army in the making, Tyrconnell returned to Whitehall in August 1686 accompanied by Richard Nagle, one of a group of Catholic lawyers who became his close advisers. His next objective was the viceroyalty itself. But while Sunderland was prepared to drop Clarendon, none of the king's advisers was willing to appoint Tyrconnell, having felt the repercussions on English attitudes of his rush to catholicise public institutions in Ireland. After weeks of intrigue Tyrconnell won full executive power in Ireland, but only under the lesser title of lord deputy and with Thomas Sheridan attached as his political secretary. The new lord deputy reached Dublin two years to the day after Charles's death. He was unique among governors of that or the next century in having no non-Irish involvements or ambitions and in the degree of his own political independence.

The previous year's religious policies were quickly extended. New appointments produced Catholic majorities in all three common law courts, and an English Catholic became lord chancellor. Remodelling the army continued: Tyrconnell favoured his own kin and gave preference to the Old English who in general were far better able financially to support their units than families of Gaelic lineage. By the autumn of 1688 the army was more than 90 per cent Catholic, and the loyalty of the remaining Protestant soldiers doubtful.

The transformation of local government had been completed during 1687. All but one of the county sheriffs appointed by government that year were Catholic (twenty of the twenty-nine having Old English names); in the event of a parliamentary election being called their influence would be crucial. As for the parliamentary boroughs, a number of their charters were adjudged defective in the court of common pleas. Some towns meekly surrendered their charters before judgment was given. On this *tabula rasa* Tyrconnell directed the redrawing of all borough charters, nominating new lists of aldermen and burgesses. For most towns, two-thirds of those nominated were Catholic.

The revenue administration lay beyond Tyrconnell's grasp. Sheridan, who had independent access to the king, had also been appointed first commissioner. Of Gaelic background, anglican upbringing, and a recent convert to Catholicism, he proved to be no mere acolyte of his immediate master in Dublin. Having had some association with Petty and Ranelagh, he was well versed in the complexities of Irish revenue and had a practical interest in the economy generally. Faced with his master's determination to catholicise the service, Sheridan stood his ground, aided by the solidarity of the commissioners and their close bonds with the English treasury. It was his distress signals regarding revenue income and the state of trade which led James to summon Tyrconnell to Chester in August 1687 to defend his policies.[28]

The meeting at Chester is poorly documented, but it was apparently a political turning point. The lord deputy satisfied James as to revenue receipts, and moved to rid himself of Sheridan. The king was persuaded to adopt a bolder land policy as likely to produce more permanent results than mere adjustments of the magistracy, bench and army, and his agreement in principle to call an Irish parliament for this purpose was a major triumph for Tyrconnell, who had played on the king's religious sympathies for his Irish subjects. In the months following, two modes of breaking the land settlement were studied in Dublin, and draft bills were brought to London early in 1688. Despite the opposition of the entire English privy council, James approved the mode preferred by Tyrconnell. Far from seeking to redress the many inequities of the court of claims proceedings of 1663, this formula simply proposed that all estates confiscated under Cromwell and not resumed by the old proprietors in the 1660s should now be divided equally between the descendants of the 1641 owners and the families then in occupation. Under such an arrangement Protestants would still have owned about 60 per cent of Irish land, for it left older plantation titles untouched. All now depended on the calling of a Dublin parliament to enact the necessary legislation, but this was impossible before all the boroughs had received their new charters. That task was completed in the summer of 1688, but James had to delay the summons, and in a complex deadlock involving resistance to James in England, it seems that Tyrconnell may have sought royal support for the repeal of Poynings's law, which had been the keystone of the Irish parliament's subservience since 1494.[29]

After Chester, Tyrconnell's control over domestic policy was complete. Catholic religious orders were encouraged to open schools, culminating in the decision of June 1688 to entrust all future teaching positions in state-endowed schools to the Jesuits. He was kept in check, however, on Presbyterian Ulster; the king, anxious for support among English dissenters and for peace in Scotland, had in 1687 expressly forbidden further disarming there. Belfast's new charter gave it the first opportunity for representative local government, and its nominated burgesses were an exact balance of Protestant and Catholic.

By the middle of 1688, James's position in England had been weakened. His pro-Catholic moves were modest by Irish standards, yet intensely unpopular there. The birth of a male heir in June opened the prospect of a Catholic dynasty, and many Whigs now looked towards Holland where Prince William was seeking ways to capitalise on the king's distress and to push England out of its alliance with France. Since April 1688 William had been seeking an invitation from James's English opponents to intervene militarily. With several Whig magnates only too willing to oblige, preparations for a Dutch invasion went ahead. Tyrconnell and others recognised the danger long before the king did, and the English army was strengthened in October by the transfer of three Irish regiments and a battalion of guards. In fact over a third of the Irish army was thus removed at short notice without any immediate effect on local public order. In England, however, the arrival of this untrained and predominantly Catholic force of 2,500 men inflamed an already dangerous situation, and in Williamite propaganda the size of this 'papist' army was exaggerated with telling effect.

It was September before the king recognised the likelihood of William's intervention, and his reactions were indecisive and self-cancelling. When a predominantly Dutch force of 14,000 men landed in Devon in November James's mental agonising became irrelevant. William publicly demanded a 'free' parliament and the dismissal of Catholic ministers, but privately he despaired of making terms with his father-in-law. He was helped by defections from James's numerically superior army across England, and this discouraged the king from an immediate attack on the invaders. Early in December, in response to Tory leaders' petitions for a free parliament and in the absence of any groundswell of popular support in England, James chose exile in France, and his son-in-law's gamble paid off.

These events helped to trigger off the wider war which William had expected and his new subjects, for the most part, had not. England had now to pay the price for choosing William over James by becoming an indissoluble part of the former's grand alliance against the French. And for one of the few occasions in the history of international conflict, Ireland became a major theatre of war.

Ireland in the late seventeenth century

2

War and Peace, 1688–1714

THE THREE-YEARS WAR

AFTER THE collapse of James's authority in England in November 1688, Tyrconnell's immediate task was to maintain some semblance of central control in Ireland. Many southern Protestants (but by no means a majority) had emigrated, gone north, or crowded into Dublin. For several weeks, Tyrconnell sought to conciliate those in the capital; mounting evidence of secret contacts with Prince William, however, led to them being disarmed. The lord deputy decided to expand the army to 35,000 but there was now a grave shortage of experienced men fit to receive commissions. Furthermore, the huge fall in exchequer revenue evident by the beginning of 1689 left virtually no funds for the new levies. The entire army had to depend on 'free quarters' which in many districts simply meant plundering wealthy Protestants of their moveable goods. Banditry increased during the winter of 1688–89, and both bandit (or 'tory') and free-quartered soldiers were now known by the common name of 'rapparee'. The Protestants who remained formed armed associations where they were sufficiently strong and flooded into defensible towns and castles. Where their numbers were few, they tried to escape, or to co-operate with the Jacobite authorities in the defence of property and local order. In counties such as Kerry, Cork and Kilkenny the Protestant landowners who stayed maintained a high profile, but elsewhere they lay low, longing for James's arrival and a drop in political tension. To many Protestants, the news from England in February 1689 that William and Mary had accepted the convention parliament's invitation to assume the throne was quite unwelcome: 'it will make this nation the seat of war'.[1] And so it did. The largest formal military operations ever to occur on Irish soil began to unfold in a five-act conflict.

Act one lasted from March to July 1689; its military concern was west Ulster and its outcome, a regional Protestant victory; its political focus lay south in Dublin in the 'patriot' parliament. Act two was more thoroughly if less dramatically a contest of arms, Schomberg's invasion of the north-east; this may be dated from August 1689 to May 1690, and its background vitally concerns James's 'brass money'. The third act centres on the Protestant hero, William's visit from June to September 1690; the battle of the Boyne is its triumphant climax, Limerick its contrasting coda. The fourth, and least familiar, act was the whirlwind campaign in south Munster in the autumn of 1690. Finally, there was a struggle for the west from June to September 1691, with the deaths of St Ruth and Tyrconnell signalling the end of Jacobite Ireland, a conclusion discernible long before the end of the drama.

* * *

(i) The transfer from Ulster to England of a large part of the Irish army in the autumn of 1688 had created a military vacuum. Northern Protestant leaders formed a number of county armed associations, and although these possessed little regional cohesion they directly challenged Tyrconnell by each declaring for the English revolution and, later, by pledging themselves to William and Mary. By March 1689 resistance was centred on the Lagan valley in the east, Enniskillen in the west and Derry in the north. While the associations grew, Tyrconnell strove to expand his army. Nevertheless the question remains whether or not he might have surrendered Ireland to William in return for guarantees of religious toleration. It is not implausible that he intended serious negotiations with William, should France fail to send military aid. But King James landed at Kinsale in March with French arms, his optimism recharged by the sojourn in France. As he began his triumphal progress towards Dublin, a Jacobite expedition of about 2,500 men was successfully challenging the county associations in the north-east. The Protestant forces retreated towards Derry, a robustly walled town and strategic port which until the previous December had been garrisoned by a predominantly Protestant regiment. The prospect of a new part-Highland, part-Ulster Catholic garrison led 'the youthhood by a strange impulse'[2] to shut the gates of Derry against the new troops.

James chose to go straight to this cockpit of the northern struggle in order to lend moral support to Hamilton, the Irish Jacobite commander, and to minimise the military action. When, against French advice and in violation of a truce, the king rode up to within sight of Derry's walls, the city's leaders were in two minds about further resistance. But the temper of 'the meaner sort' in a city filling with refugees was defiant, and the discovery that James lacked siege weaponry encouraged resistance.

Before leaving for Dublin, the king ordered an encirclement of the city, and this was completed by a French-designed boom across the river.

It was a very long siege. As the hundredth day approached, the case for surrender grew more popular, but Jacobite morale was also sapped as the stalemate dragged on into its third rain-sodden month. There had been relief food-ships from England lying downstream, frustrated by the boom, and when they finally sailed away Hamilton negotiated an agreement which would have conceded free exercise of religion and a general pardon for the besieged. But men from the relief ships were landed in neighbouring Lough Swilly, and Derry, despite its diet of vermin, held out. On 28 July, the English commander breached the boom and two food-ships reached the city under ineffectual Jacobite bombardment. Two days later, the Jacobites were marching away from a defeat which had massively wasted their resources.

Meanwhile, west Ulster was proving stubborn. Areas where Protestant tenant-farmers and small gentry were fairly numerous had remained under the control of their armed associations. At first the threat they posed seemed minor, even when they gathered in the island town of Enniskillen. However, guerrilla raids into firmly Jacobite districts forced Dublin to act. Early in July MacCarthy (now Viscount Mountcashel) was despatched with some 5,000 men. He was confronted by Protestant frontiersmen, aided by English officers from Lough Swilly, who exploited the drumlin topography of south Fermanagh: two-fifths of the Jacobite government force were killed at Newtownbutler, and Mountcashel was captured. This ferocious slaughter of Munster Catholics by third-generation Ulster settlers now made it truly a civil war.

As west Ulster was being irretrievably lost, the Jacobite parliament assembled in Dublin on 7 May. Two-thirds of the 240 MPs were Old English, many of them in fact nominated by Tyrconnell. No returns were made from west Ulster, and only six Protestants sat in the commons. In the lords, Old English Catholics also predominated, but as the 'spiritual peers' were the Church of Ireland bishops, there was a small but vigorous opposition. To later nationalists, this was the first 'patriot' parliament; to many Catholic contemporaries it was a lamentable distraction from the urgent business of Derry and Enniskillen. Without the war, however, no parliament would have been needed; James required its consent for a subsidy (in effect, a land tax) to pay the army. This was granted. But four other legislative proposals were far more controversial.

Two of these had previously surfaced in 1640–41 and in the 1660s: a bill to repeal Poynings's law and the powers it gave the privy council to draw up and amend Irish legislation; and a declaratory bill asserting the autonomy of the Irish parliament from Westminster, and thus the invalidity of English legislation purporting to bind Ireland, and of English appellate jurisdiction in Irish suits. First the king agreed that Poynings's law should go, and that the vetting of Irish parliamentary bills should be left to the viceroy. Then he backtracked, and the bill was lost in the lords. The declaratory bill passed, but received only very reluctant royal consent.

The other two items related to land and disloyalty. Repeal of the Restoration land settlement was for most of the Catholic MPs the burning issue. James found his English advisers and even some in the Irish governing circle strongly opposed to such a move, knowing that this would destroy residual Protestant support for the legal *status quo*. The French ambassador however supported a radical readjustment. But in the commons there was an enthusiastic majority for Sir Ulick Bourke when he proposed the complete expropriation of new landowners, holding under the 1663–65 acts. The spiritual peers warned against such a policy, and Tyrconnell's 1688 formula for an equal division between 'old' and 'new' proprietors was introduced in the lords. Even there it failed to get a majority. A bill was introduced in the commons to revert to the 1641 pattern of ownership but it was considerably delayed. Only after rowdy joint conferences and some strong talk from the commons about 'the heart and courage of the whole nation' being dependent on total repeal[3] did the commons' bill reach the king in late June. Once again very reluctant assent was given. Implementation was to be by a new court of claims, but this did not materialise. However, there were soon reports of the descendants of former owners hurrying to view their patrimonies, of informal possession of land, and even of the levying of nominal rent from sitting tenants. Old English rather than Gaelic families stood to gain by this anti-Cromwellian settlement. The whole of County Derry was to be repossessed from the London Companies as well as other 'rebel' Ulster estates, but these lands were not going to be restored to the Gaelic families expropriated seventy years earlier, but used to compensate Jacobite loyalists, mainly Old English, who had bought Cromwellian properties now scheduled for repossession. In addition, an Act of Attainder was adopted late in the session which listed about 2,400 Protestants – peers, lesser landlords, clergy, merchants, even a Dublin upholsterer – who had fled to England. Their exile was deemed rebellion and their possessions stood forfeit unless they made immediate submission in Dublin. Enforcing confiscation, properly the business of the revenue commissioners, become a cover for private despoliation and cattle rustling.

God and Mammon were not of course ignored by the 'patriot' parliament. There was disagreement over religious policy, but the legislation ultimately adopted declared for total liberty and a reorganisation of tithes so that ministers and clergy were to be entitled only to the tithe paid by members of their own congregations. The Church of Ireland's property – the parish glebes and the huge episcopal church-lands – was not touched. As with all other reforms demanded by the Catholic gentry in the commons, James resisted drastic changes in religious policy in order to keep alive the latent Protestant support presumed to exist in England for his return. For the same reason, Protestants in the Irish parliament enjoyed unusual access to the king. His essentially English loyalties also conditioned the commercial legislation. A navigation act was allowed, restoring such Irish access to the English colonies as had existed up to 1663. Commons bills seeking to give France special trading privileges (e.g. in wool) were quashed in the lords on James's instructions. His non-Irish entourage was in general appalled by the acrimony stirred up at the assembly, for its proceedings exposed the division between the king and Tyrconnell's supporters and, less visibly, between the Old English and Gaelic leaders. The actual legislation reveals much of the political mentality of Old English Ireland.

(ii) After William's accession the combined navies of England and Holland roughly equalled that of France, but neither power fully exploited its naval strength. James had been ferried to Ireland uneventfully, but a follow-up French expedition was intercepted by an inferior English force in May 1689, just after some 2,000 men had landed in Bantry Bay. What was by Irish standards a major sea-battle involving forty-two ships ensued. Its most important consequence was to deter French naval operations in the Irish Sea. There was no Irish navy, so only fear of the French and tight Jacobite policing of the Irish ports restricted Anglo-Irish communications. The English ships relieving Derry had run no dangers at sea, and when a far larger English force assembled at Chester in the early summer of 1689 the risks of Williamite defeat did not lie at sea.

The elderly duke of Schomberg was its leader and his remit was the destruction of Jacobite authority in Ireland. About 14,000 men were involved, about half of whom were newly recruited in England; many officers were Protestant Irish – refugees or soldiers purged by Tyrconnell. When the greater part of the expedition sailed across to Bangor two weeks after the relief of Derry, Jacobite forces near Belfast retreated tactically, leaving only the garrison at Carrickfergus to confront Schomberg.

James's non-Irish advisers advocated the abandonment of Dublin and a general retreat to the Shannon until French reinforcements arrived, but Tyrconnell's advice prevailed. By late September, when all Ulster was in Williamite hands and Schomberg was establishing camp near Dundalk, James had gathered a force larger than the Williamites' and was moving north through Louth.

The great battle was not yet to be. James sought an engagement but Schomberg held back – for reasons no one entirely understood. This, together with news of a health crisis in the Williamite camp and the inexperience of some Anglo-Irish regiments, boosted Jacobite morale. By the following spring over a third of the invasionary force had died in camp. James's army suffered less severely, but the civilian population in Ulster endured food shortages and epidemics so severe that the surge in mortality was described in February 1690 as 'scarce to be paralleled in the history of former times'.[4] Over the southern half of the country, limited economic activity continued in the shadow of the war. The haemorrhage of specie out of the country and the disastrous state of the treasury had led the government to set up a mint in Dublin using, instead of gold and silver, bronze and brass alloys. These coins were declared legal tender, and issued with the promise that, when conditions permitted, they would be redeemable for gold and silver. Until the spring of 1690 they circulated without hindrance, but the sheer volume minted (the official value was £1.1 million) greatly exceeded the value of the coinage in circulation a few years previously. In consequence prices rose, and the new coinage was exchanged for older specie at a huge discount. Soldiers, landlords and merchants had little choice but to accept these tokens, and it is a measure of continued public confidence in the Jacobite cause that they circulated to the extent they did. But when William's landing at Carrickfergus in June 1690 became known in Dublin, James's 'brass money' was immediately less acceptable.

(iii) In the late winter of 1689–90 both sides replenished their armies, the Jacobites exchanging 5,000 Irish troops for over 6,000 veterans in the pay of France, the Williamites being strengthened by an even larger number of Danish, Huguenot, Dutch and English troops. By the following spring King William had decided on personal intervention in Ireland, despite the political tensions in England and the wider war against Louis; the Irish problem threatened to drain his resources and to remain a permanent challenge to his regime.

William landed at Carrickfergus on 14 June 1690. His retinue of more than five hundred ships brought many commodities which Schomberg had been short of – ordnance and powder, 450 bread-wagons, 9,000 horses with fodder, fifteen tons of small coin – not to mention 15,000 further troops. With an army superior in quality as well as equipment to that of the duke, William lost no time in moving south, reaching Dundalk in a fortnight and the Boyne three days later. On the morning of 1 July, the largest military confrontation in Irish history began. William's united army of 37,000 faced James's of 25,000.

Jacobite strategists were in well-practised disagreement, and the Irish among them urged the more offensive option. It was however Williamite tactics which determined the outcome of the battle. One-third of William's army moved upstream as if to cross, and two-thirds of James's (including all the French) made to intercept them. The main Williamite thrust below the Jacobite camp was met by the remaining 8,000 Irish troops under Tyrconnell, whose skill and courage saved a defeat from becoming an ignominious walk-over. When the Williamite cavalry took control of the south bank, the road to Dublin was virtually theirs. No line of further defence was possible in that open countryside, even though Sarsfield was among one of several Jacobite commanders who wanted to regroup. For Protestant generations to come, the Boyne crossing became the moment when Catholic ascendancy was defeated.

The immediate aftermath was the rushed departure of James for France, embittered and unpopular after his sixteen-month stay in Ireland, and the abandonment of Dublin by the government and by wealthier Catholics. In the city nine prominent Protestants formed themselves into a governing committee with the senior member of the Kildare clan, Robert Fitzgerald, appointed governor. Two days later, the first Williamite soldiers entered the city to the frenzied delight of the still numerous Protestant population. Dublin had changed hands without suffering physical damage, though months elapsed before civil government returned to the Castle.

From his camp at Finglas William issued remarkably unattractive terms to James's supporters in arms. Men of little property were offered a general pardon, but there were no inducements for 'the desperate leaders of the rebellion'. Richard Cox, a Bandon lawyer and assistant to William's secretary, drafted the royal declaration and doubtless supported its uncompromising terms. For William, it may have been a tactical move, with kinder terms to come for the Catholic gentry as the military situation became clearer. The wealthier Protestants, liberated by William's troops, found themselves the object of some suspicion, and the Church of Ireland bishops who met the new king at Finglas were coolly received when they tried to explain why many anglicans had remained in public office under James for as long as they had. There seemed a real prospect of a major change in the constitutional status of the Church of Ireland. But the skilful propagandist writings of Dean William King, twice prisoner in Dublin Castle, did much to restore the reputation of those Protestants who had remained in Tyrconnell's Ireland.

William planned to take Waterford and then leave his commanders to finish the job. But it fell without a siege, and despite alarms in the English Channel, he decided to complete the Irish business himself. The Jacobites still controlled most of Munster and all of Connacht; Tyrconnell had chosen the walled city of Limerick as the best rallying point for the Jacobite army after the Boyne. William reached Limerick two months after the Jacobites had begun modest refortifications, and his army outnumbered the defenders. But Sarsfield's brilliant destruction of an ordnance convoy at Ballyneety, followed by weeks of heavy rain, led to the siege being raised. William returned frustrated to London, leaving two provinces still in Jacobite hands. The stalemate had also proved Tyrconnell wrong, and he too departed and sailed for France where he hoped to recover his influence with James. He was accompanied by the French army which Louis had withdrawn.

(iv) The second expedition of 1690 was distinctive in several ways. English-led and English-manned, it totally and swiftly succeeded in its aims. The plan had been advanced by the earl of Marlborough, backed, it seems, by influential Munster Protestant exiles. His force of 5,000 men set sail after William's return to England, and landed in Cork harbour in mid-September. Jacobite control of this area was weakening, for Williamite troops from Waterford had just taken Youghal. Danish and Dutch cavalry working south from Tipperary had wreaked havoc on an Irish force near Mallow, and were reaching the northern extremities of Cork city just as Marlborough was ready to take the southern approaches.

The 4,000-strong Jacobite garrison in the city was covered by enemy artillery. Within the modest walls there was a large and part-Protestant civilian population – and little ammunition. Negotiations began within days, with Marlborough pushing for unusually harsh terms. After a double assault the garrison surrendered as prisoners of war. Jacobite commitments to defend both Cork and Kinsale were proving over-ambitious, and in October Kinsale fell after a two-week siege. But had Orrery's great citadel been manned with a larger garrison, Marlborough could have been held down for much longer. A Jacobite relief force from Limerick was not far away at the time of the Kinsale surrender; ironically, its main achievement was the burning of Orrery's private palace and the town of Charleville. Marlborough was lucky, and this lightning campaign laid the basis for his future reputation.

After the south Munster sieges, the territorial holdings of both armies remained virtually unchanged for eight months, with the Jacobites in control of Kerry, most of Limerick and all of Connacht, and Williamite garrisons unchallenged in east Munster, most of Leinster and all of Ulster. Sarsfield as the *de facto* Jacobite leader based himself in Athlone during the winter of 1690–91, and not only protected the Shannon but encouraged forays across it. He also re-established a Leinster garrison in Westmeath.

The 'rapparees' came to notice during these months; equipped with half-pikes, they operated within Williamite areas as the guerrilla wing of Sarsfield's operations. Much of the wartime destruction of houses and livestock seems to have been the responsibility of this motley force of old tories, regular soldiers and mere adventurers, though the undisciplined behaviour of Williamite garrisons, badly paid and living off the country, contributed mightily to the same effect. The new Williamite government established its most effective militia (outside Ulster) in County Cork where a large Protestant force was mobilised by Cox. Between May and October 1691, the Cork militias killed 'not less than 3,000' of the vagabond parties attached to the enemy and took 'in cattle and plunder at least … £12,000' from them.[5]

Bitter divisions persisted behind the Jacobite lines. Late in 1690 the Dutch commander, Ginkel, hinted at an offer of something more than the Finglas declaration: religious liberty and the restoration of Catholic property as enjoyed in 1685. This prospect was attractive to Catholics who had been restored in the 1660s or had later purchased confiscated property. But the peace party, though strong especially in Galway, was overwhelmed by Tyrconnell's return from France with full viceregal powers. Promised fresh support from France, the viceroy now believed in a long war and the full recovery of his status, even in the face of Sarsfield's hostility. Many distrusted the old schemer since his espousal of surrender after the Boyne and his drastic devaluation of brass money. Sarsfield's circle also wanted to mount a 1691 campaign, but to be led by a French commander. The subsequent arrival of St Ruth and other French officers in Limerick was therefore particularly welcome to them. St Ruth brought large supplies of arms, clothing and provisions, but no more French soldiers.

(v) England's commitment to ending the war was far stronger than France's to its continuation. Ginkel favoured a direct attack on Athlone, then an advance west to Galway, leaving Limerick till last. Despite the heavier artillery now at his disposal, he took ten days to cross the Shannon; the Jacobite defence in Athlone was so effective that the Williamite assault was nearly abandoned. But with a salient established in east Galway, Ginkel issued a proclamation seeking peace, less generous than the private offer of the previous autumn but designed to undermine resistance: pardons to officers surrendering with their soldiers, a guaranteed restoration of their properties, and rather vague undertakings on religious liberty. This had no immediate effect on Jacobite dispositions, but it prompted Protestant Irish leaders to whip up opposition to such a compromise peace.

Sarsfield in the field and Tyrconnell in Limerick both urged St Ruth to pull back to the strongly fortified centres of resistance. Sarsfield also envisaged extending the guerrilla attacks of the winter, whereas Tyrconnell pinned all on substantial French reinforcements. But St Ruth was determined on a formal battle. It was not a bad decision in itself for he was able to draw up his army on an excellent site at Aughrim, fifteen miles west of the Shannon. Ginkel advanced slowly, and was surprised to find a Jacobite army equal to his own in size ranged along a two-mile ridge, and with first-rate natural cover. He too was determined on a decisive confrontation, and took his men straight into battle. It was a costly decision: his attacks were completely repulsed. However in the early evening all was changed by the death of St Ruth and the disablement of his French deputy. Sarsfield – for whatever reason – failed to take control, and this (together with the probable treachery of a few Jacobite officers) turned the battle into a rout. The Jacobite army fled, and seven thousand men – over a third of the total – were slaughtered in probably the bloodiest single encounter in Irish history.

Most Jacobite regiments were now thoroughly demoralised, though Galway, Sligo, Limerick and Killarney still stood firm. Ginkel moved up to the walls of Galway within a week of Aughrim, and negotiated a surrender on terms far easier than those Marlborough had forced on Cork. Catholic civilians and clergy were not dismayed by these: a pardon for all property owners then within the walls, religious toleration, and the right to bear arms. Ginkel had concluded the negotiation without consulting his superiors, such was his anxiety to reach Limerick before autumn.

The end of Sligo came through the conversion of the Ulster Gaelic leader, Hugh 'Balldearg' O'Donnell, to a Williamite pension and his exit to return to the Spanish army. Meanwhile Limerick was under siege again, garrisoned by twenty thousand discontented and ill-paid troops.

Then Tyrconnell died suddenly amid the siege. Yet this changed little: the Jacobite leaders were as divided as ever, but the argument was now left to weaker men. The French favoured total resistance because they knew supplies were on their way from France, while the Irish commanders wished to seek terms. Limerick was in fact stronger and better provisioned than it had been a year previously, and Ginkel was loath to commit himself to a long or hard-fought siege. Thus he renewed the post-Athlone proclamation. Some Jacobites began private negotiations with him, but others were deterred by the fear 'of the parliament not making it good'.[6] Ginkel's caution infuriated Protestant Irish leaders, and William himself demanded a more aggressive approach.

Though a few may not have realised it, the five-act drama was now over. The negotiations at the end of September covered all districts still outside Williamite control. Initially, the Jacobite party demanded a general Catholic pardon, religious liberty and the right to full membership of corporations. These were refused, and Ginkel's own conditions – with some limited amendments – were accepted within a few days. They were close to the terms privately offered a year earlier: the enjoyment of 'such privileges in the exercise of their religion as are consistent with the laws of Ireland; or as they did enjoy in the reign of King Charles II'; specific pardons to property-owners who surrendered, the pardons now offered being far more general, extending to all propertied soldiers and civilians within the areas still controlled by the Jacobites. What was novel was not these 'civil' articles, but the military articles, which proposed to allow those who wished to continue in James's service to go to France and maintain the fight, the men choosing this option to surrender all claim to property in Ireland. From the French point of view, the extraction of the Jacobite army as intact as possible was the outcome they desired. For other gentry who opted for pardon and security of their 1685 property a simple oath of allegiance would be obligatory, nothing more. There would be an explicit undertaking that the king and queen would use 'their utmost endeavours' to get parliamentary ratification. On 3 October 1691 the Jacobite commanders, Ginkel, and the Williamite lords justices signed the Treaty of Limerick.

The speed with which peace came, and Sarsfield's prominence in negotiating it, surprised many. The prospect of a free exit to France for a still formidable army was extremely attractive to a commander who saw his continental prospects as preferable to a further year of, at best, military stalemate. And at the time it was this concession to Sarsfield which upset William's advisers, not the civil articles. It was later claimed that Tyrconnell would never have concluded on such terms 'because he expected to retrieve the country by spinning out the war,[7] but no Irish leader involved challenged Sarsfield's settlement. This aspect of the military articles was immediately implemented, and within ten weeks some twelve thousand Irish troops had sailed into French service, many with wives and children, from Limerick or Cork. The less palpable civil articles had a different history. They had been hastily and ambiguously drafted, and their partial implementation spanned a dozen years, with a number of key aspects being set aside by the once again all-Protestant Irish parliament.

The outcome of the war has often been presented as inevitable, the Catholic defeat comprehensive. This is misleading. The result in Ireland was determined by the course of a wider struggle, and William's strategic position had often been very vulnerable. French naval initiative could have prolonged the Irish war, and a French military command united in its interpretation and direction of the campaign could have ensured that a larger part of Ireland was in Jacobite hands when negotiations commenced. Conversely, spared Ballyneety, William would have taken Limerick a year earlier, and nearly all Catholic property would have been obliterated. At no time was there any substance to the Jacobite dream of a kingdom autonomous in relation to England yet under French protection. What was at issue was how the four 'nations' and three main religious denominations would fare relative to one another at the resolution of the crisis.

Deaths in battle and skirmish probably amounted to less than 25,000, but mortality from disease in camp and among a population affected by food shortages and property destruction was much higher. The unprecedented loss of livestock to rapparees, soldiers and impartial rustlers bankrupted landholders, large and small, and helps to account for the slow re-tenanting of estates in the 1690s. The imprecise evidence of hearth-tax yields points to a contraction of about one-third in the number of households able to pay it between 1687 and 1694;[8] the worst affected counties were in north Munster, south-west Ulster and the north midlands. The 'marcher' areas of the war were, it seems, the most devastated.

PROBLEMS OF PEACE

The three years of war in Ireland cost in excess of six million pounds, over twice the value of all Catholic property on the eve of the war, or over eight times the amount finally realised by the sale of forfeited property in 1702–3.[9] The Irish war and the subsequent continental war had to be financed by new and higher taxation in England, and by loans underwritten by the English parliament with its now much enlarged authority. But the new shift in the political centre of gravity in London from crown to parliament was at least as much a product of the colossal financial strains of war as of the constitutional crisis of 1688.

Parliament's enhanced role affected Ireland in a number of ways. It reduced the crown's ability to pursue Irish policies independently. It allowed Westminster to behave more explicitly as an imperial parliament able to legislate for dependent territories. It provoked the Dublin parliament to a new assertiveness vis-à-vis the crown's representatives in the Castle. Finally, it transferred a new factionalism across the Irish Sea, so that conflicts even in the 1692 Irish parliament were directly influenced by party struggles in London. Even the composition of this first Williamite Irish assembly was governed by *English* legislation, for a Westminster law of 1691 specified that no MP could sit in an Irish parliament (or hold public office) who had not sworn oaths against transubstantiation and the pope's temporal powers; this more effectively excluded Catholics than Restoration limitations had done, and contradicted the terms of the Treaty of Limerick. The assembly of Irish gentry in 1692 was as a result even more uniformly Protestant than the 1689 parliament had been Catholic – though a handful of peers and MPs sat in both.

Within months of civil government being restored in Dublin, plans for a parliament had been under way, for William had promised to call one and local Protestant leaders were strongly in favour. But given Westminster's new role, an Irish parliament was neither a political nor, arguably, a legal necessity. During 1692 there were signs of backtracking, for unpopular office-holders as always resisted such things. But pressure from London resulted in elections, and parliament met in October 1692.

The lower house was left with too much time on its hands; mismanaged by Speaker Levinge it began to inquire into government corruption. Moreover, lawyer-members sought to establish a more positive constitutional role for parliament than that desired by government. So the commons came to discuss whether its function was merely to reject or assent to legislation drawn up by one or other of the privy councils, or whether it should not have the right to initiate its own legislation, albeit following the letter of Poynings's law and framing draft bills ('heads of bills') for vetting by the privy councils. It is not clear how far opponents of the government hijacked the commons through techniques they had lately learned at Westminster. But as there was no organised court group, the 'opposition' went virtually unchallenged and most of the government's bills were thrown out.

The opposition had made its first stand against two money bills: drawing on Restoration precedents, the commons asserted that legislation relating to new taxes should be initiated by their house, as heads. In the event, they sanctioned a 'short' money bill for just two-thirds of the tax revenue the government sought. Then by an unprecedented motion, the house claimed for itself the *sole* right to draft the details of proposed financial legislation, even that arising at the beginning of a parliament. The constitutional implications were starkly obvious: if the commons were to control 'supply', i.e. non-hereditary revenues, then regular meetings of parliament would be unavoidable, with a consequent increase in its power over the executive in all matters of public policy.

Sydney, the lord lieutenant, was highly embarrassed by his own misjudgment. But the 'sole right' claim had given him an excuse to prorogue parliament after just one month, thus avoiding a debate on corruption and a resolution to impeach his friend, Vice-Treasurer Coningsby, for grand embezzlement.[10] The corruption charges had some foundation, but a belief that Catholics had been treated with excessive leniency by the government – at the surrender of Limerick and after – was harder to sustain. Both issues had contributed to MPs' anger, but the heat was fanned by a number of members who were associated with the 'country' opposition in England.

Shortly after parliament had been prorogued, some of these members sought Sydney's permission to petition the king about their grievances. His indignant refusal provided them with further complaints which they duly brought to Westminster. There their evidence fuelled the 'country' majority's campaign against William's mixed ministry, and this in turn led to Sydney's recall during 1693 and the subsequent dissolution of the Irish parliament. Three lords justices succeeded Sydney at the head of the Irish government, and after two years one of them, Lord Capel (younger brother of the earl of Essex who had been Charles II's most effective viceroy) emerged to become lord deputy.

Capel pioneered a style of political management which was to last seventy years: he negotiated an understanding between the Castle and some 'sole right' advocates, notably the Brodrick brothers – government posts for several of them, a slice of patronage, and official support for legislative proposals popular among MPs, in return for their securing parliamentary majorities for government measures. New parliamentary elections were held in the summer of 1695, and a compromise over 'sole right' was devised: the precedent was set for the initiation within the commons of the main supply bills but not the symbolic opening one. In addition, the session of 1695 saw Irish MPs use their expanded financial role to investigate and audit treasury accounts for the first time.

The 'sole right' issue was probably less important to MPs than securing tighter control over Catholics. An English commons committee had in 1694 called on an Irish parliament to pass 'such laws as shall be necessary for the security of Protestants',[11] and Capel willingly complied. And despite the qualms of Lord Chancellor Porter, a Tory supporter of the Treaty of Limerick and its ratification, anti-Catholic bills were easily passed in the Dublin parliament: these prohibited Catholic parents from educating their children abroad, Catholic teachers from opening schools at home, Catholic gentlemen from bearing arms without licence (unless they were 'articlemen' covered by the Treaty), and any Catholic from being recruited into the army or owning horses worth five pounds or more. Alan Brodrick observed that 'the country hath had such laws passed as they have long wanted and wished for'.[12]

These were the beginning of a series of comprehensive anti-Catholic measures which the parliament enacted over the next thirty-nine years. The 'penal code' has often appeared to later generations as a coherent corpus of law. But as in the evolution of English mercantilist legislation, the original rationale was substantially different from the arguments made later to elaborate and preserve the code. There seems little doubt that, had the Irish parliament sat in the 1670s or early 1680s, anti-Catholic legislation would have been attempted then. The events of the later '80s only seemed to confirm Catholic Ireland's remarkable regenerative potency, and so the case for strong restrictions was popular among the anglican gentry, especially in the light of the limited post-war Catholic forfeitures. With the example of the swingeing new laws against England's small Catholic population, the 1695 legislation restricting Irish Catholics in areas not directly covered by the Treaty was neither controversial nor unexpected in London. The principal argument for the disarming and 'dismounting' of Catholics was a security one, the pressing need to disable the 'internal enemy' during wartime. Catholic student or seminarian contact with Europe could also be represented as militarily dangerous insofar as it provided the cover for Jacobite correspondence. When the parliament went on to draw up heads of a bill to banish all 'regular' Catholic clergy it may have been in breach of the spirit of Limerick, yet Capel was happy to forward it. Only diplomatic pressure from the Habsburg emperor led to that bill being abandoned.

A surprising degree of support for Porter emerged in the commons when an attempt was made later in the session to impeach him as 'generally in favour of Irish papists'. Despite the efforts of 'the most considerable gentlemen of the house' and the covert support of Capel, the impeachment failed.[13] In this we find a measure of the independent political power and patronage of a lord chancellor and the existence of a large bloc of moderate, Tory-inclined gentry representing Leinster, Connacht and some Munster constituencies.

When both Capel and Porter died in 1696, the dominant lord justice was the Huguenot commander, the earl of Galway, but the new lord chancellor, John Methuen, had the job of managing of the Irish parliament which reassembled in 1697. The first piece of government business in the lords was the bill, shelved in 1695, to banish the regular Catholic clergy. As the Catholic church authorities were still actively committed to a Jacobite restoration, government and parliament were united in assuming that the only way the state could police the Catholic church and steer it away from political subversion was to remove the friars, Jesuits and other regulars with direct continental links, and to keep tabs on the secular parish clergy. Even the prospect of European peace (the treaties of Ryswick were agreed in September and October) did nothing to reduce local pressure for the banishment bill.

Several amendments of English origin led to the Irish lords rejecting the draft. The Irish privy council then inserted clauses banishing all Catholic bishops and diocesan dignitaries, with death the penalty for those who returned. Though there were precedents for much of this, the statutory ban on bishops implied a more comprehensive suppression of Catholicism; even diplomats in London and The Hague lobbying against the bill failed to register its full scope until it was passed. Yet the Irish council's decision to enlarge its provisions seems to have been only tactical, designed to acquire parliamentary support for the politically more sensitive issue of ratification of the Treaty.[14] The immediate impact was very serious for the Catholic church: five bishops were already on the continent, and of eight still in the country in 1697, four went into exile over the next four years and four remained in precarious circumstances. The threat of rigorous enforcement of the act was real enough to undermine Catholic ecclesiastical authority and administration in most dioceses for more than two decades.

This was the price for confirmation of the much-hated Treaty of Limerick by the Irish parliament in 1697. Passage of time had not rendered it less noxious to Protestants: the recent military successes of the Irish Brigade were well known, the vagueness of the religious articles a threat that had already encouraged the pre-emptive penal legislation of 1695 and 1697. In the bill to confirm the civil articles, all reference to the first article was omitted. The articles relating to the property of those who had surrendered at Galway and Limerick were embodied except for a clause relating to the status of non-combatant landowners within Jacobite territory in September 1691; this clause had been accidentally left out of the Treaty as originally signed, but its authenticity had been subsequently acknowledged by the king. The exclusion of this clause in 1697 was a calculated political judgment – with the clause in, the whole bill would probably have failed; the matter was referred to William in Holland who did not press for its inclusion. And it was because of this particular exclusion rather than the omission of religious toleration that the bill was very nearly lost in the lords; seven lay peers and seven bishops protested that the bill did not accord with the Treaty. Some of the protesters were recent converts affected by family ties, others by links with Coningsby and the second duke of Ormond. Some like William King (now bishop of Derry) feared that the 'missing clause' would open the way for more forfeitures, and thus more land would be disposed of in England. Many exaggerated the entire issue, for few of the western gentry whom the clause was intended to protect had been outlawed in the first place. It was in the same sessions of the house of lords that a unique attempt was made – by Bishop Foy of Waterford – to move a bill to outlaw the use of the Irish language; the bishop, an educational enthusiast, failed in his endeavour.

The ratification of the Treaty of Limerick benefited the many Catholic proprietors who had been in Limerick and Galway in 1691, and who still awaited formal reversal of outlawry in order to recover their estates. In 1692 and 1693 the privy council had accepted the claims of all but eight of the 491 petitions to benefit under the peace terms. The hearings were then suspended – due to Protestant reaction to these decisions – until ratification of the Treaty. So in 1697–98 a further 791 petitions were heard, and again only eight failed. These judgments stabilised Catholic landowning at *c.*14 per cent, roughly two-thirds of the 1687 level.[15]

Economic reconstruction was still not complete by 1697. Land values in most areas were well below pre-war levels. It had taken many landlords four to six years to complete the re-leasing of their estates, for large numbers of Catholic families failed to return after 1690 and countless Catholic petty landholders had lost their worldly substance in stock. Inland counties, from Tyrone to north Cork, suffered greater dislocation than those maritime districts where the army presence had been slighter and the local power structures less disturbed. The tillage counties of east Leinster were indeed exporting cereals to France and Britain by the mid-1690s. North and east Ulster also recovered quickly after July 1689, for refugees had returned promptly and local merchants played an important part in provisioning the Williamite armies during the war. By fair means or foul much of the displaced southern cattle stocks were brought into this region. And throughout the decade there was a large immigration of lowland Scots, initially into north and east Ulster, later further west. Most of the 'yeomen' migrants of the early 1690s arrived with some resources, being drawn by the prospect of cheap farms on estates where the former tenantry, Irish, Scottish or English, had disappeared. The later migrants, fleeing from the Scottish famines of 1695–98, were much poorer. In 1698 the first wave of migration was estimated at a minimum of 30,000, and the second at 'not less than 20,000 poor'.[16] These figures are probably inflated, but they were believed at the time. The sharpened hostility of the anglican establishment towards Presbyterianism in the 1690s is obviously related to this perception. The growth in number of Presbyterian congregations at a time when the king remained cool towards the established church made its bishops more intolerant of dissent and more strident in defence of their own status.

Francophone Protestant refugees had been entering Ireland since the early decades of the century, and numbers had risen steeply in the 1670s. Persecution in France after 1685 led to a further influx in the 1690s. Some came as skilled artisans from London or other English centres of refuge, but a large proportion of the Irish Huguenot population of 1700 were officers from William's disbanded French regiments. The earl of Galway was both patron and, for many veterans, landlord of an exotic colony that developed around his new town of Portarlington. However, most Huguenots settled in the capital where they may have constituted as much as 5 per cent of Dublin's population by 1710. The veterans blended into the city's upper-class social and religious life, but the Huguenot merchants and artisans of Dublin remained apart, many of them members of non-conforming Calvinist congregations, unique in the legal toleration they enjoyed.

The war at sea hindered the recovery of foreign trade before 1697, and inland trade suffered as the official valuations of coins and their supply became unreliable. After a large inflow of coin in the early 1690s, a discrepancy between English and Irish valuations of the guinea caused a serious outflow of silver specie in 1694–95. A reduction in the official value of the guinea in England in April 1696, with no change in its Irish rate, led to a reversal of the pattern. The coinage in circulation rapidly increased again, but no inflation of prices resulted as there was a sharp recovery in farm output. This short-lived conjuncture made Irish exports very competitive at a time when international trade was itself recovering.

The last four years of the century produced circumstances very favourable for economic expansion. Few expected the high Irish currency valuations to last, and expectations of devaluation fuelled speculation in land and commodities in 1699 and 1700. As prices were raised the physical recovery was itself levelling off, with the effect of a further increase in inflationary pressures.[17] These facts need to be kept in mind when interpreting the political crisis of 1698–99, a crisis triggered by the rapid revival of the Irish woollen industry.

Fine woollen cloth had for centuries been the leading English export. The West Country, a notable woollen manufacturing region, was badly hit in the mid-1690s by the war and the English financial crisis. Before the war south Munster had sustained an export trade in West-Country types of cloth (bays and serges), using English techniques and immigrant workers for the most part. This Irish industry recovered in the mid-1690s precisely at the time when the parent region declined. John Cary, Bristol merchant and economic pamphleteer, was not alone in arguing for the Irish industry's suppression, nor in suggesting public encouragement of the nascent Irish linen industry instead, a policy first explored by Wentworth sixty years earlier. In 1696 the English duty on linen from Ireland was abolished, not – it seems – as part of such a substitution strategy but as the outcome of Capel's efforts to win concessions which would boost his popularity in Ireland. The abolition was ultimately to be of great consequence.

Early in 1697 a bill prohibiting Irish woollen exports was introduced in the English commons but failed for lack of official support. Nevertheless, the English government accepted that Irish woollens were a threat, to be phased out by the encouragement of flax and linen. England was a net importer of linen, and wartime access to the main continental sources was difficult. Such considerations influenced the new English board of trade where several members, including its secretary, the West Country man John Locke, drew up plans to mollify the English cloth lobby by diverting Irish energies into linen.

The demand in Westminster for a woollen act became louder as the opposition recognised a large stick for beating an embattled administration. In the ensuing pamphlet war, the first to treat Irish policy extensively, English writers attacked the Irish parliament while emphasising Ireland's subordinate role. Irish authors defended the woollen trade, played down its wider significance and stressed its importance to the English interest in Ireland; they also rightly represented weaving as an enclave activity, mainly confined to Protestant towns in Counties Cork and Waterford and to Dublin itself. Meanwhile, Methuen was having some success in persuading the English house of lords – until, that is, the circulation in London of a Dublin-printed book by William Molyneux: *The case of Ireland being bound by acts of parliament in England, stated* caused an uproar, and although Methuen managed to block immediate passage of a woollen act, the English parliament was stirred to address the king on the need to curb both Ireland's wool trade and the pretended freedoms of its parliament.

A Dubliner, Molyneux belonged to the Church of Ireland, represented the university in parliament, and was more scholar than politician. His book argued that Ireland was a separate kingdom under the crown, that the only legislation binding the king's subjects was that of an Irish parliament, that the Irish house of lords was the supreme court of appeal for Irish suits, and that recent instances of English legislation and adjudication relating to Ireland were exceptional and did not overturn the five-hundred-year-old Irish constitution. Attempts to suppress the Irish wool trade by English statute (and the concurrent case in the English lords over salmon fishing rights near Derry) made the question of the Dublin parliament's constitutional status highly topical. Molyneux was indebted to the unpublished work of his father-in-law, Sir William Domville, prepared for the Irish convention in 1660, and to the tract published by Patrick Darcy, the confederate lawyer, in 1643. One ingredient in Molyneux's argument revealed a greater intellectual radicalism. Drawing on Locke's *Two treatises on government* (1690) he referred in passing to 'self-evident' truths, asserting for example that 'the right of being subject only to such laws to which men give their own consent is so inherent to all mankind ... that 'tis not to be alien'd, or given up, by any body of men whatever'.[18] This natural-right argument formed a small element in his book, but it was eventually to influence eighteenth-century Irish political discourse.

Molyneux's constitutional arguments can easily be misinterpreted. He did not seek to abolish Poynings's law nor to lessen the crown's prerogative in Ireland. He was in no sense a separatist, his defence of the Irish parliament being essentially a defence of the liberties of the king's subjects in Ireland. (Most of these, he held, were the descendants of free-born Englishmen.) He saw a parliamentary union with England as an ideal but probably unrealisable arrangement, and until that came about the subject's rights could only be protected by a self-sufficient Dublin parliament. He was silent on the rights of Catholic Irishmen.

Such criticism was therefore directed towards Westminster and especially towards the view (increasingly common in the 1690s) that it was an imperial parliament with full powers to legislate for all the king's dominions. In this perspective, Ireland was as much a dependency as Virginia, being either a colonial plantation or a conquered nation. But one constitutional fact that Molyneux failed to register was the significance of 1689: Westminster, by formally determining that William and Mary were rightful rulers of Great Britain and Ireland, had become the ultimate locus of sovereignty.

Ironically one argument that had been used by those in the Church of Ireland morally uneasy about the transfer of allegiance from James, held that William and Mary had a right to their allegiance simply by the fact of conquest under divine providence. As Bishop Wetenhall put it in 1691, 'I do aver us in Ireland conquered, and with my heart bless God for it'.[19] Molyneux's invocation of contract theory and its subsequent attractiveness closed down that line of argument in Protestant Ireland. In the longer term, the *Case* laid the foundations for the patriot ideology of the 1750s and 1760s. But in the short term it was regarded as badly mistimed and highly embarrassing by leading politicians in Dublin, including Molyneux's friends. And rightly so: his attempt to weaken the woollen prohibitionists' case was to be entirely counterproductive, for he had underestimated the sensitivity of the English parliament at a time when relations between Westminster and the crown were under extreme stress. An attack on the competence of the English parliament in Irish affairs was easily interpreted as an attempt to bolster the crown's position, and several of Molyneux's arguments were unfortunately the arguments used by William himself. In addition, the assertion that it was up to the Irish parliament to decide how England should be repaid the monies outlaid on the Williamite campaigns cut directly across anti-court plans for the Irish forfeitures.

The failure of the Irish parliament to act decisively on the woollen question, coupled with the improved political position of the opposition at Westminster, made a woollen ban almost inevitable. The new English bill proposed a prohibition on the export of all types of woollen cloth except to England itself, and placed what amounted to a penal tariff on all Irish woollens entering England from Ireland except coarse frieze. Royal assent was granted in May 1699, and the news was greeted dismally in Ireland: 'had they made an act to have hanged us all it had been better for us to die martyrs than to live slaves'.[20] Constitutional shame as much as economic consequence wounded Ireland's political elite. Yet the effects were real. Two-thirds of the country's fine woollen exports and one-third of the frieze had been despatched through Cork ports in 1698; now in south Munster some eight hundred weaving families were reported emigrating from the region – 'there are no common English left … at all'.[21] However, the long-term impact of the prohibition was small, despite what pamphleteers and critics of English policy asserted in the next century. For all the talk, exports of fine cloth had been modest, being worth about £57,000 in 1698, with frieze exports worth £46,000 – in all about 10 per cent of the total value of exports in a decade when overall volumes and values were volatile. The affected areas diversified fairly easily, Munster and west Leinster into the large-scale production of woollen and worsted yarn for England, Dublin by increasing its share of the home market for high quality cloth.

In Ireland, extreme reaction to the English woollen act included the criticism by prominent anglicans that it had betrayed the English interest in Ireland, undermining in particular the economy of Church of Ireland (and Quaker) urban communities in the south. Official encouragement of linen was seen as no compensation because flax and linen were already associated with a different part of the country, the north, and with Presbyterians. Such views were exaggerated: Catholic tenants grew most of the flax, and anglican Armagh was soon to grow wealthy on linen-weaving and bleaching. The end of the very old frieze trade hit not new English but Catholic Irish weavers in the hinterlands of rural Waterford and Cork.

* * *

Post-war tension between William and the powerful country opposition in Westminster centred on the issue of the 90,000-strong English army. Ever suspicious of French intentions, William had no wish to disband it, but public opinion in England demanded a return to the very modest scale of Charles II's army in the 1670s. By a formula worked out in the commons, Ireland became in effect a reserve camp where extra regiments, beyond the minimal 7,000 men left on the English establishment, were to be maintained – at Ireland's expense. The year 1691 had seen the end of a distinctive Irish army, and these arrangements in 1699 (by which 12,000 men were normally to be garrisoned on the island) did not create a separate Irish command but involved the maintenance of a small general staff and ordnance in Dublin, accountable to London, with the Irish regiments freely available for overseas service. The existing garrison, much of it in place since 1692, included several Huguenot and Protestant Irish regiments and these were all to be disbanded – much to royal and Irish chagrin. Veterans from the continental war made up the new 'Irish' army.

These momentous decisions affecting Ireland's defence, the Irish budget and the careers of thousands of Irishmen were all made at

Westminster, during a period when the Irish parliament was for the most part not in session. Yet among the Irish gentry these were not unpopular decisions; in 1697 the Irish parliament had allocated funds for a major barracks-building programme, and between 1698 and 1701 over £100,000 was spent on about one hundred barracks of greatly varying size. One explanation for this precocious Irish initiative lay in the residual problem posed by rapparees, another in the shortage of inns suitable for garrison accommodation. The new deployment differed from the arbitrary Restoration arrangements: the cavalry were to be concentrated in purpose-built inland barracks, with the infantry fairly evenly distributed. Thirty-six redoubts, small fortified forts in remote places 'for securing the dangerous passes (and bridges) from tories and rapparees' were concentrated in two areas – the south Ulster/north Connacht counties, and north-east Munster. By the 1720s the rapparee threat was a thing of the past, and these redoubts were by then nearly all abandoned.[22] At the other end of the scale was the huge military complex on the north-west edge of Dublin. Completed in 1708, the Royal Barracks was one of the largest in Europe. Symbol of a new age, it was a formidable but open citadel.

The army, wool, and the unfinished business of the confiscated Jacobite estates were the three Irish-related issues which swirled and eddied through English politics between 1697 and 1700, and the dispute over Jacobite forfeitures brought the most bitter clashes between Westminster and the king. Until 1697, William had evaded the issue, attempting to grant as much as possible of the Irish properties deemed forfeit to close Dutch and English supporters, to soldiers prominent in the Irish war, and to political creditors. Delay in ratifying the Treaty of Limerick rendered many of these grants provisional. With the backlog of petitions from ex-Jacobites cleared by 1699, the future of those estates confirmed as forfeit had to be decided. Pressure from army debenture-holders seeking redemption at par from Irish land sales, and a wider antagonism towards what were seen as William's excessive grants, resulted in the appointment of an English parliamentary commission; this was to inquire into the outlawry procedures, the pardons, and the king's use of the royal prerogative to cut large slices out of the now diminished forfeitures. The commissioners were nearly all Irish MPs, and the majority report was damning. It claimed that the forfeited lands were worth £1.5 million, but this was an overestimate both of acreage and value. More important, though, was the report's fairly explicit criticism of the royal grants.

The English commons decided to challenge the crown and to 'resume' without compensation all the Irish properties assigned by William over the previous decade, and to appoint trustees to sell these properties and the unapportioned part of the Jacobite forfeitures. Parliament's assertion of power over the king succeeded, and the new forfeiture trustees arrived in Dublin in June 1700 to hear all claims on the 620,000 acres (Irish) still deemed confiscated, and to sell those lands which were clearly forfeit.

As a judicial body acting by English parliamentary authority the trustees were coldly received in Dublin, despite the Irish connections of several of them. To Methuen and the lords justices, they were an unwelcome intrusion and a challenge to the royal prerogative in Ireland. Government officials and leading MPs were among the potential victims of the trustees. William Conolly, a Donegal lawyer already famed for an astonishing ascent to riches, had been the largest purchaser of grantees' land, and in 1701 he rallied about half the other purchasers to urge the gentry of every county to petition the king on the dire effects of the resumption on all Protestants. The future Speaker's campaign did not wholly succeed, but terms were improved and Conolly with many others was able to reacquire the disputed land on fairly easy terms. He went on to invest heavily in further forfeited estates in 1703.

It took two years to process 3,140 claims made by the relatives and creditors of forfeiting owners and by others disputing the ownership of land deemed forfeit. By the time the residual half million acres (Irish) were put up for sale in the autumn of 1702, land values had fallen, so that the results were very disappointing for the trustees. By new English legislation only Protestants could buy, and the three hundred and sixty who did so were mostly Irish gentry or large merchants. Less than half the land offered was however sold, and the unsold properties passed to a London consortium; they soon regretted their investment. With the end of the trustees' business in 1703, the Williamite land settlement was completed. As no further outlawries or pardons occurred, landlords gradually ceased to worry about the durability of their titles. For the Catholic gentry, the settlement ultimately reduced their pre-war property by a third. Half the residual 14 per cent of Ireland still owned by them had been secured through the favourable terms negotiated at Galway and Limerick.[23]

The economic recession which damaged the trustees' auctions had begun in 1701. The next five years were among the most difficult of the new century. Perceptive contemporaries saw it as due 'to a concurrence of accidents'.[24] A post-war recovery in north-west Europe had petered out in 1701, and in June of that year the Irish government lowered the exchange rate of the guinea coin within Ireland by more than 11 per cent, bringing it closer to the English value of 1696. This was in effect a revaluation of the Irish money of account, making Irish goods significantly less attractive to outside buyers (until domestic prices fell back). Then war returned in 1702 between France and the allies, and with it the disruption of Irish trade with Spain and Portugal. Finally, at home, the Woollen Act and the forfeitures business helped to reduce economic activity, the latter by drawing nearly £300,000 out of the country. Between 1700 and 1703 agricultural prices fell between a quarter and a half, and exchequer receipts by a third. Markets were 'dead' and merchants ceased trading. By 1703 landowners were feeling the effects of what in some regions amounted to a rent famine, but tenants who had taken leases in the deceptive prosperity of the later 1690s were the main victims.

No parliament had met for four and a half years after 1698 as pressure on the exchequer was relieved by very high revenue yields in 1698, 1699, and 1700. The Irish government passed into the hands of the Tory earl of Rochester in 1700, an appointment reflecting the party colour of William's last ministry. Remembered for his activities in the 1680s, Rochester made little mark in Ireland. For three years politics were dominated by the public and private conflicts surrounding the forfeiture trustees. Their occupation of the parliament house to carry out their business had been most apt. Outside the building, the first of Dublin's great statues, King William on his horse, was unveiled on the anniversary of the Boyne in 1701. Within a year, both William and his royal adversary in exile were dead.

THE SPIRIT OF PARTY

Late in the summer of 1703, over a year after Queen Anne's accession and at a time when Irish state finances were sharply deteriorating, parliamentary elections were held and an unprecedented number of seats were contested. A new 'spirit of party', in essence a stronger identification by candidates with national policies supported or opposed by the government of the day, was beginning to emerge; the labels 'Whig' and 'Tory' were applicable to a growing number of MPs. In England the Tory faction was dominant at court and in parliament, with the 'high church' wing assertively defending the anglican church and radiating hostility towards its enemies, especially Protestant dissent. The Whigs defended the right to religious dissent, and celebrated the constitutional and personal liberties secured in 1688. And – unlike some Tories – they adopted an unambiguous position on the question of who was to be the childless Anne's successor. They were committed since 1701 to Prince George of Hanover, no matter what inducements James II's son in France might offer. In Ireland such factions had emerged more slowly: men divided less sharply upon policy and more obviously upon family connection and religious origin than was the case in England.

The new lord lieutenant was the second duke of Ormond, grandson of the old cavalier and a professional soldier. Given his standing at court and his family's influence in Ireland, he came to Dublin with real advantages over his predecessors. But he possessed more of the first duke's weaknesses than his strengths. He sought to use his local cross-party popularity to soothe divisions and secure a pliant parliament. Thus Ormond supported Alan Brodrick for the commons speakership despite the latter's anti-Tory background.

Before parliament met, the Irish council in consultation with London had prepared a legislative programme. A new popery bill was proposed which would curtail the inheritance rights of the Catholic gentry and prevent Catholics purchasing any 'Protestant' land or leasing it for terms longer than 31-year tenancies. As proposals these were not without Irish precedent, but their passage onto the legislative agenda was assisted by the example of a Westminster law of 1700: an anti-court measure initiated by the radical Jack Howe MP, this had prohibited English Catholics from buying any land whatever. The Irish council draft also proposed to ban Catholic residence inside Limerick or Galway cities (a small number of merchants *in situ* excepted). London queried this detail among others, with the result that no draft was ready when parliament met. The task of devising heads for such a bill now passed to the Irish commons. The government saw the bill (and parallel ones that would prohibit the entry into Ireland of foreign-educated secular Cathlic clergy, and oblige existing parish clergy to register formally) as the means to an immediate political end – the winning of majority support among MPs for urgent revenue measures, at a time when the gentry were highly discontented at the state of the economy and the state of their purses. Neither Ormond's circle nor others with Tory links in England were wholly keen on such severity, and resistance to it was expected in the Irish lords.

Before the popery bill made headway in parliament, the assembled gentry turned to a more fundamental question, the case for abolishing parliament itself. Ever since the wars, legislative union had been repeatedly raised by Protestant politicians – Brodrick, Cox, and Molyneux among others – and there was cross-party willingness to petition the queen for such a measure. Renewed economic crisis and the growing likelihood of an Anglo-Scottish union were now the catalysts acting upon a sharpened perception that the English parliament was behaving in a predatory manner towards Ireland, subverting Protestant liberties and damaging the economy. Some feared that Westminster might soon tax Ireland directly and so eliminate the necessity for Irish parliaments. And it was in this parliamentary session that the rhetorical link between Irish poverty and English policy was truly forged. But the near unanimity of lords and commons for Anglo-Irish union found no response in London. Union remained a fond Irish cause for the rest of the decade yet it never reached the government's agenda.

In this context Ormond's sponsorship of the popery bill was designed to win goodwill in a distracted commons, and the house found itself considering an English privy council draft.[25] Clauses were added obliging Catholic landowners to abandon primogeniture and to divide their estates equally among male offspring (except where the eldest son conformed, whereupon the reversionary interest of the whole estate passed to him), and forcing Catholic freeholders to take an oath of abjuration before parliamentary elections. In this form the commons' heads went to England. In response, a lobby at the English privy council representing the Irish Catholic gentry was organised, and England's Catholic allies were stirred to make diplomatic approaches. The new popery bill was returned to Dublin not diluted but strengthened. It was now proposed to ban Catholics from purchasing or long-leasing any land, Catholic or Protestant, along the lines of the English act of 1700. Moreover, Irish Protestant dissenters were also to be placed under further disabilities; only those prepared to take a sacramental test would in future be permitted to hold public office, receive a military commission or sit in a municipal corporation. The 'test' clause resembled the English Test Act of 1673 which was currently in abeyance there because of the Toleration Act. Its inclusion was probably designed by Ormond's English allies to increase support for the popery bill in the Irish lords.

This, the most important of the penal laws, met little opposition in its formal passage. However, a team of Catholic lawyers including the two law officers of Tyrconnell's government appeared both before the Irish commons and the lords as counsel representing a group of Catholic peers and gentlemen to make submissions against what was represented as a direct breach of several articles in the Treaty of Limerick. Recent Catholic behaviour, it was argued, gave no cause for such a new departure, but as long as Catholic spokesmen had to admit conscientious objections to any oath abjuring James's title to the throne their loyalty was in doubt, and the return of war and the fresh possibility of a Jacobite invasion closed the case in Protestant eyes. There was apparently no opposition to the Catholic clauses of the bill, and only twenty (mainly Ulster) MPs voted against the act as a whole in protest at the sacramental test. Furthermore, Irish MPs greatly resented suggestions made in England at the time of the wool controversies that Irish Protestants had been peculiarly lenient towards Catholics, had aspirations of 'independency', and were in many cases covert Jacobites. The radical 1703–4 popery act disposed of that myth. Indeed, among some Protestants, particularly Church of Ireland clergy, the dormant commitment to a general conversion of Catholic Ireland was once again coming to life.

The government's principal concern in 1703 was to secure additional taxes at a time of falling revenue. Ormond had sought a three-year supply, but even with the prospect of a popery bill anti-court sentiment prevailed and supplies for only one year were offered. Brodrick, despite being Speaker, led the 'country' and whiggish opposition, talking of a need for frequent parliaments to redress economic grievances. Government then sought a two-year supply and this compromise was carried by only three votes. After the session closed, Ormond dismissed Brodrick and his troublesome allies, and constructed a more thoroughly Tory administration.

In the course of the 1703–4 parliamentary session the Church of Ireland bishops and representatives of the lower clergy had met for the first time since 1666 in 'convocation'. Government had summoned it in 1703 – but only under pressure from the church itself, backed by powerful high church interests in London. Their demand for strong crown leadership of an authoritarian established church in England found warm support in Ireland among the embattled (and in many cases impoverished) anglican clergy. The revival of convocation by the state was seen by some as the first step towards restoring the church's role as a distinct corporation with a moral mission to all of Irish society.

The Church of Ireland's position was indeed peculiar. The new penal legislation reflected the overwhelming anglicanism of the political elite, and offered the prospect of enlarged membership for the future. Yet the dismal internal state of the Church of Ireland had attracted little notice in the Irish commons. Its financial resources were in many dioceses inadequate to rebuild churches destroyed in the wars or even to support the clergy. Bishops' incomes varied widely, and parochial clergy depended on the tithe paid by all landholders, yet in about a quarter of the parishes the clergy's right to rectorial tithes had long since been alienated to local landowning family. This led to many of the 600-odd incumbents – the younger sons of Protestant merchants, big tenants or small landowners, usually graduates of Dublin University – taking several parishes in order to sustain the kind of life to which they were accustomed. The resulting pluralism was made worse by the indifferent quality of the bishops, even the new Williamite appointees. Foy of Waterford and King of Derry were almost alone among the twenty-two on the bench in actively lobbying for reform in finance and appointments procedures, and in trying to instil a sense of collective religious purpose. The convocations of Anne's reign were very disappointing for those who sought major changes. Emerging when the status of the established church was perhaps the most highly charged issue in English domestic politics, the Irish convocation was quite unable to divorce genuine ecclesiastical problems from party politics.

Irish politics between 1704 and 1710 proceeded in the shadow of a slow-moving continental and naval war. English war aims now determined alliance strategies, turning the European struggle into one for commercial and colonial ascendancy, especially within the Spanish empire. A French counter-move in the form of a Jacobite invasion was attempted in 1708 when the weather and the British navy combined to prevent James II's son, the Stuart claimant James III, from landing in Scotland. By then however a Jacobite restoration was more likely to occur through a Tory government's repudiation of the Hanoverian succession than by military action.

War kept the Irish economy in the doldrums throughout the decade, with some signs of recovery appearing after 1707. Harvests were very bad in 1708 and 1709, but famine in parts of western Europe made for far worse conditions there. Irish economic grievances were kept in the background of parliamentary politics by religious and party controversy. Ormond's administration was becoming vulnerable as high church influence waned in London, being undermined by Whig politicians who promised stronger backing for the war. Whigs began to influence policy from about 1705, and in the Irish context this held out promise of a less partisan viceroy and repeal of the 1704 test clause – thus Ormond's abrupt replacement by the moderate earl of Pembroke in 1707. This altered style rather than policy, for it soon emerged that Pembroke had no desire to repeal the test. Indeed a large majority of Irish MPs opposed the relief of dissenters, which led English politicians mistakenly to assume that the Irish gentry were uniformly Tory.

Loosely defined ideologies rather than concrete programmes divided the parties in Ireland. Whigs developed an exaggerated reverence for William's memory and for 'revolution principles'; the protection of individual liberties and of Protestantism overrode any royal hereditary principle, and thus the Hanoverian succession had their total support. Protestant unity against a still potent Catholicism was often invoked by Irish Whigs, though links with dissenters were played down by many Irish anglican Whigs, and test repeal was only supported by those Whigs from mainly Presbyterian constituencies. Irish Tories answered with an extreme loyalism towards Anne's person, were committed to defend the Church of Ireland's privileges (though not to its reform), and to the rigorous enforcement of the law against dissent, portraying Presbyterianism and all things Scottish as subversive of episcopacy and of monarchy. James II's removal in 1688 was seen as an unfortunate necessity, and most Irish Tories regarded the Hanoverian succession in a similar light; their aim was not to defeat it but to build Tory political control while their patron Anne was still on the throne. And just as politically active Whigs were for the most part not dissenters, a majority of Tories were not pro-Catholic, despite Whig propaganda. The 1703 anti-popery bill had been introduced by the Tory MP for County Louth, Henry Tenison, and towards the end of the reign the aggressively Tory regime in Dublin Castle made no effort to repeal anti-Catholic legislation. New penal proposals were however opposed by Tories, and the increasingly explicit support of Catholics and nominal conformers for the Tories gave their opponents a stick to beat them with. It was no coincidence that the Tory gentry in many counties were descended from pre-1641 settlers or from Old English families, whereas Whigs had stronger Cromwellian origins.

The parliament of 1703 remained in existence till 1711. By 1709 the two groupings seem to have had fairly even support. Pembroke was replaced by the earl of Wharton, as strong an advocate of the Presbyterian interest as Robartes or Essex forty years before, and perhaps the most anti-Catholic governor since Orrery. Wharton's larger than life personality stirred up Irish politics: the administration teemed with Tory dismissals and Whig appointments. A popery bill, set aside in 1707 because of successful Catholic lobbying in London, reappeared in 1709 with Wharton's endorsement, its many clauses designed to close the loopholes of 1697 and 1703–4, with lavish inducements for 'priest-catchers' and discoverers of property illegally obtained or held by Catholics. Tighter tests for conformers were proposed, and all priests registering under the 1704 act were now to be obliged to take an oath abjuring James III. Wharton's personal involvement and the shock of the Jacobite expedition to Scotland ensured a large local majority for what was to be the last of the major penal laws, and no trouble in London.

When Wharton planned to introduce a toleration bill along English lines, the Presbyterians showed remarkably little interest. The Irish government had failed to get such a bill through in 1692 or in 1695, when Presbyterians had pressed for such a concession. Now they turned down the offer lest it delay the removal of the test – though the virtual disappearance of any harassment of Presbyterians also played its part. The number of Presbyterians returned to parliament fluctuated between five and nine in the general elections between 1703 and 1727, but the number of Presbyterian voters, especially in urban boroughs, fell sharply.

Nearly all Ulster Presbyterian congregations at this stage belonged to the General Synod of Ulster, established in 1690 from five pre-existing presbyteries. This well-organised body witnessed institutional growth through the huge Scottish immigration of the 1690s and through the extension of congregations to districts where dissent had previously no formal presence. Between 1707 and 1716 the number of Irish congregations rose by nearly 30 per cent,[26] helped by support from the newly established Presbyterian Church of Scotland and its academies. In the next generation, the fall-off in immigration and the eruption of a series of doctrinal disputes was to make Presbyterianism far less menacing to the anglican elite. That was in the future: in 1710 Wharton's support for the already vigorous institutions of dissent seemed sinister and perverse to his many enemies.

A moderate Tory administration under Robert Harley was appointed by the queen in August 1710. His sudden elevation alarmed Irish Whigs. Speaker Brodrick felt that matters were now 'just as in the beginnings of eighty-eight, before any news of the Prince of Orange's expedition'.[27] But to Irish Tories, memories of the revolution seemed relevant: the prompt replacement of Wharton by Ormond seemed like another Williamite deliverance, this time 'from presbytery and the insults of a dissenting faction just going to devour us and all kingly government'.[28]

By the time Ormond reached Ireland again in mid-1711, the reins of government were effectively in the hands of a high church barrister, the new lord chancellor, Sir Constantine Phipps. His abrasive Tory partisanship reminded older Whigs of Tyrconnell; Phipps's object, however, was merely to revive the battered Tory party. It was he rather than Ormond who was responsible for the abnormal purge of office-holders, the privy council, the revenue commissioners, and the magistracy, and he gave Irish Tories their head in pursuing legal vendettas against prominent Whigs. A bitter parliamentary dispute broke out in 1711 over the inclusion or otherwise of 'revolution principles' in the commons' resolution granting money towards the university's new library, and for most of the session a war of transparently coded words raged between the mainly Tory upper house and the increasingly Whig-dominated commons. With government losing control of parliament, a general election and the creation of a Tory majority seemed necessary before parliament could meet again.

Phipps as the dominant lord justice remained in control throughout 1712, tightening the Tory hold on the judiciary and central government. Interference in the boroughs for party advantage was now blatantly pursued in preparation for a general election. Phipps's enemies noted that many recent converts from Catholicism were associating with the government. Harley (now earl of Oxford) planned to replace Ormond but long delays in finding a suitable moderate left Phipps to his own devices. In the most public battle – between the Whig-dominated Dublin corporation and the Irish privy council – the city fathers had refused to accept a Castle-imposed Tory mayor in 1711. The dispute became a stalemate in 1713, and in protest local government of the city virtually ceased. This Dublin piece of farce received wide attention, even in London, being seen as a trial of strength between Phipps and the Whigs, and an indication of how far Whitehall would back the strong Tory programme. The political prize, control over the forthcoming parliamentary election in the capital, was almost forgotten.

The extreme polarisation of Irish Protestant politics between 1711 and 1713 was viewed with alarm by Oxford and most of his government in London. Preoccupied with negotiations for a controversial peace with France, he had no wish to humiliate the Irish Whigs. In 1712 he tried unsuccessfully to persuade an ex-Whig ally, the duke of Shrewsbury, to take over from Ormond. Shrewsbury eventually agreed to take up the viceroyalty in 1713, with instructions to settle the Dublin city dispute by compromise and to prepare for a new parliament.

Phipps had already laid the foundations for a Tory victory by the widespread appointment of Tory sheriffs and the intimidation of those who controlled borough constituencies to ensure that they returned Tory members, and Church of Ireland bishops and clergy were enthusiastic partisans. There was an unprecedented number of contested elections – in at least two-thirds of the counties and nearly half the boroughs.[29] Dublin was not alone in having a violent riot during polling. Whigs exaggerated the importance of Catholic support for the Tories, making much of the dozen-odd Tory MPs who were recent converts. Both sides in fact indulged in fairly crude electoral malpractice.

The results were taken as a modest Tory victory: in only ten counties had Whig-connected candidates taken both seats, while in fourteen, two Tory MPs were elected. The strong Tory showing in south Leinster and Tipperary, Connacht and the north midlands suggests a positive correlation between Tory success and the relative survival of Catholic voters. But Shrewsbury failed to translate Tory electoral strength into government majorities: the litmus test was the speakership, and having first hesitated he backed the colourless Sir Richard Levinge, Speaker of the disastrous 1692 parliament. Alan Brodrick won over a disaffected group of Tories and his election by four votes set the tone for the session. The Whig group in the commons seized the initiative and investigated a number of 'excesses' of the Tory government over the previous three years. Gaining momentum they had no difficulty in securing a majority for an address to the queen demanding Phipps's dismissal, particularly pointing to the Dublin mayoralty. A supply bill was postponed until political scores were settled.

At the beginning of 1714, there was total political deadlock on the question of Phipps's future; parliament had to be prorogued. This left the viceroy with the practical problem of running a government without the normal 'additional revenue'. State expenditure was clipped back, the *regium donum* cancelled, and customs duties lapsed in what was the first year of peace, thereby accelerating the recovery of trade and creating a short import boom. During the early summer of 1714 Bolingbroke began to get the upper hand over Oxford at court, and this had immediate repercussions in Ireland: a drastic Schism Act, intended to suppress dissenters' schools and colleges, included Ireland in its scope, and some Irish Tory justices of the peace (JPs) tried to enforce it. But for all their partisan fury, the Tories in the three kingdoms were riven by factional strife when the queen died in August.

Anne had taken little interest in Irish affairs and, at a personal level, contributed little. But by her death and particularly in its timing, the old politics of party predicated on uncertainty in the overlapping spheres of religion and the succession came to an abrupt end. The roller-coaster politics of the previous ten years did, however, leave important Irish legacies. The institution of parliament (especially the commons) had been strengthened through use and by party tensions. Between 1703 and 1713 there had been seven sessions, each lasting several months. Procedures became more sophisticated, the use of committees more extensive, and the origination of legislation through heads of bills in the commons now far more frequent than the drafting of bills in either Irish or British privy council. Without this training, the Whig resistance to Tory executive power in 1713 would hardly have been so successful.

With greater *de facto* influence, the College Green parliament saw the aspiration for union wither; one should not, however, exaggerate the loyalty of either warring faction to a separate, self-sufficient Irish parliament. Even Brodrick, the great survivor since 1692 and a most effective faction manager, was prepared to lobby for a Westminster act in 1708 to overturn the test when Pembroke had failed to push for its repeal in the Irish parliament. At the constituency level, the recent growth in contests led to a more careful approach to borough management by patrons and, in Irish counties, to more tightly organised political networks among the gentry.

A second political legacy lay in the manner in which the new penal legislation was to be enforced. In the area of Catholic property restrictions, inadequacies and loopholes in the initial 1703–4 legislation were quickly spotted; amendments were drawn up in 1707 and enacted in 1709. The mechanism for discovering concealments was from the start the private informer, but only in the 1709 act were the rewards sufficiently handsome to bring results. A related statute in 1709 led to the establishment of a national registry of deeds where records of all property conveyances had to be entered for public inspection. Such legislation governing property was in the short term fairly successful in changing the nominal religious affiliation of many Catholic gentry. In the years after 1704 there had only been about six legal conformities a year whereas in the two decades after 1709 there were about 500 in all, a significant minority of whom were substantial landowners or heirs to property. Laws directly excluding Catholics from political power, such as the bar on entering municipal office and parliament, predated the 1690s; they were easy to enforce and were now rigorously observed. Laws relating to the visible symbols of power – possession of arms and fine horses – were used far more occasionally. Implementation of the purely ecclesiastical legislation was spotty, being dependent both on government or parliamentary action, and on the willingness of JPs and county grand juries to apply the full extremes of the new laws. And despite the rewards for arresting unregistered clergy, the gentry in the later years of Anne's reign exerted themselves only when prompted by government proclamation, as in 1708 after the Jacobite scare and in 1712 when Ormond became alarmed at possible clerical involvement in a cattle-maiming campaign in Connacht. For the most part, even with the army dispersed round the country, rural magistrates were wary of mounting local offensives against their Catholic tenants' clergy. This pattern of 'connivance with menaces' was to become the norm as government interest in priest-hunting subsided after 1720. The clause of the 1709 Popery Act extending the oath of abjuration to parish clergy was the most obvious example of the law running ahead of the means – or the will – to its enforcement. Over a thousand priests had been prepared to register under the 1704 legislation, less than a hundred agreed to swear the 1709 oath.

As for converting the Catholic laity there was a brief flurry of interest after 1709, mainly among Ulster Church of Ireland clergy, and a new evangelising mission using Irish-speaking preachers was equipped with an Irish-language Bible and *Book of common prayer*, helped by the London funds of the Society for Promoting Christian Knowledge. The project was supported in innocuous resolutions in the convocation and in the commons, but quickly disappeared from view in the larger debates on church, state, and dissent. Neither party and no major politician was at this time prepared to champion the general conversion of the Catholic masses through the vernacular. And while there were many more churchmen who saw an opportunity to protestantise Catholic Ireland through the aggressive provision of anglophone education, even they found no strong political current on which to swim.[30]

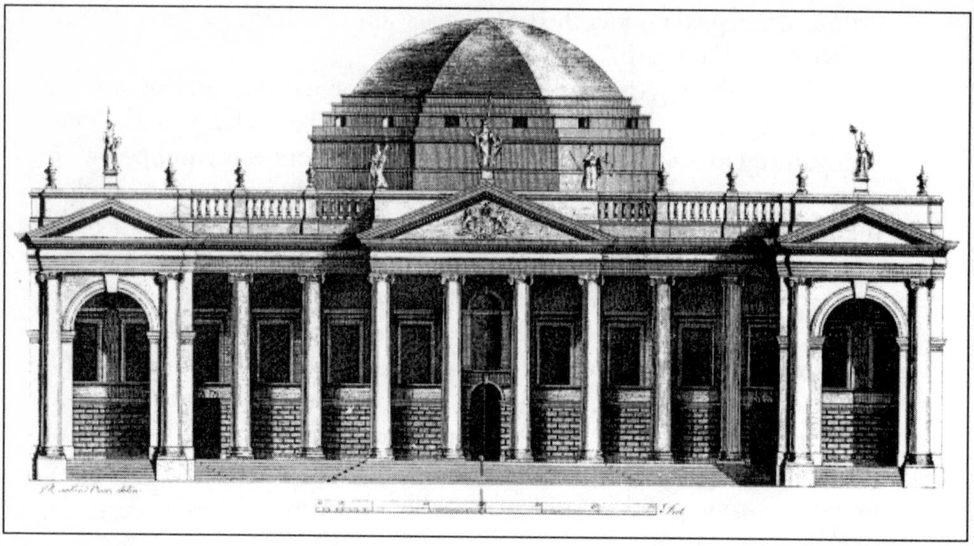

Elevation of the College Green facade of the new Parliament House, designed by Edward Lovett Pearce and first used in 1732. It was recognized as one of the most imposing buildings erected anywhere in *ancien regime* Europe to house a *parlement*, a diet or any form of legislative assembly, and was a physical affirmation of the status and pretensions of the Irish institution. (Engr. by Patrick Halpin, 1767)

3

Hibernia Anglicana, 1714–60

THE HANOVERIAN REGIME

FIVE YEARS of extreme parliamentary volatility and constitutional uncertainty were swiftly terminated in August 1714 by the successful legitimation of George, elector of Hanover, as sovereign of the three kingdoms, and by the emergence of a firmly Whig government in London, allied to the court but to a novel degree independent of it. 'This miraculous lucky turn of the public affairs'[1] (as Irish Whigs saw it) ushered in a period of unmitigated disaster for the Tory party, in England and in Ireland, but however inevitable the demise of the Tories might appear in retrospect, it was the immediate events surrounding the change of dynasty that brought to an end the two-party character of Irish politics, and ensured 'the Whig ascendancy'.

The behaviour of the Irish Tories, following the return of Dublin Castle into their hands in 1710, had done much to inflame partisan passions and certainly invited some measure of retribution when the tables were turned. Before 1714 Whigs had come to believe their own propaganda concerning the Jacobitism of leading Irish Tories. Their suspicions were to be sensationally confirmed a year after George I's accession when the former lord lieutenant, the duke of Ormond, followed Bolingbroke and fled to France. Neither politician had been a full-blooded opponent of the Hanoverian succession, and persecution by the new Whig regime more than commitment to the house of Stuart drove both men to James III's court at St Germain. Indeed the great majority of Protestant Irishmen who had voted for Tory candidates in the 1713 general election – whether on the grounds of religious sentiment or because of political connections – can only have been relieved in the autumn of 1714 that the Protestant succession was secure. Few anticipated so total an eclipse of a party that had appeared to have such a strong electoral base in the three kingdoms, or of the ministers who had secured an end to the long war with France, a commercial recovery at home, and the protection of the established church from its theological enemies. However, within a few months of the queen's death, in Ireland as elsewhere, a total purge of Tories from the Irish privy council, the judiciary, the magistracy, the army, the revenue and from offices of state held 'at pleasure', had begun. Events in the following year – explosive Jacobite risings in Scotland and the north of England against the new dynasty, and Ormond's defection to France – reinforced trends under way: the political victimisation of those in church and state who were strongly identified with the Tory cause, and a more general withering away of the 'Tory interest' within Protestant Ireland. Many seats went uncontested in the Irish general election of 1715, but where identifiable party contests occurred the Tories suffered. The Irish house of lords, with its large complement of Tory-inclined bishops, was soon sorted out by the new government; it secured control with the unprecedented creation of eleven peers in 1715, all drawn from Whig landowning families.

The arrival of the new dynasty on the British throne was, on the face of it, of little relevance for Catholic Ireland. One Tory Church of Ireland cleric, commenting on Anne's death, reassured his English correspondent that there was 'not the least motion from the Papists who … are contented with their potatoes and buttermilk and hard labour, and look no further …'.[2] More whiggish Protestants may have been less confident, but the Jacobite risings across the Irish sea in 1715 – in which English and Scottish Catholic involvement was so pronounced – helped to demonstrate the relative military security of Ireland. No Irish-based complicity in these eruptions was revealed, and there was no Irish echo of what were spontaneous risings in the Tory heartlands of northern Britain. Indeed there was greater rioting and public expression of support for the Jacobite cause in London during the winter of 1715–16 than in all Ireland (the only reported disturbances being in east Ulster, apparently between Presbyterians and supporters of the Church of Ireland). Yet the collapse of the Jacobite challenge in 1716 certainly registered among the Irish-language literati north and south, and the mixture of despair and providential expectation, already established in seventeenth-century Irish writing, was refashioned to look beyond the Hanoverian present. The prospect of a Jacobite restoration, whether expressed explicitly or allegorically, remained the most powerful theme resonating in Irish-language political poetry for the next fifty years. But to those who were actually in James III's confidence, Ireland was never seen as an inviting launch-pad for a military challenge to the Hanoverian regime, nor was its particular status a dynastic priority. A swift attack on the centre of British power was to be the consistent preference of Jacobite planners and their backers.

Although Irish Catholics were passive in 1714 and 1715, the events of those years did have their impact on the Catholic elite. The political eclipse of the Tory interest in Ireland was a major reverse for the surviving Catholic gentry. The willingness of Irish Tories before 1714 to mobilise Catholic electoral support, to oppose at least some of the anti-Catholic legislation, and to draw support from ex-Catholic *converso* lawyers and others of ambiguous religious loyalty, had offered some prospect to propertied Catholics of a re-entry into the political nation. The new configuration of Irish politics and the effective end of ideological discord within Protestant Ireland was far less promising.

The two most striking tendencies in Irish politics under George I were the growth in the number of English-born and, in some cases, English-based office-holders, privy councillors, judges and Church of Ireland bishops; and in the Irish house of commons the replacement of ideologically committed party blocks by a number of 'factions' or informal associations of MPs, which were held together by family connection or personal loyalty to the leading member, the common objective being to maximise the group's access to government patronage.

At first the reconstituted privy council was dominated by local Whigs. Their leader in the Irish commons, Alan Brodrick, was made lord chancellor, and most of the immediate judicial appointments went to Irish Whigs as well. But things began to change even before the first Hanoverian parliamentary session; on the resignation of the earl of Sunderland (lord lieutenant 1714–15), two English-based lords justices were appointed to manage Irish affairs, the earl of Galway and one of Charles II's natural grandchildren, the duke of Grafton. From thenceforward the appointment of Englishmen to key positions in the government of Ireland became more common, although not as prevalent as some protested. Without exception, those holding the viceregal office itself were senior English peers connected with the Whig magnates – Viscount Townshend (1716–17), the duke of Bolton (1717–20), the duke of Grafton (1720–24) – although Townshend never reached Ireland, and Bolton and Grafton only took up residence during the biennial parliamentary sessions. The practical responsibility for executive government was left to those who were appointed lords justices, key Irish-based office-holders such as Brodrick (now Viscount Midleton), Archbishop King and William Conolly (Speaker of the commons from 1715), but they had little scope to exercise independent patronage.

The ease with which Whig supremacy had been secured in Ireland led successive ministries in London to undervalue their Irish allies and tempted them after 1715 to reward certain English supporters with offices and 'places' in Ireland. The reaction to this and to other mishandling of Irish sensitivities provoked growing resentment in the Irish parliament and helped to ignite the two most important political crises during George I's reign, in 1719–20 and 1723–25. These incidents gave a different motive for placing Englishmen in strategic positions of power: the need to make secure 'the English interest', i.e. Whitehall's interests, in Dublin Castle and in the College Green parliament. In addition, Sir Robert Walpole, firmly established as first minister in 1721, was personally committed to centralising key government decision-making throughout the three kingdoms as far as circumstances would allow.

The first political crisis after 1714 revived the unresolved issue of the constitutional relationship between the Irish and British parliaments. Despite the passage of several pieces of crucial legislation relating to Ireland through the Westminster parliament during William's reign, few Irish parliamentarians – whatever their party loyalties – were prepared to accept the logic of these precedents. Where British legislation had served the interests of Protestant Ireland (as in 1691) the precedent was ignored, but where legislation had seemed to benefit England at Ireland's expense (as in 1699) it was remembered as a case of the British parliament acting *ultra vires*. Molyneux's arguments of 1699 in defence of the autonomy of the Irish legislature were easily revived, as in 1719 when another aspect of the Irish parliament's independence of Westminster came into question, its role as supreme court of appeal. Since the 1690s the English house of lords and its Irish counterpart had on several occasions become embroiled in civil appeals where rival litigants exploited the constitutional ambiguity as to where the supreme court for Ireland was, in Dublin or London. The judgment of the English house of lords prevailed in one instance, that of the Irish house by default in another. A direct constitutional clash came when a complex dispute (Annesley v. Sherlock) over the ownership of property in Kildare had gone on appeal to London. In August 1719 after the judges in the Irish exchequer court had sought to enforce the *British* lords' ruling, they were placed in custody by the *Irish* lords for betraying 'the undoubted ancient rights and privileges of this house and of the rights of the subjects of this kingdom'.[3]

The Irish commons played no direct part in the subsequent proceedings, and it was the small upper house, still heavily populated with Tory bishops appointed before 1714, which decided by a large majority directly to address King George, justifying their actions. This communication, almost certainly drafted by Archbishop King, was despatched in November 1719; besides reciting the history of the case at issue, it asserted quite explicitly Ireland's constitutional integrity along the lines Molyneux had argued:

> this Kingdom, being of itself a distinct dominion, and no part of the Kingdom of England, none can determine concerning the affairs thereof, unless authorised thereto by the known laws and customs of this Kingdom, or by the express consent of the King.[4]

The uncompromising tone of the address provoked a severe reaction from the British lords in January 1720, leading to the initiation there of legislation denying *any* appellate rights to the Irish parliament and, more fundamentally, stating without much elaboration the British parliament's superior status and its competence to legislate for Ireland. What had been implicit in the constitutional relationship was thus made explicit in what came to be known as the Declaratory Act (6th Geo. I, c. 5), and its passing embittered Protestant Ireland. Jonathan Swift, the Tory dean of St Patrick's Cathedral, brought out a satirically effective pamphlet, *A Proposal for the universal use of Irish manufactures*, which endorsed the idea of a law to burn everything from England except its coal and its people (and they should stay at home). Meanwhile the Whig Lord Molesworth warned in the Irish lords of the threat of direct taxation from England which, if imposed, would mean that the British parliament would 'but use us like those slaves which at present they declare us to be …'.[5] This was more than rhetoric for, as all knew, the political power of the Irish parliament rested on its ability to maintain control over much of Irish taxation and the Irish budget. There were private thoughts in London during 1720 as to what the costs might be for the Exchequer if the Irish parliament was in future not summoned on a regular basis; the loss of 'additional' revenues that were authorised by parliamentary money bills would immediately lop 2,000 men off the military establishment. By that calculation, College Green was still an imperial necessity. However the practical results of the Declaratory Act were limited: the Irish house of lords lost its judicial functions, but Westminster legislation binding Ireland remained unusual and of little importance. The Church of Ireland, in and out of the house of lords, remained the cockpit of tension between the new Whig and English bishops and resentful Irish ecclesiastics: both factions puffed up the constitutional significance of what in many respects was a grand dispute over 'preferment' and patronage.

The second and more spectacular crisis of the reign centred on a monetary issue, the decision by the British government – without consulting Dublin Castle – to have a patent issued in 1722 for the private minting of copper halfpence and farthings for circulation in Ireland; a similar patent authorising small coin for America was passed about the same time. The offending patent had originally been granted by the king (under the great seal of Great Britain, not of Ireland) to his mistress, the countess of Kendal, and she had immediately sold it to a prominent Wolverhampton ironmaster, William Wood. It was a quite unexceptional political proceeding as seen from London: a royal favourite was receiving a handsome *douceur*, while the much complained-of shortage of coin in Ireland would be relieved.

There had indeed been serious scarcities of the types of silver coin necessary for retail transactions in the early eighteenth century, particularly in the wake of domestic food shortages when heavy food imports upset the trade balance. The effects of the 1701 revaluation were still felt, and the failure to follow the British lowering of gold coin in 1717 only exacerbated matters. Other causes of Ireland's coinage difficulties – some fanciful, some contributory – were identified in the early eighteenth century by pamphleteers and parliamentarians, and most diagnoses had political undertones. An Irish mint had been repeatedly called for since the 1690s but London resisted, not least because such an institution might threaten monetary stability within England and, more basically, because possession of an official mint was now seen to carry connotations of political sovereignty. Another increasingly popular Irish explanation for the shortage of coin was the presumed financial drain created by the remittance of salaries and pensions from the Irish exchequer to English-based court favourites, 'place-men' and others, and the sizeable transfer of Irish property rents to English-based landlords. The Irish balance of payments and, indirectly, the money supply was certainly affected by the flow of remittances to England, but the significance of absenteeism was colourfully exaggerated.

By the early 1720s the real need was for a substantial increase in the amount of silver coin in circulation; more copper might actually drive out the already depleted quantity of silver coin. When the scale of the new copper coinage to be minted became known – roughly equivalent in value to one quarter of the coin then in circulation – nearly all Irish-based government officials including, significantly, the revenue commissioners opposed the scheme as commercially counterproductive as well as being politically insensitive.

The coinage issue became the immediate centre of attention in the parliamentary session which began in the autumn of 1723 – after Wood's coppers had begun to circulate. The commons investigated both the patent and the actual coins, and each house sent addresses to the crown, setting out a number of grievances – the resort to private minting as a procedure, the means by which Wood had secured the patent, the profits which he was making by the coinage and, finally, the damage his poor quality pieces were going to have on trade and state revenue. Walpole in London was quite unsympathetic, blaming the rumpus on mischief makers who had been encouraged by English opponents of his ministry. There were in fact grounds for such suspicions: Midleton had close links with Walpole's rivals – notably Carteret – and he was not disposed to help in dampening down the flames; his son, St John Brodrick, was actually leading the commons' protests at this stage. The hapless lord lieutenant, Grafton, after early tactical errors managed to buy time in December 1723 by undertaking to have the operation of the patent examined in England, and by giving the impression that he would secure its revocation on his return. However, he was unable to persuade any of the public critics of Wood to cross the Irish Sea and give evidence, and he failed to explain to his colleagues the genuine character of Irish opposition. At this stage even the Irish privy council, including all the newly reappointed lords justices, declared against the coin and sent over an address to London setting out the *economic* arguments for withdrawing it.

In July 1724 a British privy council committee cleared Wood of the Irish parliament's charges of fraud, indeed found the coin superior to all earlier Irish copper money, and attacked the Irish revenue commissioners' alleged lack of co-operation. Their only concession was a proposal to reduce greatly the amount of coin Wood was authorised to issue. With the confirmation of the patent, orders came from London to ensure the unhindered distribution of the new coin through official channels – the revenue commissioners and the army – but neither lords justices nor the Irish privy council showed any willingness to follow such a course. The revenue commissioners (of whom Conolly was chief) questioned the authority of the treasury in London to give specific orders relating to the coin. The unprecedented executive rebellion, for so it was seen by Walpole, led to the unscheduled despatch to Dublin of a new lord lieutenant, Walpole's formidable ministerial opponent, Lord Carteret, in October 1724, almost a year ahead of the next parliamentary session. With the kingdom united 'from the herb women to the nobles'[6] against the coinage, Whitehall sensed a growing political challenge to the royal prerogative and to the authority of the king's ministers. A more conciliatory approach by Carteret failed to soften political or public hostility towards the coinage, and his position was not notably strengthened when he obtained Midleton's resignation from the lord chancellorship in January 1725. However, with the reassembly of parliament imminent, the prospect of a totally unmanageable session and the denial of supplies concentrated minds in London and – to the king's personal chagrin – the patent was revoked in August.

Two factors help to explain the unremitting two-year opposition to the coinage in Ireland. First, there was the very real fear that by accepting Wood's coppers in a transaction, one would be taking a rapidly depreciating currency, and as the coins were never strictly 'legal tender', no one could be obliged to receive them and no one stood to suffer by participating in the boycott. Secondly, public opinion (meaning the explicit sentiments of literate Irish people) was excited in a quite novel way by a series of inflammatory pamphlets, in all over forty, the most important group being the four *Drapier's letters*,[7] written as most knew by Dean Swift. Both constitutional and economic grievances had featured in the pamphlets that appeared many months before Swift published the first letter purporting to come from a Dublin shopkeeper in February 1724, but his contributions were to be quite exceptional in their quality and popularity: two thousand copies of the first letter 'laying the whole villainy open, and advising the people what to do ...', were within a month 'dispersed by gentlemen in several parts of the country'.[8] It savaged Wood, his patent and everything to do with it.

The unfavourable judgment of the British privy council committee on the Irish case prompted Swift's second and third letters in August 1724; both ran quickly to several editions, and in these Swift urged public bodies to pass declarations not to handle the coinage. His proposed wording influenced many such declarations in the following two months. Then in October the fourth letter, 'to the whole people of Ireland', reached the streets of Dublin to coincide with Carteret's ominous arrival. Rumours that the new lord lieutenant would force the government to accept the coinage were ridiculed by Swift: no political authority could compel the king's subjects to accept what was not coin current in England, and what could never be legal tender in Ireland. He dwelt on the critical distinction between a rejection of the prerogative authority of the crown, which was indeed treason, and a rejection of the constitutional arguments underlying the Declaratory Act, which was justifiable:

> a depending kingdom is a modern term of art; unknown ... to all ancient ... writers upon government ... I have looked over all the English and

> Irish statutes without finding any law that makes Ireland depend upon England, any more than England does upon Ireland ... I declare, next under God, I depend only on the king my sovereign, and on the laws of my own country.[9]

This was a heady restatement of Molyneux's arguments in 1698, but in so far as he based his case on common law and precedent, Swift was re-entering a previous battlefield, and contesting the final outcome: the Declaratory Act had ended an old debate, and created a new precedent. However, he provided a further justification for Irish resistance to English government actions; he incorporated the line of argument that had only been marginally present in Molyneux's work:

> in reason, all government without the consent of the governed, is the very definition of slavery ... by the laws of God, of nature, of nations, and of your own country, you are and ought to be as free a people as your brethren in England.[10]

Swift was thus deploying the Lockean natural-right argument by which specific English actions in the past, however authentic as legislative precedents, could be presented as fundamental violations of Irish rights – insofar as Irish consent had been lacking.

The lord lieutenant found allies within the Irish privy council when he sought a prosecution of Swift and his printer for their 'seditious and scandalous paragraphs'.[11] The strong men of the government, Midleton in particular, were only too anxious to silence Swift's embarrassing indiscretions which weakened their more limited objections to the patent. Some privy councillors, notably Archbishop King, refused to sign this proclamation, fearing it would confuse the opposition campaign, but as it turned out Swift's language and political reasoning had immediate appeal outside Dublin Castle. Attempts to get the grand jury of Dublin to indict the printer backfired, the jury was dismissed, and a new jury not only refused to bow to judicial pressure but instead issued legal threats against any who introduced Wood's coppers into circulation.

This protracted affair, ending in total victory for Irish arguments, revealed the limit of London's executive power in Ireland. The non-co-operation of key elements in the Dublin government had come as an unpleasant surprise, and this, more than the mobilisation of Irish public opinion, impressed London. It has often been suggested that the affair forced a reassessment as to how Ireland should be governed; this was supposed to have led to the emergence of what was later called the 'under-taker' system, the arrangement whereby leaders of one or two dominant factions in the Dublin parliament were allocated a fat share of patronage in return for their undertaking to secure parliamentary majorities for motions and legislation sought by the lord lieutenant. Certainly there is a contrast between the turbulent parliamentary history of the first quarter of the century and the relatively crisis-free sessions of the 1730s and 1740s. Constitutional issues became less important and political controversy was more successfully contained. The management skills of the new parliamentary leaders helped to keep the Irish commons a less unpredictable assembly during George II's reign than it had been in his father's time.

But just how novel was this political arrangement? The evolution of parliamentary management by faction leaders can be traced back to the second Williamite parliament when Alan Brodrick emerged as the commons vote-broker willing to co-operate with Capel and able to mobilise parliamentary support for government – in return for office and influence. The 'Munster squadron' of MPs loyal to Alan and his son, St John Brodrick, were to remain the dominant Whig group until the 1720s. The family's power extended well beyond the coterie of MPs directly dependent on them for election and patronage, and they repeatedly demonstrated their ability to draw on the temporary loyalty of a much wider circle of MPs in times of conflict. They were unusual in having close links with leading Whig politicians in England – Alan and his brother were at different stages also MPs at Westminster – and when they had friends in office at the Castle their access to patronage was unrivalled. Conversely, during periods when the Tories had been in control before 1714, Alan Brodrick's rhetoric and mastery of parliamentary procedure had made him a highly effective opposition leader.

A commons faction of a different sort had developed behind William Conolly, Brodrick's contemporary of rather humbler origins. Conolly, the successful speculator in forfeited Jacobite estates, had initially led an Ulster grouping of MPs, and as the most energetic member of the Irish revenue board since 1709, he demonstrated for the first time the political leverage that such bureaucratic power bestowed.

By 1715 the two Whig groupings were clear rivals for power: to some extent this was an Irish reflection of tensions among the Whig grandees at Westminster, with the Brodricks linked to the fortunes of Sunderland and Stanhope, and Conolly closer to Townshend and Walpole's friends. But the vacuum created by the eclipse of the Tories in Ireland after 1714 also heightened the probability of a squabble over the spoils of victory. Conolly replaced Brodrick as Speaker of the commons in the first Hanoverian parliament after Brodrick had chosen to be elevated to the lord chancellorship, and Conolly's close relationship with the chief secretary between 1715 and 1717 widened Conolly's influence over patronage decisions. In reaction St John Brodrick, Alan's son, led commons opposition to government in this session, whipping up parliamentary resentment at the growing burden of absentee pensions (i.e. annuities drawn on the Irish exchequer and granted to non-residents), and in this he secured support from the attenuated Tory element in the house.

The tables were turned in 1717 when, after English ministerial changes, the Brodricks had the ear of the Castle; Midleton became Bolton's key adviser in his management of parliament, and supported the government line in 1717 and 1719. The demise of the Brodricks' London allies – in the wake of the financial scandal of the South Sea Bubble during 1720 – and Grafton's appointment to the lord lieutenancy led to the consolidation of Speaker Conolly's position. However, Grafton's failure to contain the Irish reaction to Wood's Halfpence, and the appointment of Walpole's outmanoeuvred rival, Carteret, to the Irish viceroyalty, once again shifted the political influence wielded by Conolly and his friends, and the Brodricks. Throughout this period of changing fortunes, Conolly and Midleton had remained in government in the sense that Conolly retained the commons speakership, Midleton the lord chancellorship, and both more often than not held executive responsibility as the lords justices. When lords lieutenants were in residence these men were leading if often dissonant voices in the Irish privy council.[12] Who then really ruled Ireland in the early Hanoverian period?

THE RULING COALITION

The government of Ireland was vested in the lord lieutenant, whose function it was to transmit and interpret 'the king's pleasure', which now meant the policies of the British ministry of the day. He was not accountable to the Irish parliament, the formal powers of which were more narrowly defined than ever. Indeed parliament exercised no legal or political control over the composition of the government, the privy council or the judiciary. The discretionary powers of the lord lieutenant were themselves restricted: the Irish revenue boards were closely monitored from London, and many decisions relating to the Irish army were taken not by its formal commander-in-chief in Dublin Castle but by the secretary of war in London.

But such evidence of dependency is only one perspective. Hanoverian

Ireland was only in a very partial sense governed from London, for however feeble the claim that Ireland was an autonomous kingdom in a dual monarchy, in practice both the structure of decision-making and the development of domestic Irish government policy were the outcome of a *coalition* of interests between the Whig ascendancy in England and that small number of loosely knit factions drawn from the politically active Protestant Irish gentry. British control of Irish destinies may have been non-negotiable, but in so far as that control was ultimately for negative reasons of metropolitan security, the form it took was always negotiable. The character of the Irish part of the coalition and the shape of political power within Ireland was of course clearly established by the military and dynastic outcomes of the previous three-quarters of a century. But the relative leverage of Irish-based interests, and the composition of those interests over time, were subject to change, thanks to forces to a considerable degree operating *within* Ireland.

In order, then, to assess the power of the Irish half of the governing equation at this stage, we must review the demands of the social group from which the undertakers were drawn, the Protestant landed proprietors: what did they want from the state and an involvement in politics, and how successful were they in obtaining it? It can be argued that Hanoverian Irish landowners sought, in descending order of priority, *collective security* of their property and social position, *private profit* from places, offices, employments and contracts in the gift of the state, *low taxes*, and what might be called *development incentives*. Between the 1710s and the 1760s they were relatively successful in achieving these ends – a reflection of their power in parliament, and of the Irish parliament's *de facto* leverage. Parliament's now undisputed control over state revenue was the foundation stone and the commons, despite the formal constitutional restraints of Poynings's law, had considerable success in determining the range and content of domestic Irish statute law.

Collective security, although the fundamental political concern of the landed class, was in many ways a reactive matter. Issues such as the defence of the Williamite and earlier land settlements from any modification, the protection of the existing corpus of land law (highly favourable to the fee-simple proprietor), and the preservation of the discretionary powers of the landlord-dominated magistracy were largely uncontentious. Even the more formal aspects of military arrangements were usually not a source of division between the Irish landed interest and Dublin Castle: the deployment in peacetime of such a disproportionately large part of British land forces in Ireland was politically convenient for Whitehall and provided most areas of the country with more than adequate armed support whenever a sheriff or magistrate might require it. In wartime, Protestant Irish fears of invasion were of course easily revived, but the residual strength of the army kept these in check. In addition, the local profits from servicing the widely dispersed barracks neutralised most objections to having such a large charge on the Irish establishment.

There was however one issue in this area where gentry and government tended to be in conflict: should Irish recruitment to foreign armies be permitted? Since the time when James II's Irish army had been despatched to France in 1691–92 there had been a large if irregular migration of Catholic recruits to the Irish Brigade of the French army, and to other Irish-officered regiments under the French and Spanish crowns. Periods of intensive recruiting (in 1721–22 for the Spanish service and the late 1720s and late 1730s for France) were greeted with particular alarm by Protestant gentry – who feared a Jacobite invasion more than a depleted labour force – yet for diplomatic reasons Dublin Castle, taking its cue from London, sought on each of these occasions to subvert or at least deflect protests from the country. Even conservative estimates of the outflow in the fifty years after 1692 suggest that in the region of 35,000 men volunteered as mercenaries, so it would seem that here at least the Protestant gentry's wishes were frustrated.

A more fundamental source of contention was the determination of the landlord class to defend the exclusive political rights of all members of the established church at the expense of both Catholics and Protestant dissenters. Although this commitment was fully endorsed by some lords lieutenants after 1714, as the century advanced Dublin Castle and British ministries became increasingly critical of the Irish parliament's disposition, not least because they were sensitive to diplomatic pressure from their Catholic allies on the continent. Sentiment in the Irish parliament in relation to the penal laws changed remarkably little for half a century – whatever about the actual implementation of the code – and nearly all the post-1714 resolutions and acts merely sought to strengthen or renew existing statutes. The only novel elements were the formal exclusion of the remaining Catholic peers from the house of lords (in 1716), the explicit removal of parliamentary suffrage from Catholic freeholders (in 1729), the ban on Catholic lawyers practising at the bar (in 1733), and the act of 1745 that made all 'mixed marriages' null and void.

Most anti-Catholic legislation after 1714 was reactive, following legal verdicts that revealed loopholes in the existing law, or after invasion rumours which gave a sinister significance to the influx of continentally educated priests. Bills in 1719 and 1723 that proposed more sensational punishments for *unregistered* clergy (in fact the overwhelming majority) – castration in 1719 and hanging in 1723 – were panic measures that failed to reach the statute book and were not revived. At least some of the credit for the very limited extension of the penal laws must go to Austrian diplomacy, aided at times (as in 1723) by the other Catholic powers who lobbied the British privy council on behalf of their Irish co-religionists; in addition, legal agents representing the Irish Catholic interest had far more success in London exploiting the obligatory vetting role of the Whitehall privy council than they had at the bar of the Irish commons. As Fagan has suggested, perhaps 'Poynings's law was a blessing in disguise as far as the Catholics were concerned ...'.[13]

The first eighteenth-century diocesan synod was held discreetly in Limerick in 1721, and very slowly the reconstruction of the Catholic church took place, interrupted at times of parliamentary enthusiasm for penal enforcement (e.g. the early months of 1734), and of international tension, most dramatically so during the invasion scare of 1744. And the fact that the ecclesiastical legislation was only occasionally implemented does not mean that the magistracy at large disapproved of the penal statutes. The enduring object of the code, particularly those statutes directed against the normal functioning of the Catholic church, was seen to be intimidatory rather than destructive; by giving considerable discretionary powers to JPs it provided additional levers of social control. The gentry had an exaggerated respect for the power of parish priests over their laity, and they increasingly used them to try and maintain communal calm and submission, and to root out troublemakers. The dormant penal legislation made priests co-operate willingly.

As for the legislation against Catholic property-owners, all recognised that the share of land owned by Catholics was slipping inexorably. However, those Protestants who expected the penal laws to transform the religious demography of Ireland were a dwindling minority; between 1704 and 1789, despite the legal incentives, only about 5,500 Catholics registered their formal conversion to the established church. And there were many who travelled the other way, although none to rival Sylvester Lloyd, son of a Tipperary minister, ardent Jacobite, and Catholic bishop of Killaloe and later of Waterford and Lismore.

Protestants committed to the idea of mass conversion, generally anglican bishops or clergy, concentrated their energies on the promotion of private and public charity schools as a means of proselytising the Catholic poor, and such free schools – using the medium of English – undoubtedly swelled Church of Ireland numbers more than adult conformities. In the case of the charter schools, first established in the 1730s as proselytising institutions providing vocational training and amply funded by donations from the political establishment, some 2,500 Catholic children had graduated into trade apprenticeships after three decades. For a generation, the belief held firm that these and other contemporary educational initiatives had revolutionary religious potential, a belief shared indeed by many fearful Catholic clergy.

The legislation constraining the dissenter population was far less comprehensive than the anti-Catholic laws, but there were underlying common elements. The key legislation affecting dissenters' status remained the test clause of 1704 which checked dissenter involvement in the institutions of the Irish state. Intensive pressure from London to repeal it was put on the Irish parliament in the early years of George I's reign (the king personally supported relief), but the commons were divided – the Whigs themselves being at odds on the issue – and the lords hostile. However, in 1719 the first of many temporary toleration and indemnity acts was passed which largely suspended the test clause's operation. But parliamentary resistance to its actual repeal hardened, if anything, in the following decades. The practical consequences for dissenters were limited enough – the 1719 Toleration Act formally recognised their educational and religious liberties, and they retained the right to vote and to sit in parliament; however, they remained excluded from county and local government and from the magistracy, which placed them at a material disadvantage in Ulster electoral contests. The threat of full enforcement of the test clause was a standing grievance among dissenters and remained so until 1780. The survival of the test certainly contributed to the remarkable decline in the number of Presbyterian gentry in eighteenth-century Ulster, as the social pressure for conformity took effect.

The second political dividend sought by the landlord interest was private profit: access to office and employment which would bring guaranteed income, status and family advancement. Between 1714 and 1760 most of the positions sought were not central government posts as such, but the long list of appointments which were in the gift of the lord lieutenant – on the judicial bench, in the Church of Ireland, in the revenue service, or in army regiments on the Irish establishment. And there were the several hundred places (mostly sinecures) and 'pensions' on the civil establishment. The majority of pension-holders were probably absentee throughout the period,[14] but a large and growing proportion of the placeholders were Irish who held their positions 'at pleasure', tenure being contingent on the holder not becoming politically obnoxious. The demand for the large number of minor positions and places came in part because of many landowners' concern to secure employment, or at least an income, for their younger sons at a time of limited socially acceptable alternatives, in part from politicians seeking posts which could be filled by their supporters and dependants, and for which they would receive the credit. The competition for higher positions was accentuated as they became more profitable with the growth of the economy. Some professional preparation and experience were obviously essential for candidates seeking church, army or legal preferment, but throughout the public service, appointment and promotion were determined primarily by lobbying and political calculation, not on individual merit.

The changing pattern of recruitment to the episcopacy and the bench under George I cut directly across the ambitions of many Anglo-Irish families. English appointees were deeply resented by the often articulate Irish-born candidates deprived of 'advancement' (e.g. Archbishops King and Synge) and, more generally, because of the political leverage that thereby reverted to what was characterised as (or rather characterised itself as) the 'English interest'. In addition, considerable independent patronage went with some of the posts that outsiders were filling: it was claimed that the English bishops were filling all vacant benefices in their new dioceses with fellow countrymen. In fact, this discrimination against Irish-born Protestants was less serious than critics maintained, and particularly during Carteret's viceroyalty Irish promotions continued: there were eleven Irish-born and eleven English bishops of the Church of Ireland at George I's death in 1727, and the number was the same in 1760. During George II's reign only nine out of twenty-three judicial appointments were drawn from England. However the English appointments, particularly to the episcopacy, tended to be to the more powerful (and lucrative) posts; the huge archbishopric of Armagh and the pivotal lord chancellorship remained in exclusively English hands until 1822 and 1789 respectively.

This denial of the commanding peaks to Irish place-seekers should not disguise the fact that the overwhelming majority of positions in church and state continued to be held by Irish-born Protestants. Nomination to all twelve hundred-plus positions in the revenue service was shared out between the active commissioners – and a majority of those who regularly attended meetings were Irish-born. This expanding bureaucracy remained not surprisingly a major source of remunerative employment for Irishmen. Moreover, army commissions, barracks masterships and positions on the army general staff in Dublin were similarly accessible to Protestant Irish families. The parliament-dominated barracks board controlled all barracks appointments, but regimental commissions were ultimately decided in London, and while many hopefuls crossed the channel to lobby for places and promotion, the lord lieutenant transmitted recommendations based on domestic political calculations. A modern suggestion that perhaps a quarter of the British officer corps (around a thousand commissions) was Irish by mid-century gives some indication of the remarkably successful penetration of the Protestant landed class in this direction, a contrast to the overwhelmingly British make-up of the recruits themselves.[15]

A persistent source of Irish complaint concerned that part of the gravy train which was out of reach, the pensions and sinecures held by non-Irish court and ministerial favourites; legislation was actually passed in 1727 imposing a 20 per cent tax on the salaries of office-holders predominantly resident outside Ireland. Its impact was severely weakened by a clause permitting the crown to grant exemptions, and the legislation was scrapped in 1753, only to be revived in more effective form in 1769. Pension-holders, however, remained outside any such restraint.

The third policy objective of Irish landlords was the maintenance of low taxation levels. In this they were relatively successful for government budgets remained small – equivalent to between 2 and 3 per cent of national income – until the 1790s. Throughout the century, the budget was dominated by military expenditure: 82.5 per cent of total state spending in the years 1715–19 was taken up by the military establishment, 75 per cent in the years 1750–54.[16] The main complaints about this military budget related to the wartime financing of 'Irish' regiments when they were moved abroad.

Military contingencies dominated the public finances and determined taxation levels, but the growth of a national debt in the 1720s and 1730s was primarily a consequence of the shortfall of revenue, just as the temporary clearing of the debt in 1754 came after several years of pronounced prosperity and higher tax yields. The structure of taxation was such that customs duties and excise contributed an exceptionally large percentage of national revenue (around three-fifths), and direct taxation was even by eighteenth-century British standards very low: the English land tax, originally a wartime measure imposed in 1697–98 and paid by landowners, had no parallel in eighteenth-century Ireland, and the 'quit' and crown rents, paid by the inheritors of certain classes of forfeited property, were a fixed and generally modest overhead. Only the hearth tax (even less important to the exchequer than these rents) survived as a near universal levy affecting mansion and cabin at rates unchanged between the 1660s and the 1790s. There was in other words no general tax on wealth or income, and while some of the excise duties and taxes on luxury goods – silks, silver plate, carriages – were clearly going to affect the propertied classes, their impact was more than compensated for by buoyant incomes. Indeed the indirect-tax burden was disproportionately shouldered by middle-income families, artisans and the urban sector generally, where the consumption of shop goods and alcohol was much higher than in the countryside. In all, the small scale of central government meant that the country was run relatively cheaply, and with imperial contributions confined to the maintenance of the 12,000-strong standing army, landowners enjoyed much lower overheads than their equivalents in England.

The fourth identifiable goal of the landed interest was the creation and maintenance of an economic order that would aid and protect their estates and their incomes. The economic order which landlords sought was one modelled on contemporary Britain where, as it seemed, a more assured prosperity was emerging based on the twin pillars of international trade (linked to the successful development of colonies overseas), and domestic manufacturing (nurtured by vigorous protection of the home market and a rational tariff structure). Recent British experience thus appeared to demonstrate the ability of state policy and statute law to stimulate economic activity, just as Ireland's relative backwardness seemed to provide confirmation through antithesis: from the 1690s the Irish political elite firmly believed that English legislation restricting Irish foreign trade was having major and generally negative effects on the domestic economy. Because of this perspective, they came to have an exaggerated estimate of the positive consequences that would flow from benign legislation and official economic incentives.

Such an analysis may have been superficial and faulty, yet the survival on the English and Irish statute books of the Woollen Act, various sections of the Navigation Acts that discriminated against Irish trade and shipping, and the Cattle Acts, remained a genuine grievance that was often aired by opposition MPs and complained of privately at more elevated levels. At no time under the first two Georges was there any prospect of repeal in Westminster: the English commercial interests that would have been affected (or feared they might be) had sufficient influence in London to stall any Irish initiative, and could use a variety of commercial arguments to justify Ireland's notionally subordinate status within the commercial empire of the Navigation Acts. So the political achievement of the Irish gentry in this area was essentially negative: the prevention of any further legislation constraining Irish trade. Many in Ireland feared that with the Declaratory Act, the British parliament would greatly extend its statutory regulation of the Irish economy. In fact, throughout the years 1720–60 only a handful of new acts was passed in Westminster 'which can be regarded as new special legislation imposed on Ireland in the interests of Britain',[17] and these mainly related to external trade, particularly in American goods; indeed the prohibition on Irish glass exports (1746) and the high English tariff on Irish sailcloth (1750) were of marginal significance, however politically irritating. More important was the defeat, after vigorous Irish lobbying, of Westminster attempts to raise duties on Irish woollen and worsted yarn entering England in 1707 and 1711, and the successful struggle for the reduction of those duties in the 1730s. And the favoured status of Irish plain linen in British and colonial markets, first conceded in 1696, was consolidated in Irish and English bounty legislation. Direct access to transatlantic markets for all Irish exporters, conceded in 1731, laid the foundations for a valuable new Atlantic shipping network for Irish merchant communities.

The economic legislation of the Irish parliament itself was, like the penal code, over-ambitious but not without practical consequences. Fifteen per cent of all public statutes between 1715 and 1760 were concerned with transport improvements, 10 per cent with trade and banking, 5 per cent with industrial development and only 1 per cent (five acts) dealt specifically with agriculture or forestry. The underlying philosophy was mercantilist – to stimulate import substitution and reduce the cost of raw materials in the export sector by rational tariff adjustment. The turnpiking of public roads and the state-sponsored construction of canals were part of this, in that parliament's aim was to cut down coal and corn imports through the lowering of transport costs between potential inland sources of supply and the (mainly coastal) city markets. And when parliament actually had a large revenue surplus to play with in the 1750s, 70 per cent of all grants went to inland and coastal navigation projects, 28 per cent to assist industrial ventures. Linen remained the great – but not the exclusive – industrial object of attention; the Linen Board, established in 1711, was always handsomely financed, and although its administrative efficiency was compromised by considerations of local and national patronage, it succeeded in its own profligate way in promoting technical innovation and in spreading linen manufacture outside east Ulster.

Much parliamentary legislation, enacted ostensibly for the public good, tended to benefit disproportionately the holders of wealth, and while stern laws relating to servants and labourers, and the tightening up of the statutory rights of property-owners and creditors were welcome to all wealth-holders, the seigneurial bias of both legislation and grant allocation was obvious. Unlike the situation at Westminster there was no countervailing 'monied interest' in College Green, and the weakness of non-landed, non-rural interests was occasionally laid bare. The defeat of the National Bank Bill in 1720–21, and the passing of the 1757 Banking Act, which shut wholesale merchants out of the business of private banking, were telling displays of the gentry's overwhelming dominance in the Irish legislature.

Engagement in public life was of course shaped by other, less concrete and less measurable considerations. A sense of family duty, a commitment to enlightenment values of civic responsibility, a practical enthusiasm for economic development, a religious belief in the moral degradation of Irish society and the individual's duty to reform it – all such considerations informed some of those public men of affairs for at least some of the time.

THE LONG PARLIAMENT

The accession of George II in June 1727 was an unsensational affair. A few weeks later a group of Irish Catholic gentry, led by the elderly earl of Westmeath, a veteran of the siege of Limerick, signed an address on behalf of 'the Roman Catholics of the kingdom of Ireland' to the new king, which was accepted by Carteret in London. Its fulsome references to 'our steady allegiance and most humble duty to your majesty's person and government', and to their 'unfeigned loyalty, which no power on earth can dispense with …' split the Catholic interest – some objecting to its failure to dwell on recent grievances, others because of their principled commitment to James III and the house of Stuart. No churchman was involved, and Sylvester Lloyd, soon to be a bishop, saw the address as 'vile and nauseous flattery'.[18] Westmeath's move was before its time.

The novelty of a general election failed to raise the political temperature, despite some lively county contests. New members were returned for about one-quarter of the seats, but this did not noticeably alter the political composition of the house of commons – although the parliamentary strength of several factions seems to have been consolidated. For most Irish people the late 1720s were years dominated by bad harvests, falling incomes and the threat of hunger and epidemic.

Archbishop King and Speaker Conolly both died in 1729. The first of a new political generation to fill their place was Archbishop Boulter; he had come from Bristol to Armagh in 1724, and his political authority rested on a personal friendship with the duke of Newcastle and on his regular reappointment as a lord justice between 1725 and 1740. After the political crisis of 1723–25 the discretionary powers of the lords justices were increased – but two of the three justices deputising for absent lords lieutenants were in future to be English-born archbishops of Armagh and English-born lord chancellors, with Boulter and his successors the stronger half of the English element. On the whole Boulter remained aloof from the parliamentary factions and was irrationally suspicious of the remnants of Irish Toryism and of any talk of parliamentary 'independency'. Within the Church of Ireland, Boulter was the antithesis of Swift; intellectually inferior to the Dean of St Patrick's, Boulter was nevertheless a formidable figure in church and state, active in funding and promoting charitable works and education, in forwarding economic legislation where English interests would not be injured, and in defending and where possible enlarging the resources of the Church of Ireland.

The Irish privy council (rather than the house of lords) was the key political arena for Boulter. The council met regularly whether or not parliament was in session, and still had both legislative and executive functions. It used its powers to initiate, amend or veto controversial heads of bills sparingly. Its powers to determine the make-up of municipal corporations were more frequently invoked; it occasionally rejected nominations to higher municipal office and arbitrated in disputed elections of sheriffs. Its most public function was in the formulation and authorisation of proclamations relating to trade and public order. From the evidence of Boulter's own correspondence the council seems to have been more successfully managed in the Castle interest under his supervision than previously, yet it was not sufficiently small or coherent to become a government 'cabinet'.

The third office-holder who for more than two decades served as a lord justice was Henry Boyle, the Speaker of the commons. The political weight of the speakership had significantly increased during William Conolly's tenure, thanks to his highly successful performance as parliamentary manager and revenue commissioner. Boyle's pre-eminence is at first sight perplexing despite his illustrious ancestry (he was great-grandson of the first earl of Cork, and grandson of Orrery). His landed estates were modest compared with those of his titled cousins and up until 1756 he did not outgrow his reputation as a mere country gentleman, an old Whig, and as essentially a spokesman for his equals in the commons. He first entered parliament as one of Alan Brodrick's 'squadron' in 1707, and achieved independence when he became in effect political manager of a clutch of Munster boroughs controlled by or at least influenced by his absentee cousin, the earl of Burlington. This 'interest' was the foundation for a mainly Munster faction, larger and more ably led than the Brodricks' grouping had been, which made Boyle the most powerful broker in the Irish commons by the time he first stood for the speakership in 1729, although on that occasion he was defeated by Ralph Gore.

For twenty-three years from 1733 Boyle retained the speakership, and for nearly twenty of these, as he later claimed, 'the business of parliament' was 'carried on with remarkable unanimity, and very seldom disturbed, never broken, by those struggles which private interest inspires, and which, while men are men, can never be totally avoided'; such management of the commons, Boyle suggested, was not the result of 'private family connections, nor mean dependence, but of a much nobler course, a sameness of principles ...'.[19] Boyle was indeed popular with his own class, carefully cultivating a large network of country gentry through his share of government patronage while remaining anchored to his Cork base at Castlemartyr. He buttressed his position by tactical alliances with lesser faction leaders – including at times even his future enemies the Ponsonbys. The relative tranquillity of English politics before the 1750s and the absence of a coherent opposition at Westminster able to stir up trouble in College Green made Boyle's task lighter. Furthermore the long viceroyalties of the dukes of Dorset (1730–37; 1750–55), Devonshire (1737–45) and Harrington (1746–50), none of whom were overly concerned to become enmeshed in Irish politics, created a congenial environment for the consolidation of the undertaker system, reducing uncertainty among patrons and clients.

Two more fundamental if negative factors contributed to the relative calm of parliamentary politics before the 1750s. First there was Protestant Ireland's recurring fear of invasion from France or Spain, a perception of vulnerability that influenced political behaviour especially when war threatened or broke out. This anxiety, strongest among rural Protestant landowners of the southern counties, helped to maintain among unaligned MPs, however heated they might become over the prerogatives of the house, finite limits to their displays of opposition. In addition, the first half of Boyle's speakership spanned a period of sharp agricultural and commercial reverses. It was becoming increasingly difficult simply to blame English government policy as the cause of the sluggish performance of the Irish economy. Depressed international prices and the dislocating effects of war meant hard times for landlord and

Patron Name:
(Surname, first name)

Date:

Staff Initial:

(MAIN COLLECTION)

REQUEST – AWAITING PICK-UP

REQUEST – AWAITING PICK-UP

(MAIN COLLECTION)

Staff Initial:

Date:

Patron Name:
(Surname, first name)

Patron Name: O'Sullivan, Ruairi
(Surname, first name)

Date: 3/3/23

Staff Initial: PL

(MAIN COLLECTION)

REQUEST – AWAITING PICK-UP

REQUEST – AWAITING PICK-UP

(MAIN COLLECTION)

Staff Initial:

Date:

(Surname, first name)
Patron Name:

landholder, and by extension shaky public finances, a situation reflected in a parliament that was rarely high spirited, often demoralised and sometimes frightened.

The concentration of power into the hands of Boyle and a few allies raises the question of the degree to which parliament's status was being subverted by the undertakers. In purely physical terms, the Irish parliament was utterly transformed in the 1730s: in 1727 the decision was taken to demolish the old Chichester town house in College Green, and the building plans of a young MP, Edward Lovett Pearce, were accepted by parliament and viceroy. Pearce was friend and architectural adviser to Speaker Conolly – which probably secured him the commission – and his *avant-garde* neo-classical design was by any measure successful. Parliament began to occupy the unfinished building at the end of the 1731–32 session, and the fact that the commons' chamber, not the lords', was the centrepiece of the new building was symbolic and reflected the old Speaker's prejudices.[20] Work on the building continued fitfully for more than twenty years, but even in the 1730s the great edifice in the centre of Dublin, busy only for six or seven months in twenty-four, was an exaggerated political statement. Its modest legislative output, constitutional subordination to the Castle and to the Irish and British privy councils, and its management by a handful of faction leaders, hardly made it a great sanctuary of liberty. Yet, that said, parliament's survival guaranteed the underlying 'coalition', and within its now established procedures and financial prerogatives lay the potential for future political movement. The behaviour and conduct of the commons helped to determine the leverage and standing of undertakers vis-à-vis the viceroy. Ironically it was a small group of normally 'anti-court' MPs, those unwilling to commit themselves to any understanding with the government of the day, who really began to exploit the potential of the house and who enlarged its functions and, in time, its *de facto* powers, notably in the area of budget control.

The most crucial procedural privilege cherished by the commons was the by now well-established convention whereby the house initiated the money or supply heads of bills at the beginning of each session. A money bill's introduction was always preceded by the formal inspection of the public accounts by MPs. From at least the 1725–26 session one can detect a growing readiness to examine government accounting and expenditure as well as the budget estimates; in every parliamentary session over the next dozen years there was conflict over the accounts submitted or over the legislative procedures whereby governments sought to raise extra revenue. The Committee of Public Accounts in 1735 sought to establish why the administrative costs of revenue collection had risen so much, only to find their enquiries sabotaged when the revenue commissioners sent into the house 'a horse load of books containing customs accounts and left it to the committee to find out ...'.[21] In Devonshire's first parliament, the committee sought to curb a different facet of executive non-accountability, the discretionary powers of the lord lieutenant to draw on the treasury by king's letter, but despite a tactical victory with the carrying of a resolution condemning future 'overdrawings', the active critics of government were finally outvoted.

Several of those who involved themselves in the more sophisticated scrutiny of government finances in the 1730s were ambitious young MPs of Tory background, men such as Sir Richard Cox, grandson of Anne's Tory lord chancellor, and the formidable new MP for Westmeath, Anthony Malone, a barrister, baptised a Catholic, who had married Speaker Gore's daughter. But there were few social or ideological distinctions between the articulate independents on the one hand and the majority of regularly attending country members who remained identified, often rather loosely, with particular parliamentary groupings. The independents could win sudden majorities when they raised the alarm about parliamentary prerogatives, although what appeared to be independents' victories in the division lobby were often covert shows of strength by the undertakers themselves.

The duke of Devonshire's long viceroyalty (1737–45) was in parliamentary terms a quiet time, the relative peacefulness of public life contrasting with the turbulence of the wider world – the outbreak of what was at first an Atlantic war between Britain and Spain in 1739, the return of territorial war to continental Europe the following year, a political hiatus at Westminster which led in 1742 to Walpole's fall from power, and in 1744 the final outbreak of hostilities between Britain and France – after several years of precarious diplomatic relations undermined two decades of *détente*.

The political stability under Devonshire was helped by a remarkable new family alliance: two of the duke's daughters were married (in 1739 and 1743) to sons of the new earl of Bessborough, Brabazon Ponsonby. The Ponsonby family had a secure political base among the freeholders of County Kilkenny and a good Cromwellian, old Whig pedigree, but neither in terms of rental income nor of control of parliamentary boroughs were they among the first rank. However, after 1714 their political influence had risen as allies of Speaker Conolly – the family's first peerage had come to Brabazon's elderly father in 1721, and after Conolly's death Brabazon, with his sons William and John, helped to reorganise the parliamentary 'friends' of the former Speaker; from the late 1730s the Ponsonby clan emerged as one of the great political families of eighteenth-century Ireland. John Ponsonby's appointment as a revenue commissioner (in Boyle's place) in 1739 marked the beginnings of a three-decade span during which the revenue service was exploited by the family as an engine of power and patronage. In 1741 the elder son became Devonshire's chief secretary. It was not long before they had become the main counterpoint to the Boyle interest within parliament. Lacking a power base in the boroughs, they remained more demonstrably allies of the Castle than did Boyle's group, which in the course of the 1740s picked up the support of erstwhile independents, notably Anthony Malone. The violent political divisions of the mid-1750s were long in the making.

Before the wars of the 1740s had made their mark on Ireland a social and economic calamity hit the country. Parliament was in session through the winter of 1739–40 when an extraordinarily intense and durable frost destroyed a large proportion of rural food stocks, but despite the personal involvement of large numbers of the politically active elite – most conspicuously Boulter himself – in raising charitable subscriptions and in the administration of private emergency food schemes, the official record of parliament is silent on the mounting crisis. A run of seven highly abnormal seasons devastated the resources of tens of thousands of poorer families. And when parliament reassembled in October 1741 over an eighth of the island's population had died from the combined effects of food scarcity and the collapse of farm incomes. But such was the class-specific character of the crisis that its political impact was negligible – perhaps a greater commitment among MPs to promote indigenous cereal farming and public granaries, to channel public funds into investment in inland communications projects, and a willingness to extend statutory controls over tenants' cultivation practices. After the climatic horrors of 1740–41 had passed, war delayed economic recovery until at least 1746. Repeated trade embargoes – mostly at the behest of London – reduced the volume of maritime trade, and a depleted army presence, increased taxation, and the unsettling effects of invasion rumours weakened the inland economy. Problems in northern parts of the country were compounded by a further severe harvest and fodder crisis in 1744–45.

Rumours of Spanish-backed invasion of Ireland circulated through the country in 1740, but more firmly-based reports of an intended French invasion of Ireland or England in February 1744, on the eve of the French declaration of war, led to drastic anti-Catholic measures by Devonshire's administration: all magistrates in the country were instructed 'strictly to put in execution' all penal laws relating to ecclesiastics and firearms. This

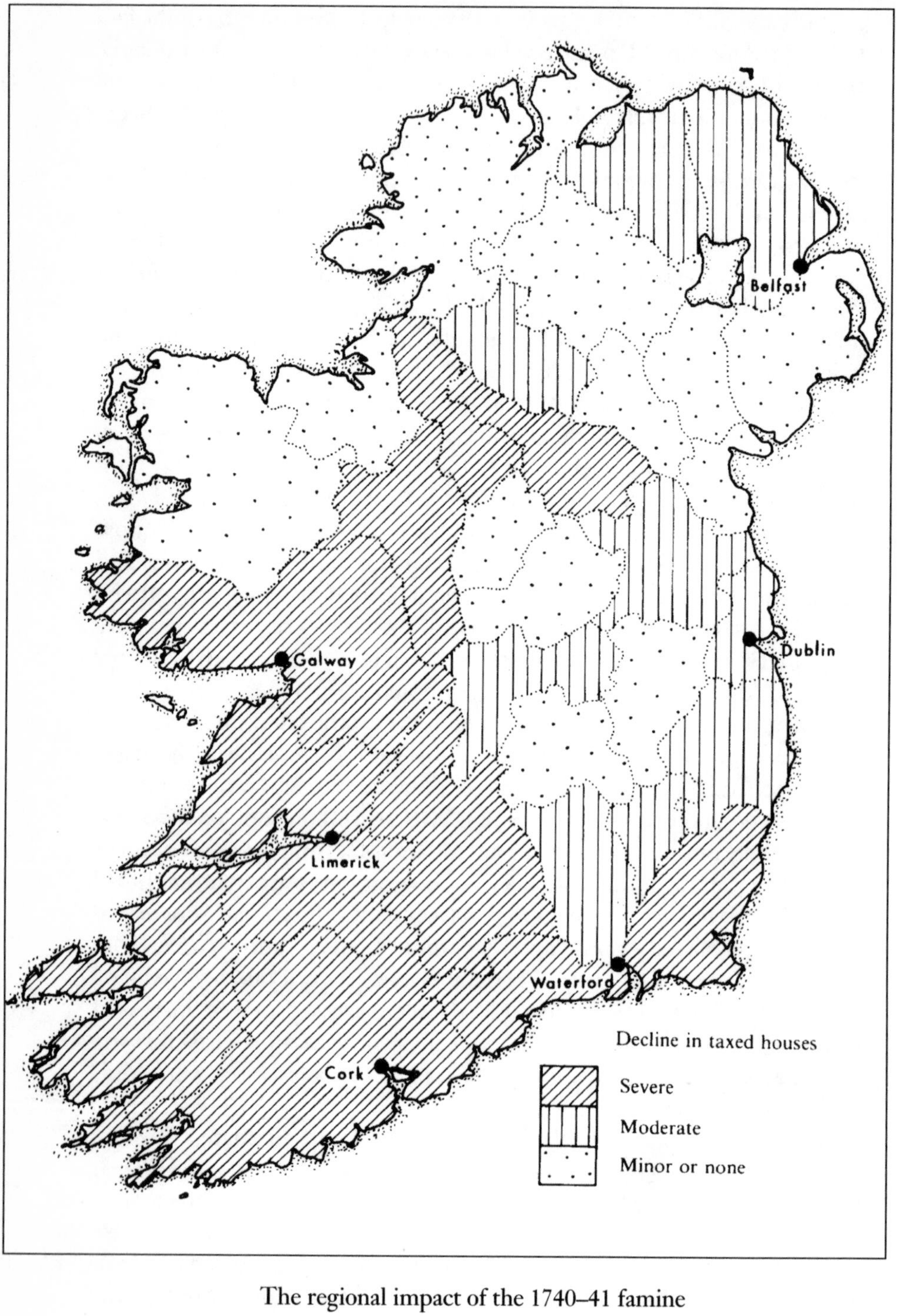

The regional impact of the 1740–41 famine

led to the arrest of some Catholic clergy, mainly bishops and friars, and to the concealment of many others, the closure by magistrates of Catholic places of worship especially in urban areas, and the harassment of prominent lay Catholics suspected by JPs of Jacobite links or of holding illegal arms. Bishop MacDonagh of Kilmore, a former confessor of James III, had to change domicile a dozen times in two months. The panic subsided fairly quickly, but only after a series of ugly incidents in Dublin and the southern cities involving displaced mass-goers.

The Continental military campaign went badly for Britain and its allies, and the great battle in southern Belgium at Fontenoy in May 1745 helped ensure that the war was largely a stalemate. Fontenoy itself demonstrates many of the ironies of Ireland's position during the war: the kingdom was constitutionally at war with Britain's declared enemies, although its governors in their official capacity had no say in British foreign policy; Irish taxes supported the 'Irish' regiments summoned across to the Low Countries, and in some of these the officers were largely Protestant Irish, as Fontenoy's victims show. Yet the real heroes of Fontenoy were in fact the 4,000-odd men in six Irish regiments fighting on the French side, regiments still largely made up of Irish recruits brought over during the years of Anglo-French *détente*. They turned the course of the battle.

Hardly three months later came word of a Jacobite rising in Scotland, gathering rapid momentum despite no direct support from France. The motley Highland army which soon formed behind Prince Charles Edward, the young Stuart heir, advanced successfully during September into lowland Scotland. In Ireland, it was obvious that the country was quite unprepared should there be a direct French landing – as was indeed being advocated by some at the French court. And fears of a secondary Jacobite move into east Ulster from Scotland led to the mobilisation of county militia in that province and elsewhere. Even in Munster, Protestant fears were again welling up. One English-born estate agent reported from north Cork in early October how

> the Irish are beginning insolencies already, they begin to steal sheep and neglect to sow and plant ... One whom I discharged told my wife he hoped soon to see the day he would not be obliged to slave for 5d a day ... Our priests and friars ... have not been known for years to preach in these parts ... yet they are grown very vigilant of late preaching frequently and earnestly entreating that none go without their beads ...

The sense that the Babylonian captivity of the children of Israel might be drawing to a close was it seems alive, in Munster at least. Slightly less millenarian behaviour was attributed to Dublin Catholic merchants who were observed to 'have drawn their money out of the banks'.[22]

The unexpected progress of Prince Charles Edward's small army into Lancashire during November caused more than a ripple of anticipation through Catholic Ireland, not least among its fervently Jacobite poets, but no resident Catholic – of either 'old family' or new wealth – compromised himself by becoming drawn into the Jacobite initiative. Émigré Irish involvement by contrast was crucial: the financial organisation of the prince's mission by the Waters family in Paris was complemented by Antony Walsh of Nantes who organised the shipping, and four of Prince Charles Edward's landing party in Scotland were of Irish extraction. One of his most stalwart aides, Col. Felix O'Neill, was a native of south Armagh. But the links between these French- and Spanish-based networks and their Irish cousins were not as strong as in the previous generation, and Catholic gentry disillusionment with the Jacobite cause had set in before 1745. The private judgment of a minor Catholic gentleman, Owen Callanan, as news of the Jacobite victories was reaching Ireland was probably not untypical of his class: 'These wicked troubles in Scotland increases [sic] our confusion. Surely there can be nothing but a chimera in it?'[23] Disbelief, rather than hostility.

The passivity of Ireland through the autumn of 1745 was also due to the behaviour of the earl of Chesterfield, whose short regime (1745–46) punctuated the pattern of long, low-key viceroyalties. Learning from Devonshire's foolish over-reaction in the previous year he resisted pressures to arrest senior Catholic ecclesiastics and to close 'mass-houses', and in so doing managed to keep the kingdom calm. The ebbing of Jacobite fortunes and Prince Charles Edward's final defeat at Culloden in April 1746 may indeed have led to 'a very visible dejection in the countenances of men … who do not expect any other so good a chance for a revolution in their favour',[24] but the clean record of Irish Catholics of influence during the crisis was in the longer term to be used as hard evidence of Catholic loyalty to the house of Hanover and of the inappropriateness of the penal laws.

Chesterfield's more relaxed view of Irish 'popery' was a sign of things to come. And in other ways his brief viceroyalty was remembered. Displaying unusual energy for a lord lieutenant he busied himself in the management of the 1745–46 session. He distanced himself from Devonshire's parliamentary managers, particularly the Ponsonbys, and sought as he later put it, to 'govern alone', at the cost of 'a great deal more trouble', and at the risk of a difficult parliamentary sessions and of a damaged reputation in London.[25] In fact the external shocks in Britain guaranteed him a fairly easy ride, but a precedent had been set. His popularity was enhanced by his active patronage of 'improving' projects, notably the Dublin Society, and long after his return to England he was remembered as an exceptional viceroy.

* * *

The political calm was broken by events in the capital. What had begun in 1742 as an internal corporation battle between the city fathers and a large section of the enfranchised freemen became a quite novel political conflict of national significance in 1748. The municipal struggle in the early 'forties had arisen from a challenge in the lower house of the corporation to the board of aldermen's almost exclusive control over office-holding and patronage. The most outspoken critic of the aldermen's supposed alienation of freemen's liberties was one Charles Lucas, an apothecary by trade and a natural controversialist; he extended the crusade in a series of pamphlets to an attack on Dublin Castle's powers of veto over proposed mayors and sheriffs. Despite strong support among the city's manufacturing and craft guilds, Lucas' attack on aldermanic privilege had seemed lost when litigation failed in 1744. However, the death of both the sitting MPs for Dublin city during the 1748–49 parliamentary recess offered the capital's radicals a fresh opportunity to challenge the position of the small network of anglican merchant and banking families who had effectively monopolised political power in the city. Lucas (in uneasy alliance with James La Touche, a wealthier and more cautious dissident) spent the fourteen months before parliament's reassembly in October 1749 attempting to mobilise the city's 4,000-odd voters to a sense of their political oppression, urging them as a first step towards national regeneration to reject the new aldermanic candidates.

The electoral battle was one of the liveliest in any eighteenth-century Irish constituency, and well in excess of 150 pamphlets were published by the candidates and their allies.[26] The campaign saw the appearance (briefly) of the first regular radical newspaper in the city, *The Censor*, edited by Lucas himself, and the politicisation of the existing city press. Lucas's own writings were the most distinctive aspect of the affair in terms both of their volume – some thirty titles and nearly a quarter of a million words[27] – and their political argument; in his twenty 'addresses' to the freemen and freeholders which appeared erratically over thirteen months, Lucas widened his attack from aldermanic usurpations and municipal corruption to a critique of the Irish government, their parliamentary allies, and the judiciary. He drew explicitly on the historic defenders of Irish constitutional liberties Molyneux and Swift, and was also influenced by more recent English radical writers, notably Bolingbroke, in their extension and application of Lockean contract theory. In terms of abstract political ideas Lucas was in no way original; he was a polemicist with little of the satirical sophistication of *The Drapier* and a great deal of his argument was pedantically concerned with historical precedent rather than with current political realities. Yet however contorted his rhetoric and inelegant his prose, his writings circulated and in a number of instances ran to multiple editions.

Lucas was demonstrably a new voice in Irish politics. And although not directly critical of the structure of parliament, the franchise or the quality of representation, his radicalism found no echo in College Green. To office-holders and to the country gentry in parliament he seemed a subversive force – not so much because he was reasserting that the British parliament's claim to superiority over Ireland's was false (which many privately believed), but because he linked this to the argument that Ireland was not a conquered nation, and that all Irish reverses, all former rebellions, had been caused by English misgovernment; the fact that such views were being applauded in parts of the public press and by a substantial section of the capital's politically active population appeared all the more dangerous. But the implications of such heretical views on Irish rebellion, his equation of the oppression of the 'ancient Irish' in medieval times with the current fate of the king's Irish subjects, and his inclusive definition of the Irish political nation were not followed up by Lucas. Yet they were later to influence Catholic apologists arguing for relaxation of the penal laws, and political radicals seeking parliamentary reform. However Lucas's own beliefs on Catholics' entitlement to political rights remained close to traditional country whiggery; he was the champion of the *Protestant* dispossessed.

By the summer of 1749 Lucas's political education of the Dublin electorate had sharply polarised the city: a majority even on the common council of the corporation distanced themselves from him, but most of the ordinary freemen in the trade guilds – craftspeople, shopkeepers, lesser merchants – were swept along. As for the parliamentary world, Lucas was the 'seditious tradesman' exploiting the printing press and the dangerously open city franchise with unforeseeable consequences. Sir Richard Cox, at this stage a friend of the Castle, took the initiative, having been stung by Lucas's insulting references to his grandfather; immediately after the viceroy in his speech opening parliament had warned of audacious attempts being made 'to create a jealousy between the two kingdoms',[28] Cox directed a commons inquisition of Lucas and his printers. The result was a series of resolutions documenting his 'scandalous' libels, declaring him an enemy of his country, and calling for his immediate committal to prison; these were passed without any opposition and Lucas promptly fled the country. A subsequent privy council proclamation for his arrest, two grand jury presentments against him and corporate disenfranchisement together ensured that his exile (in England and beyond) was to be a long one.

The city election went ahead and the more moderate La Touche and another Lucas-endorsed merchant received the support of roughly half the city's voters. The commons' committee of privileges then held a lengthy enquiry into the election, and despite the sheriffs' return of La Touche and one of the aldermanic candidates as topping the poll, the committee invalidated La Touche's election – ostensibly because of the methods La Touche and Lucas had employed to influence voters, but in fact because La Touche was damned by association with the unacceptable Lucas.[29] Not for the last time parliament and government had united in attacking the uncontrollable petty politicians on their doorstep.

Chesterfield had been followed in the Castle by his weaker step-brother, the earl of Harrington. His position was greatly compromised by the Lucas affair; when parliament, led by the Speaker, had removed the political embarrassment, it held the initiative. Within days of Lucas's flight, a money bill, drafted by Boyle, Malone and their allies, was introduced into the house, and it used a form of words that implied parliament's right to have a formal say as to how surplus funds in the exchequer should be disposed of. It was a nice constitutional point, touching on the crown's prerogatives and on the actual ownership of public funds once they had been collected; the issue had suddenly been made relevant by the lift-off of the economy and by the unexpectedly buoyant customs and excise receipts. Harrington was obliged to accept the bill in the form proposed and then attempted to play down the precedent that was being set.

In the following year, 1750, the duke of Dorset resumed the viceroyalty after a thirteen-year absence. From the beginning he was less well disposed towards the old Speaker than he had been in his first administration. The reason for this was not a little to do with the growing influence of the English cleric, George Stone, whom Dorset had brought over as his youthful chaplain two decades previously. Stone had stayed in Ireland and, with the patronage of Dorset and Newcastle, had risen rapidly through the ecclesiastical ranks of the Church of Ireland; in 1747 he secured the see of Armagh. Like Archbishop Boulter he became a willing arm of civil government, but unlike him Stone obviously relished political power and from the late 'forties built up a network of personal supporters in the commons. Whereas Boulter's defence of 'the English interest' had been quite sincere and his involvement in church and social policies fruitful, Stone's attack on the overmighty Irish politicians was at least partly self-interested and his commitment to such public issues as financing turnpikes and canal construction superficial.

Stone and the Ponsonbys were firmly in alliance by the time of the 1751–52 parliamentary sessions, united in their aim to clip Boyle's power, and although there was no break between the Castle and Speaker Boyle, he was privately resentful of Stone's influence and ambitions. His ally Malone drafted a new money bill to authorise the allocation of the treasury surplus to the national debt, which once again failed to recognise in specific terms the king's prerogative. This time the preamble was altered by the British privy council so as to acknowledge the *prior consent* of the crown to parliament's financial decision. And again in the 1753 parliamentary sessions, almost the first business was another controversially worded money bill, which passed through the commons and was transmitted unaltered by the Castle to the British privy council, Dorset being unwilling to struggle for its amendment within the Irish privy council. Before the money bill arrived back from London – inevitably amended – Stone had scored an unexpected victory over the Speaker; it concerned a disputed election result for County Armagh, and Stone's protégé was confirmed as victor by one vote. Such electoral reverses put the Speaker's standing in the commons in some doubt; it was the first occasion in twenty years that an election vote had gone against him. The evenness of parliamentary forces and the challenge to Boyle's status restricted his room for manoeuvre and forced him into an uncharacteristically defiant posture.

In the days leading up to the debate on the amended money bill in mid-December 1753, parliamentary and public excitement in the capital rose to new levels. Boyle was later accused of 'inflaming the minds of the common people of Dublin, and making the lord lieutenant believe that the same spirit prevailed through the whole kingdom'.[30] The popular perception of the contest was not so different from the way Stone sought to portray it to the English government – a clash between those who sought to restore English authority in Dublin, and those who sought to protect and if possible enhance the Irish parliament's powers. Yet it is quite clear that to Boyle himself the struggle was essentially a political one – the preservation of his own sphere of influence from encroachment – but to some of his allies, notably Anthony Malone, the issue was more fundamental.

Between October and December several dozen topical pamphlets were published, nearly all supporting the Boyle party. These ranged from the obscurely allegorical to viciously satirical attacks on the archbishop. The leading critics of 'prior consent' were cast as 'patriots' both in the old Whig and English sense, opponents of venality and a potentially tyrannical executive, and, in an Irish sense, champions of Hibernian constitutional liberties.

The money bill, once amended in London, could of course only be accepted or rejected *in toto* on its return to Dublin. And after a debate continuing to midnight on 17 December, it was thrown out by 122 votes to 117, a result literally trumpeted about central Dublin so that 'the blaze of more than 1,000 bonfires illuminated our streets'.[31] Within a fortnight of the commons' vote, the English ministry responded. With the encouragement of an angry king, Newcastle instructed Dorset to dismiss Malone and Thomas Carter, master of the rolls, together with lesser office-holding relatives of the Speaker, because of 'their endeavours to alienate the minds of his majesty's faithful subjects of Ireland from that subordination and dependence upon this country which is the security of Ireland, as well as the right of this kingdom'.[32]

The essential legislative business of parliament, including a supply bill, was completed without any hold-up and parliament was then abruptly prorogued early in the new year. Subsequently the treasury surplus was transferred as the commons had intended but by king's letter, not by statutory authority. The outstanding question for the Castle was whether Boyle would now be sufficiently chastened to seek terms and, if not, who should act as lord justice in his place during the lord lieutenant's year-and-a-half absence. By April, Dorset's cautious approach to the crisis and his soft handling of Boyle had achieved very little, and so a second round of dismissals included Boyle's removal from the chancellorship of the exchequer. More galling for Boyle than that was the appointment of his old rival Bessborough as lord justice in his place.

By the following autumn the lords justices were anything but confident of their position. Stone pleaded with the English ministry to extend the dismissals to Nathaniel Clements, teller of the treasury, whose proclaimed loyalty to Castle policy was belied by his private behaviour; he was evidently exploiting his control over treasury cash and credit to consolidate support for the opposition cause. Clements's 'backstairs' influence at St James made the king reluctant to agree to his removal, and his survival in office was perceived by the lords justices as a serious weakening of their authority.

For reasons as much connected with English high politics as Irish circumstances, Dorset was replaced in February 1755 by the duke of

Devonshire's heir, the marquis of Hartington, a political figure of even greater weight than Dorset. With his strong Irish connections – brother-in-law of two Ponsonbys, nephew by marriage of Boyle, and heir to the huge Burlington estates in Munster – Hartington was determined to re-establish normalcy by a mixture of firmness and compromise, and to reduce the power of the undertakers and of the commons speakership. In the months between his appointment and the new parliamentary session Hartington resided in Dublin and laid the ground for the rehabilitation of the 'patriot' leaders. The danger of a new war with France gave an urgency to his task of pacification. However it took a difficult parliamentary session before a comprehensive peace was agreed with Boyle in the spring of 1756. Stone was not to be reappointed as a lord justice, and Boyle was to retire from the speakership and to support the nomination of John Ponsonby; in return Boyle was to receive remarkable compensation by any standards, the earldom of Shannon and a £2,000 p.a. pension to run for 31 years; Stone received nothing, underlining his weakened influence on both sides of the channel. The deal with Boyle was no bad investment for the Castle: Boyle's inflated public reputation as a 'patriot' leader was punctured, and some measure of political stability was restored.

Despite the extraordinary heat that the Money Bill dispute generated, it is a difficult affair both to unravel – much of the public rhetoric was coded – and to assess as to its consequences. Boyle's uncharacteristic behaviour was governed primarily by his anxiety to demonstrate his strength and indispensability – before handing over his interest to family or allies. But he was forced into such a demonstration by the policies and actions of Dorset, Stone and their parliamentary supporters. As Malcomson has observed, 'his delicate and difficult task was to defeat his enemies without at the same time surrendering to his new "patriot" friends'.[33] Whatever about the motives of the earl of Kildare and of Cox, it does appear that Malone and perhaps Carter were hoping to turn a political victory over Stone into a constitutional one, the reassertion of the Irish commons control over financial policy and taxation as a means of buttressing the autonomy – albeit weakened – of the Irish parliament. However, because the British government had throughout the affair privately accepted the more cynical reading of the situation, their response (particularly after Newcastle became prime minister in 1754) was ultimately conciliatory. This political flexibility reflected the personal and political links between several of the executive rebels and Westminster leaders, notably Kildare with Henry Fox and Boyle with the duke of Devonshire. Nevertheless, the exploitation of anti-government and by extension anti-English sentiment by Boyle's allies, encouraging 'disaffection in the lower people, who understand what they say and not what they mean',[34] and the pointed celebration of earlier challenges to English authority, however much they were only tactics of parliamentary warfare, opened a Pandora's box. The rhetoric of Lucas was borrowed by pamphleteers who now reached a wider audience of country gentry and county freeholders, and by larger-circulation successors of *The Censor*, such as Dunn's *Universal Advertiser*, which popularised the sense of a black-and-white political firmament, filled by virtuous patriots struggling against a venal Castle administration, corrupt placemen, and an English ministry intent on further subjugating the Irish parliament and draining the Irish treasury for non-Irish purposes.[35]

The settlement of 1756 in a sense only reinforced the position of the Irish parliamentary leaders in the country's administration as Hartington's successor, the duke of Bedford, discovered when he sought to dominate the 1757–58 sessions of parliament. Bedford had initially tried to woo the earl of Kildare and some of the unconnected parliamentary members, but their support was insufficient against the combined blocking power of the existing parliamentary factions; in the end Bedford came to terms with the Ponsonbys, Stone *and* Shannon: *plus ça change*. In one perspective the 1753–56 crisis had been a succession battle between two Irish-based groups, one wearing Castle costume, the other 'national' emblems, from which neither side emerged triumphant: John Ponsonby, the new Speaker, did not possess the hard core of dependent MPs that Boyle had always had, and relied on his control of public service patronage, especially the revenue. Boyle's eldest son and heir lacked his father's canniness but he inherited the unpopularity which his father's rehabilitation had earned him in 1756. Furthermore, the problems of parliamentary management for all faction leaders were increasing in the late 1750s as political demands from electors in the open constituencies began to build up, with calls for fixed-term parliaments and a reduction of the civil list.

Such tendencies meant that Whitehall was forced to examine the terms of the old governing coalition. Given that the effectiveness of the leading families as brokers between the British government and the Irish gentry was in decline, successive English ministries went in search of new means of achieving a working relationship with the Irish parliament and the Irish ruling class. Parliamentary union was canvassed by some in London, but unfounded fears of a sudden move by government in that direction triggered rioting in Dublin in December 1759, and the brief occupation of the parliament house (principally by the denizens of the

Liberties). This, 'the most spectacular popular political demonstration to be staged prior to the rise of the Volunteers', eloquently demonstrated the public sense of ownership of College Green.[36]

OUTSIDE THE POLITY

The final years of George II's reign were a critical transitional period in the slow reincorporation of propertied Catholic families into the Irish political world. 1748 had witnessed the final attempt by Irish MPs to strengthen penal legislation against the Catholic laity (in the form of a revised foreign education bill). The initiative collapsed, not on this occasion because of diplomatic pressure in London but as a result of discreet but successful lobbying of the Irish house of lords. Even more significantly, the old advocate of last resort for Irish Catholic interests, the Habsburg monarch, switched alliances in the diplomatic revolution of 1756, and for the first time in more than a century Austria became Britain's enemy with the outbreak of the Seven Years War (pitching Britain and Prussia against Austria, Russia and France). The return of Anglo-French hostilities that year inevitably raised the spectre of an attack on Ireland: thus on the eve of hostilities the Catholic archbishop of Armagh and several priests were arrested at Dundalk on suspicion of raising money for James III, but they were quickly released. In truth, the elderly Stuart claimant was no longer a potent threat; indeed he had never had any particular interest in uprooting Protestant Ireland, and his dissolute heir Prince Charles Edward was fading from the reckoning.

By coincidence the magistrate involved with O'Reilly's detention was the earl of Clanbrassill: in the previous parliamentary sessions he was the instigator of an attempt in the Irish house of lords to secure support for a registration scheme legitimising the secular Catholic priesthood, while at the same time confirming and enforcing the banishment of the always suspect regular clergy, The initiative divided both the pro- and anti-reform camps, and was unsuccessful. The registry bill was revived in 1757 with further concessions designed to win Catholic compliance but, despite the explicit support of the duke of Bedford, it was thrown out in the Irish privy council by a narrow margin. The bill was remarkable for proposing a simple oath of allegiance for diocesan priests which had been devised quarter a century earlier by Cornelius Nary, Catholic theologian and independent-minded parish priest of St Michan's in Dublin. But even if the bill had been successful, the scruples of too many Catholic clergy, in particular those in the religious orders, would have been offended by Clanbrassill's compromise formula.

In discriminating against the regulars, the registration bill would only have done more brutally what was implicit in the sweeping measures of ecclesiastical reform decreed by Pope Benedict XIV in 1751: all new Irish recruits to the religious orders were henceforth to go to Europe for their education; all regulars on the Irish mission were to live in community and be under the authority in many respects of the local bishop. The pope's restrictions on the religious orders were based on a faulty assessment of their discipline and of the pastoral role they played in eighteenth-century Ireland, but the restrictions were not rescinded. In consequence there was a drastic decline during the following decades in the number of friars (from around 700 *c*.1750) and of religious houses, and the consequential strengthening of diocesan and parochial structures, thereby helping to shape the strongly episcopalian Irish Catholic church of the future.

Against the background of these events, the return of war was the catalyst for the formation in Dublin of a Catholic association in the summer of 1756. It seems that it was city merchants, not church leaders or Catholic gentry, who made the first move in establishing this, the first explicitly Catholic public organisation in Hanoverian Ireland. The bishops, in particular the tough new archbishop of Dublin Richard Lincoln, were uncomfortable with such innovations, and hopes by Catholic gentry that this new body would sanction an address of loyalty (echoing that of 1727) were dashed. Attempts in 1757, co-ordinated by the Catholic peer Lord Trimleston, to get clerical support for one element of the proposed registry bill, the regular offering up of prayers for George II, ran into trouble after initial support and the plan was lost in fratricidal acrimony. It was only with the more proximate threat of a French invasion in the autumn of 1759 (in which the hero of Fontenoy, Lord Clare, was to have had a commanding role) that several groups of Irish Catholics felt compelled to declare their loyalties: some 300 Dublin-based merchants and gentry presented Speaker Ponsonby with an address of loyalty and support for 'this just and necessary war'. Similar Catholic addresses were sent up from the southern cities that winter, the declaration from Cork warning France of its 'imaginary hope of assistance here from the former attachments of our deluded predecessors ...'.[37] No Catholic cleric was involved in these public declarations, but they were a timely gesture. In February 1760 a force of over 600 Frenchmen under François Thurot entered Belfast Lough, captured the ill-fortified castle at Carrickfergus, and held it for some days. It was a sign of the times that in the embarrassed aftermath there was no crackdown on prominent Irish Catholics.

The most solid evidence of a fresh turn in Catholic affairs was the fraternal network that emerged around John Curry, leading Dublin physician and man of letters, and Charles O'Conor, Roscommon landowner and antiquarian. O'Conor was a Janus-like figure who kept a diary in Irish and yet was widely read in the new philosophy emanating from France, and once contrasted his own politics with his mother's Jacobitism. Through his writings and social contacts he played a key role between the 1740s and the 1770s in quietly opening up a civic space for secular Catholic loyalism to the house of Hanover.[38] It was a process predicated on finding common agreement among the contending parties on a civil oath of allegiance, while at the same time generating broad-based Protestant support on pragmatic 'modern' grounds for religious toleration. This fledgling post-Jacobite Catholic intelligentsia were somewhat ahead of their bishops (about whom they expressed much private frustration) in the search for rapprochement with official Ireland and for a formal discarding of links with the Jacobite court. Indeed their agenda was primarily a lay agenda, seeking the relaxation of the penal laws as they affected their secular world. But they were greatly helped by the decision of the pope in 1760 – after the death of George II – to omit James III's name in all future briefs of appointment of Irish bishops. And on James' death in 1766 the non-recognition of Charles Edward by the papacy was the vital next step, ending the 75-year long status of Irish Catholicism as literally an established church in exile.

Despite this new configuration, the Catholic *politiques* of Dublin were at that stage disregarded by, and quite disregarding, the powerful 'hedge-Jacobitism' of the Irish-language poets whose writings old and new circulated widely in manuscript and resonated in the southern countryside. But even within the political sphere a fundamental philosophical rejection of the penal code was possible: the best-placed London ally of the Irish Catholic leadership, the aspirant politician Edmund Burke, put forward (but did not publish) the argument in the 1760s that the penal laws 'contradict nature and the end of law itself', and offended the principle of rational utility. And that explosive line of argument based on natural rights theories, when taken to its logical conclusion, was to unite elite and popular challenges to the *status quo* a generation later.[39]

* * *

At first sight there were striking common elements in the position of Catholics and of Presbyterians at mid-century: in both cases the wealthy and ambitious among them were denied full participation in public life by the law of the land – unless they chose to conform to the established church; in both communities religious authority was contested and subverted, internal dog-fights consuming much of the energies of their respective clergy, and this was at least in part a consequence of the absence of state endorsement or of strong public patronage; and in both cases their intellectual leaders, their clergy, were educated abroad, Trinity College Dublin remaining an almost exclusively anglican institution. For prospective Presbyterian ministers Edinburgh and in particular Glasgow were as much the centres of their educational universe as were Paris, Bordeaux, Toulouse, Louvain, Salamanca, and the two dozen other continental Irish colleges for the streams of Catholic seminarians. Lowland Scotland may not have been an entirely unfamiliar world for the *Scoti-hiberni* (as Glasgow University described them) but these Presbyterian migrants did not regard themselves as expatriate Scots. Scottish theological divisions were however responsible for some of the institutional fragmentation in eighteenth-century Irish Presbyterianism. But not dissimilarly, the old French debate on Gallicanism – on the relationship between church and crown – cast a long and awkward shadow across the Irish Catholic church.

But in many other respects Irish Presbyterianism was the polar opposite of Irish Catholicism – in its Calvinist theological tradition, in its decentralised administrative culture of kirk session and governance by lay elder, in its attitude to the comprehensive scriptural education of the laity, and in its geographical concentration, mainly but not exclusively, in the nine counties of Ulster. By the 1750s Presbyterianism was far less formidable politically than it had been half a century previously, thanks to the haemorrhage of its gentry into the ranks of the Church of Ireland, and to its own bitter doctrinal divisions over whether or not ministers should subscribe to the 1642 Westminster Confession of Faith. Yet socially and economically the quarter of a million Irish Presbyterians were as a community far better off than their Catholic neighbours, and as an interest group they exerted greater influence, a consequence both of the Ulster economic take-off in the previous generation and of the strategic position of Presbyterian families in the trading towns of Ulster and in Dublin. The Ulster north Atlantic migration, principally of Presbyterians, which had started in the 1710s and 1720s in years of real economic difficulty, was by mid-century no longer a sign of hard times at home but of well-advertised opportunities for the footloose in north America – among their kith and kin. Indeed the scale of this Ulster out-migration (averaging about 1,000 p.a. at this period) was often exaggerated by contemporaries, as was the role of religious persecution in triggering it.

The hybrid influences of English non-conformity and Scottish Presbyterianism created a singular culture of dissent in Dublin, which in turn permeated Irish Presbyterianism at large; a remarkable succession of theologically independent and philosophically innovative ministers passed through the capital, most notably the Ulster-born Francis Hutcheson who in the 1720s had attracted the patronage of the radical peer Lord Molesworth and of the viceroy Lord Carteret; his later academic career in Glasgow as 'father of the Scottish Enlightenment' was truly Dublin's loss. But the Dublin Presbyterian world continued to be a small but important crucible for the development of ideas and movements that would challenge the *status quo*.

What best captures the gulf between the wider Presbyterian and Catholic worlds of the 1750s is the contrasting public profiles of their leaders. The Catholic bishops, compromised by the Vatican's continued refusal to recognise the Hanoverian succession and understandably anxious to give no ammunition to their enemies in College Green, were determined at all costs to stay out of Irish public notice and to keep their 'flocks' quiet. Presbyterian ministers, as befitted a far more consensual church polity and a self-confident and educated laity, adopted a variety of public postures on matters of theology and, less often, politics. Most striking were the handful of clergy, mainly it seems 'New Light' men, who were prominently involved in the 'patriot' clubs of Antrim and Down in 1753–55, men who had passed under the influence of Hutcheson: 'if ever one had the art to create an esteem for liberty and a contempt for tyranny and tyrants, he was the man'.[40] The influence of such principled advocacy resonated in countless Ulster sermons and was reaching as far as the thirteen colonies. But as a political language it was not yet available to the Catholic clergy of Ireland.

'*The farmer's daughter's return from Dublin*' *c*. 1760. The new tyranny of fashion – in dress, in food, in reading, in manners – was diffused socially downwards from the gentry world to the 'comfortable' farming classes, and geographically inland from the port cities. Dublin's role was critical, both as the centre for luxury trades and crafts, and as the social stage for conspicuous display, not least on the part of the marriageable daughters of the gentry. By the 1760s the stage was larger and the actors were being drawn from a wider circle. (Engr.: B.L. Dept. of Prints & Drawings)

4

The Economic Base

LONG TERM TRENDS

POPULATION IN early Restoration Ireland had at most been around 1.5 millions; a century later it was slightly over double that figure, with the rate of growth accelerating. The level of economic activity grew more strikingly; in 1664–65 the volume of Irish exports had been barely one-fifth of the level being recorded in the 1770s.[1] The livestock population in the 1660s had also been much smaller, and the proportion of land surface waste, i.e. unable to support regular grazing of livestock, far higher. Reclamation of bog, marsh and 'mountain' was one of the great economic achievements of the intervening period. In the 1660s the only roads sufficiently durable to withstand wheeled traffic were a series of ill-maintained trunk routes linking Dublin with the outports; by the late eighteenth century a complex web of carriage roads criss-crossed the country (apart from the western peninsulas) and Dublin was the pivot of a growing public coach network.[2]

The scale of Irish towns had also been far smaller in the 1660s; apart from Dublin, already containing a population of *c.* 30,000, there was no city of any consequence by European standards. A century later there was an impressive series of large provincial ports – Limerick, Cork, Waterford and Belfast – with a combined population of perhaps two-thirds of Dublin's 150,000. The total number of urban settlements did not, however, increase over that period. The great era of village and market foundation had been in the first half of the seventeenth century, and many of those plantation seedlings failed to mature. But in the north, the west and parts of the south numerous landlord villages, mostly of seventeenth-century origin, blossomed in the first two-thirds of the eighteenth century, very often aided by the siting within them of textile manufacturers and dealers, or of an army barracks.

Irish society became qualitatively more commercialised over the period. Judged by the standards of the late eighteenth century, Restoration Ireland had hardly constituted an integrated market economy. The small port cities each had roughly defined hinterlands, long-established spheres of economic and social influence. And although the growth of seventeenth-century Dublin and the rise of cattle exports were breaking down the autonomy of these market hinterlands, the process of economic integration was only really beginning in the 1660s. Inter-regional trade was then of very little importance, and regional agricultural specialisation was very limited. One indication of the decidedly primitive structure of the economy was the small number of fairs around the country – and their uneven distribution: Bourk's *Almanack* of 1684 lists some 503 fairs, 43 per cent of which were in Leinster. Aside from their social and carnival functions, the quarterly or twice yearly fairs were the main conduit for cattle exchanges and the occasion for retail purchases of non-local commodities. By the 1770s there were nearly 3,000 advertised fairs around the country, only 27 per cent of which were now in Leinster. Sites where weekly markets were authorised also grew in number, but many of those already patented in 1660 (notably some of the 500-odd new markets created between 1600 and 1641) remained paper creations, and others, though initially successful, withered as the village settlements around them atrophied. By the mid-nineteenth century there were only 349 active market sites in the whole country.[3]

Agricultural sales throughout the period were predominantly for overseas markets. Exports as a proportion of national income in the 1660s have been tentatively estimated at 5 per cent; by the last quarter of the eighteenth century the proportion had probably doubled.[4] And if we allow for the great expansion of the non-farmer population over the intervening period – in the successful urban communities, in rural handicraft industry and in agricultural labour – then it can be assumed that the overall proportion of agricultural output sold, bartered or exchanged had increased much more. At its simplest this meant that by the later eighteenth century there were far more households in regular contact with the market, transacting either food sales or food purchases. However, even in the 1660s the use of money in the settlement of commercial deals and in the payment of agricultural rents was already firmly established through the greater part of the country. Most householders probably had several cash transactions every year, although relatively few people outside the towns would have handled coin or promissory notes even once a week. A century later the greater wealth of the country was reflected in the much larger and more regular circulation of coin, in the diffusion of private-bank notes for wholesale and bulk transactions, and in the greater acceptability of small denomination inter-personal credit notes. However there was still a large fraction of the population who were only marginally involved in the cash economy.

The existence of such a subterranean stratum introduces the third contrast between Restoration Irish society and that of the late eighteenth century. Sir William Petty, our only contemporary source for seventeenth-century social statistics, delineated a community with a highly unequal distribution of wealth: in 1686 he suggested that 'above 100,000' houses, containing perhaps 40–45 per cent of the population, were worth less than 10s (50p) each, the owners of which held no land to speak of, and possessed perhaps two or three head of cattle; in other words they were servants and labourers.[5] Petty's rough estimate is not so different from a more sophisticated one for contemporary England, where Gregory King calculated that 47 per cent of families were headed by a labourer, an out-servant, a 'cottager', a pauper, or a vagrant.[6] However, the material resources of the Irish poor were clearly less, in terms at least of housing and furnishings, than their English peers and, with no equivalent to the parish poor law of England, years of bad harvests or other adversity wreaked a greater havoc among the Irish poor than their English counterparts. Petty had estimated in 1672 (perhaps rather conservatively) an average per capita income of £2.60 p.a. for 86 per cent of the Irish population (i.e. his near landless families plus small farmers) and £10.00 p.a. for the residual 14 per cent of the population (in England in 1688, even King's labouring and servant families were credited with an income of £3.12 per capita – and £12.65 per capita for the other 53 per cent).

By comparison (although the data are not strictly comparable), in 1791–92, 11 per cent of the Irish population had a gross per capita income in excess of £20 p.a., while 59 per cent were surviving with less than £5 p.a., some much less. The really significant new element was the increase of those strata in Irish society who were neither at the minimum subsistence level nor demonstrably wealthy: the 30 per cent whose per capita income in 1791–92 lay between £5 and £20 p.a.[7] Admittedly Petty's tantalising occupational estimates of 1686 imply that even by then there was perhaps 55 per cent of the population (as estimated by him) above the level of servant and labourer, but insofar as most of these were part of the 86 per cent with an income of £2.60 (following his 1672 estimate), the only conclusion that one can draw from Petty's analysis is that even the small landholders and cattle-owners of Restoration Ireland appeared to be little better off than agricultural servants and day labourers. The relative importance in statistical terms of the near landless was in fact exaggerated by Petty (generalising from his Munster perspective), for the composite picture of rural society that we get from other late seventeenth-century sources suggests a relatively homogeneous 'peasant' class, Irish-speaking and illiterate, consisting mainly of 'labouring farmers' who owned or hired small herds of livestock and who rented land in partnership with their neighbours, usually for short periods, the rent for which was paid off in money, labour or a mixture of the two. The real poverty of this smallholder majority of the population was demonstrated by the devastating effects of bad grain or fodder harvests and of cattle epidemics: under stress such tenants simply took their movables and fled.

There was of course a veneer of 'strong' farmers with large flocks of sheep and extensive herds in the 1660s. Many of these graziers were themselves landowners or freeholders (i.e. tenants holding very long or perpetuity leases) who were directly managing at least part of their properties. Other large stock-owners were members of the dispossessed clans whose metamorphosis from landlord to tenant had been more legal than economic; and some big farmers were first- or second-generation immigrants, often enjoying a privileged relationship with their ground landlord.

By the final decades of the eighteenth century the stratification of rural society was considerably more complex. The descendants of the large farmers of Restoration Ireland, if they were still in possession, had in many instances become under-landlords or 'middlemen', renting out most or all of their pastures to small farmers, and enjoying genteel status as *tiarnaí beaga*. Only in prime grassland parishes did large farms tend to remain relatively intact as production units. As for the rest, their fate depended even more on local land quality and on distance from major towns and ports. In upland districts, on poorer soils and in areas away from major centres of demand, the small-farmer stratum had, on balance, recovered and increased in numbers, benefiting from a growing involvement in market production as the eighteenth century progressed, from the rising profits from young stock, and from the widening opportunities for supplementary income from spinning and weaving. However on the better soils of Munster, Leinster and east Connacht, overseas demand for beef and butter, coming at a time when the profits from cereal farming were poor, had led to a drastic change in farm size: part-subsistence small farmers had all but disappeared, and large empty grazing ranches or dairy farms dominated the naturally lush and well-drained pastures from Westmeath to north Kerry. In these areas a large under-employed labouring population survived, clustering on the more marginal soils and above the 150-metre contour, sustained by an uncertain mix of domestic industry, intermittent local agricultural employment and seasonal migration. In Ikerrin barony (north Tipperary), which was by no means an extreme demonstration of these tendencies, the wealthiest 25 per cent of Catholic householders in 1750 occupied over 80 per cent of the (non-Protestant) farmland, while the poorest 25 per cent held only 2 per cent. By comparison, in Culdaff parish in north-east Donegal, where flax cultivation and spinning, barley growing and illicit distillation, fishing and cattle rearing all coexisted, the distribution of land (in 1773) was decidedly less unequal: the top 25 per cent held just under half the profitable land surface, the poorest 25 per cent around 11 per cent.[8] In south-east Ulster, the almost uniformly small size of farms was a function of manufacturing prosperity and population growth, with agricultural production an ancillary to the extraordinary industrial expansion; on the Brownlow estate in the Lagan valley, the mean size of new tenant holdings had fallen from 72 acres (statute) in the 1660s to a mere 8 acres in the 1790s; conversely, new rent levels on the estate rose over the same period from £0.08 per acre to £0.94.[9]

Over Ireland as a whole, the most important structural change was the emergence of medium-sized independent farming families, approximating to the 30 per cent who occupied the middle category in the 1791–92 survey. The resurgence of commercial tillage farming in the last quarter of the eighteenth century increased both their numbers and their wealth, but even by the 1750s the importance of modest cattle-owning and lease-holding farmers had been growing, families with sufficient resources to buy consumer goods as well as to sell farm produce at the fair or market, and able in a modest way to respond advantageously to market opportunities.

The evolution of exports between the 1620s and the 1790s highlights very starkly the two supports of the commercial economy: cattle production and domestic linen manufacture. Fishing, for instance, which was regionally very important in the plantation period, dwindled as European markets were supplied more cheaply from across the Atlantic. As for grain, international prospects were generally depressed up to the 1760s in what was an era of historically low prices, with market opportunities only for the best located or best cosseted producers – the middle colonies of north America or the innovating districts of south-east England. Irish iron production and timber processing were also condemned to a marginal role by the operation of the laws of comparative advantage: in the eighteenth century when cheap timber from New England and cheaply smelted pig iron from Scandinavia and Russia was available to Britain, the conservation of Bannside or Munster Blackwater woodland made little commercial sense; profits lay in the maintenance and extension of pasture ground. Sheep farming and wool processing were of course of strategic regional significance for much of the period, and large-scale sheep production remained profitable in shallow-soiled limestone districts throughout the eighteenth century, but after the 1720s, it was the state of British, Continental and Atlantic markets for beef, butter and linen that between them determined the health of the Irish economy. The successful expansion of the linen trade was undoubtedly the most remarkable economic achievement of the period. It was an Ulster-centred activity, but neither the ingredients nor the results of that success were exclusive to the province; the pronounced rise in incomes and population of the north-east quarter of the island had strong spill-over effects that reached Mayo, Waterford and Cork.

VALUE AND STRUCTURE OF IRISH EXPORTS 1626–1796/7

	Official value of exports (1664/5 = 100)	*Cattle and cattle products (per cent)*	*Grain and grain products (per cent)*	*Fish (per cent)*	*Hemp, flax and linen (per cent)*	*Sheep, wool and wool products (per cent)*	*Iron, timber and misc. (per cent)*
1626*	55*	53.4	8.2	21.7	1.9	8.8	6.0
1664/5	100	62.0	1.6	6.0	4.5	24.8	1.2
1700/1	167	53.7	2.2	2.8	8.4	30.2	2.7
1725/6	247	50.9	1.9	1.8	33.7	9.6	2.2
1750/1	481	36.5	1.2	0.4	49.4	10.6	1.9
1775/6	807	38.8	3.8	0.8	51.6	4.5	0.6
1796/7	1126	34.5	6.5	0.1	56.5	1.2	1.2

Sources: 1626 – P.R.O.(L.), CO/30/389; 1664/5 – R. Dunlop, 'A Note on the Export Trade of Ireland in 1641, 1665 and 1669', *Eng. Hist. Rev.*, XXII (1907); 1700/1-1796/7 – P.R.O.(L.), CUST/15.

Note: *Omits figures for Derry and Coleraine; all 1626 exports valued at the official prices for 1664/5.

Four stages can usefully be identified in the country's trade-centred economic evolution between the mid-seventeenth century and 1800.

(a) 1652–90: after the plague-torn and destructive Cromwellian reconquest, there followed a thirty-year period of economic expansion frequently interrupted by external war, crop failures (notably in the mid-1670s) and trade disruption (such as the Cattle Acts). The production levels of the late 1630s were probably surpassed by the mid-1660s, but the striking growth in dairying, the development of wool processing and fine cloth-making, and the beginnings of commercial linen production only really occurred in the prosperous late 'seventies and early 'eighties. Three specific factors underlay Restoration economic growth: the new momentum of English commercial involvement in the Caribbean which, despite restrictive Navigation Acts, led a number of Irish ports into Atlantic ventures and greatly widened the demand for salted beef, butter and ship biscuit; relatively free access to the French market which became the single most important source of demand for Irish butter and hides; and the continued inflow of migrants from Britain (now increasingly from the north of England and Scotland) which strengthened in particular the rural economy of central and east Ulster, making the small town of Belfast the fourth busiest port in Ireland by the 1680s. With the growth of political tensions in the early stages of James II's reign, business confidence and land values began to decline across the country, and the Williamite war witnessed massive livestock losses and some population movement.

(b) 1690–1730: economic recovery in the 1690s spanned the whole decade and was particularly powerful in the final years of the century, with strong external demand for Irish grain and animal products. However, the new century began on a very sour note with depressed export prices, unfortunately timed currency adjustments and bad harvests. Dairy, beef and linen production grew in short bursts during the second decade after the Peace of Utrecht, but the benefits were unevenly spread. Indeed throughout this phase, the concentration of economic power – geographically on the larger ports, socially in the hands of the big graziers and the master-dairymen – was the price of commercial growth. Ulster's distinctive 'proto-industrial' economy was emerging, but the region was still backward enough to be convulsed by the run of wretched harvests in the later 1720s. Those years and the epidemic-torn early 1730s represent an historic trough, a time when both Ulster and the grassland economy of the south were profoundly depressed, when population was probably falling, and when the lot of the lowland poor was visibly deteriorating. This black conjuncture prompted some of the most acute economic writing of the century – by Sir John Browne, Thomas Prior, Arthur Dobbs, Samuel Madden, Francis Bindon and George Berkeley – and led to the founding (in 1731) of the most successful eighteenth-century agency promoting Irish economic development, the Dublin Society.

(c) 1730–1775: these were the critical years of economic growth, although outside Ulster there was very little sign of it before the mid-1740s. However, the mid-century upswing between 1747 and 1752 was of unprecedented strength and affected nearly all sectors of the economy, and there was another surge forward in the 1760s. The dynamism of the British Atlantic economy, the more positive effects of war on the Irish economy, and the strengthening of domestic British demand for Irish foodstuffs, accelerated all the slow-maturing processes evident since the mid-seventeenth century – capital formation, population growth, rural industry, urbanisation and social stratification. In addition grain (and therefore bread) prices began their long-delayed recovery in the early 1760s, and rising profits from cereal farming were to have profound effects both on the landscape and rural society. The upward drift in the cost of living also subverted settled relationships in urban society, as the purchasing power of skilled artisans began to weaken.

This cycle of national expansion was ending in the early 1770s with the Atlantic provisions trade reaching never to be repeated levels, with a serious crisis of over-production in the linen trade, and with other signs of speculative overheating of an economy that had perhaps grown too fast for its own good. Contemporary observers in the later 'seventies made conflicting diagnoses on the state of the economy; the most famous and best travelled one, Arthur Young, observed that Ireland since 1748 had 'made as great advances as could possibly be expected, perhaps greater than any other country in Europe',[10] and he was probably not far from the truth.

(d) 1775–1800: despite the wider commercial opportunities offered by 'free trade' and American independence, the economy became more completely interlocked with that of Great Britain in the last quarter of the eighteenth century. The rise of British domestic demand for Irish food dictated a change in the composition and quality of agricultural exports. Linen, however, remained the leading export, and the last great spurt in output for nearly half a century occurred in the late 1780s and early 1790s. These were years of visible expansion throughout the economy, a time of cheap money and investment starts in many sectors; they coincided with an exceptional industrial advance in Britain. The new textile and metallurgical technologies across the water had at first generally benign effects on Ireland, but urban textile handicrafts were seriously damaged. The upward drift in food prices, more pronounced in the 1790s, greatly benefited the Irish farming classes but compounded the difficulties for the urban artisan and the rural labourer. Behind agriculture's responsiveness and the continued spread of rural industry was the basic fact of a buoyant labour supply. The acceleration in population growth since the 1740s had virtually no impact on rural mortality levels; the rate of population growth was by this stage unprecedented and, even within contemporary Europe, unusual. The rapidity of economic change and of population growth, coupled now with price inflation, contributed not a little to the social and political crisis of the 1790s.

LANDLORDS AND TENANTS

The pattern of land ownership which stabilised after the Williamite forfeitures was to remain intact for nearly 200 years: an untidy patchwork of over 2,000 large private estates, a few quite compact, some broken up into non-contiguous parcels, covered most of the land surface. The majority of these fee-simple properties were in the range 2–4,000 acres (statute). They were owned overwhelmingly by members of the Church of Ireland (some of Gaelic or Old English patrilinear descent, most of New English), surprisingly few by Presbyterians, and a small and declining residue by Catholics – notably in Counties Galway, Dublin, Meath, Louth, Antrim and Kerry. Already in the early eighteenth century there was a tendency for the very large estates to fragment over time, as sections were sold off or let on perpetuity terms, generally to existing smaller landowners. The great patrimonies of the early seventeenth century – the Ormond, Boyle, Chichester, Antrim and Thomond estates for example – were nearly all being attenuated by a combination of debt-induced sales, partible inheritance and bad management (itself usually a consequence of the owner's non-residence). However, there were still several dozen great estates of more than 50,000 acres each in the late eighteenth century. A few of these had been built up during the period by canny land dealers and speculators when property was cheap and title uncertain – the most important example of course being the estates of Speaker Conolly – but the general eighteenth-century tendency was towards the consolidation of the medium-sized estate. Few freehold properties as small as one or two townlands (i.e. less than 500 acres) seem to have survived; the majority of the minor Cromwellian grantees were bought out by their more tenacious neighbours, while the Restoration land settlement had almost completely overlooked the claims of the very small Catholic property owners who had been so numerous before 1641 in Gaelic areas of the country.[11]

Irish estates in the new order of things did not become distinct production units; landowners rarely adopted an active programme of development embracing all their property, and only involved themselves directly in investment and production in rather special circumstances. In the later seventeenth century the commercial involvement of landowners was declining; larger proprietors everywhere, and smaller owners in the more advanced regions of the country, received most of their income in the form of twice-yearly rent payments from farming tenants, and by the early eighteenth century landlord participation in commercial agriculture was of little significance except in the wool-producing areas of Tipperary and Connacht. Demesnes – the land kept by resident gentry in their own hands – rarely exceeded one or two townlands in size, and they were used to provision their own extended households as well as for recreational and ornamental purposes. There was really no possibility that an eastern European or plantation-type of production system would develop, given the relatively large size of Irish property units and the density of rural population. If Irish landlords wished to use their properties for more than just provisioning their own needs and paying crown rents and taxes, and if social necessity required them to consume non-local commodities in large measure, they had perforce to let out most of their land to tenants. But to what type of tenant?

Landowners by the late seventeenth century had in practice complete freedom to choose whatever type of tenant they wanted (despite the formal obligation in many older plantation patents that a specific number of British tenants should be introduced).[12] And all other things being equal, landowners preferred to let their land to individual tenants who owned enough livestock to fill a townland, i.e. 200–400 acres (statute), and who were able to withstand the violent fluctuations in farming profits. But small 'partnership' or labouring tenants, often forming a kin group, were the usual, albeit less desirable alternative; they were, it was assumed, more likely to go into arrears and to default, leaving no assets; by their very number they were more troublesome to deal with; and they were less likely to 'improve' their farms. This concern with 'improvement' was present throughout the period, and yet the meaning of the concept remained ambiguous: it had evolved from the early seventeenth-century assumption of government and settlers alike that British colonisation was synonymous with agricultural transformation, that New English tenants would establish a new order of agriculture, commercialised and technically superior to indigenous systems. This assumption that persons of recent English (or, less emphatically, Scottish) origin, or simply Protestants, would be more inclined to divide and enclose land, plant orchards and gardens, and build solid farmhouses lingered long after 1700 in gentry thinking, and even in the newspapers of the third quarter of the eighteenth century advertisements of farms to be let quite often expressed an explicit preference for Protestant applicants (although by that stage local electoral considerations were an additional factor influencing some landlords). This prejudice against Catholic tenants in general was based on a faulty assessment of their willingness to participate fully in the market economy, but it does seem that substantial Catholic tenants, persons of 'old' family – the class whose social values were reflected in contemporary Gaelic poetry – were indeed more reluctant to engage in new forms of farming than at least some larger tenants of recent British origin. But evidence from later in the eighteenth century suggests that Irish small farmers had been discriminated against primarily because of their lack of inherited resources.

In devolving the management of their property onto tenants, landlords sought to control (a) the size of holdings, (b) the length of the contract, (c) the manner in which a tenant used the land, and (d) the level of rent. Until well into the eighteenth century the townland was the normal tenurial unit, although most estates had a few large tenants who rented whole groups of townlands; such persons might be the owners' relatives, or descendants of old owners or of early settlers holding very long 'beneficial' leases. The move to smaller individual tenancies of less than a single townland was usually a sign of local economic advance – the intensification of commercial tillage or of textile manufacturing – and was becoming much more common by the 1790s. As for the length of the contract, normal practice changed here also; in the later seventeenth century farm tenancies were usually for a maximum of twenty-one years, often for as little as seven years, and some were simply 'at will', i.e. from year to year. However very long or perpetuity tenancies at fixed rents were occasionally given where land was hard to let or where the owner's financial needs were pressing. But after the difficult early years of the new century, thirty-one years or (for Protestants) three-lives leases[13] became the standard demand of prospective tenants, and by the 1720s the thirty-one year farm lease became the conventional arrangement in most parts of the country.

The income which landowners sought from their tenants was spelt out in cash terms in the lease. Rents were agreed with prospective tenants by a variety of means, and much depended on the lessor's knowledge of the productive potential of the land being leased and the would-be lessee's ability to discourage competitors from bidding against himself. Even before 1641 it had been apparent that where there was competition for farmland, indigenous Irish bidders would offer more than tenants of British origin, but the advice offered to one young landlord by his guardian in 1702 had become almost a conventional wisdom: 'English tenants are best and safest for you even at ten in the hundred cheaper than the Irish'.[14] In other words, the financial security for a landlord of taking on a Protestant tenant was worth the lower rent; indeed the general bias towards Protestants where they were present in a district gave such applicants a lever in lease negotiations that was frequently abused. Where a tenant was committed to extensive improvement clauses, the rent was, in theory, adjusted proportionately; in practice the size of the discount depended on the prospective tenant's credibility and the strength of the landlord's own commitment to such improvements.

Land values between the 1660s and the 1790s rose spectacularly across the country, rents per acre growing by a factor of ten or more. This upward movement in the rates at which new leases were set reflected four distinct processes: the growth in external demand for agricultural goods; improved rural access to wholesale markets; productivity improvements in farming; and, after the 1740s, population growth – which stimulated the demand for small holdings and accommodation plots (usually not directly rented from landlords) and boosted the relative value of poorer quality land. The continued success of landowners in tapping the profits of Irish agricultural commercialisation was of course the foundation of their political strength as well as the means by which they left such a visible mark on the physical landscape. But it is important not to exaggerate their economic role; the lease terms that became standard, even the thirty-one-year maximum that Catholic tenants could hold after the 1704 legislation, were long enough to give many tenants ample opportunity to augment their wealth: rent payments remained fixed for the term of a lease, and while farm incomes may have fluctuated, in the long run they were rising – and visibly so from the mid-forties. Broadly speaking most of those who secured full-term leases in eighteenth-century Ireland stood to improve their circumstances. Conversely, the long leases that remained in vogue until the late eighteenth century meant that actual landlord income per acre owned was much below current letting levels; there was for some owners a frustrating delay in securing the benefits of a rising market.

If tenants are to be cast as the 'improvers' who got on with the business of farming behind the shield of long leases, were landlords simply irrelevant parasites? In this era at least, the answer must be a negative. First, the very creation by the landed class of a competitive market for farmland pushed agricultural output to levels far beyond what would have been produced if rents had been frozen, or if some form of 'peasant proprietorship' had emerged in the eighteenth century. But given the relatively large proportion of gross income siphoned off by landlords – more than one-third – it appears that the proportion of rent receipts actually ploughed back into productive investment was very small, seldom more than a few per cent; administrative costs (primarily the agent's salary) were usually a larger charge. Many landlords were admittedly involved in wetland reclamation projects on otherwise valuable farms out of lease, but dryland reclamation – the clearance of scrub, rocks and the conversion of poor hill land to permanent grass – was for the most part done piecemeal by tenants and cottier subtenants.

Landlords were more heavily involved in infrastructural improvements. These included the laying out of village sites, the purchase of patents for holding fairs and markets, the construction of market houses, the patronage of urban industrial projects – usually linen manufacture, and the provision of a rent-free site for barracks. Landlords also invested much energy and some capital in road improvement; local political influence was used to determine parish and, after 1709, county grand jury decisions as to the allocation of funds for road and bridge repair, and for new construction; they also subsidised the building and improvement of farm access roads which encouraged farmers to turn to wheeled transport. The turnpiking of trunk roads, which began in the early 1730s, reduced long-distance transport costs, particularly between Dublin, the midlands and Ulster, and was financed with local gentry funds. Some new trunk roads, such as the turnpike between Cork city and central Kerry initiated by Kerry landlords in the 1740s, were specifically intended to improve market access for producers, and were immediately successful. Landed interest in river navigation and canal projects – if rarely profitable – was also widespread from the time several Armagh proprietors investigated the possibility of linking Lough Neagh and Carlingford Lough in the 1690s. That idea was realised in 1742 (financed by parliament rather than local landlords); it contributed little to reducing the nation's coal imports but boosted land values in the Newry region. The other major canal scheme, the Dublin-Barrow-Shannon link that became the Grand Canal, was for many years a public works project before private investment by landlords and merchants in the 1770s; it began operations in the next decade, to the eventual benefit of several tillage areas in south and west Leinster. The public funding of this and other infrastructural projects rested of course on the wishes of the Irish commons, and these decisions reflected the power of particular regional interests in parliament; the very large grants for improving the lower Shannon navigation and for public works at Limerick in the 1760s were, for instance, a measure of the future Speaker Pery's influence. But perhaps the most remarkable demonstration of landlord investment indirectly benefiting agriculture was towards the end of the period, in the 1760s and after: the involvement of several dozen landowners in building and in some cases actually managing the multi-storied flour mills that appeared in half the counties of Ireland as wheat cultivation began to spread; their investment, in early instances prompted directly by the 1758 parliamentary bounty on grain sent to Dublin, encouraged local farmers back to the plough.

Property sales and marriage settlements tended to make Irish estates more and more fragmented. This, and the relatively large mean size of Irish estates even at the end of the period, made 'absenteeism' inevitable up to a point. However most Irish gentry families had a country base somewhere, usually consisting of a distinctively large house, a demesne farm, gardens, orchards, and parkland, often adjacent to an estate village or on the site of a former castle. Many landlords lived out their adult lives in permanent country residence, but the wealthier gentry and their families migrated to Dublin or farther for part of most winters. The largest landowners were the ones most likely to live outside Ireland altogether, and many of these rarely visited their Irish properties, although they kept themselves surprisingly well informed. For the tenants on an estate where the owner resided permanently, the regular consumption demands from what was invariably the wealthiest local family reverberated through the community, giving employment and a doorstep market for food and fuel. Where major building projects were under way or where there was ornamental landscaping of the demesne, the local demand for labour and building materials could for a few years transform a parish economy.

Insofar as the interests of landlords and large tenants diverged in this era, it is clear who prevailed: the obligation on all tenants to have domestic meal ground at the manorial mill and to attend the manorial courts fell into almost complete disuse by the mid-eighteenth century; lease clauses forbidding alienation (the sale of a lease to a third party during its term) were rarely enforceable despite landlord efforts to control the make-up of the tenantry; clauses introduced late in the period against subletting all or a part of the property were mostly disregarded; and only those improvements that offered the prospect of profit or short-term comfort were as a rule carried out by tenants. The willingness of larger tenants to thwart their landlords and run the risk of non-renewal was predicated on the belief that they were indispensable. Given the shortage of families able to stock grazing farms and weather the twists of economic fortune, the strong farmers of both lowland and poorer districts had indeed more economic power than was apparent, and were partners with the gentry in transforming agricultural activity.

These 'gentlemen' farmers, the men who rented one or more townlands, invariably owned their own cattle and/or sheep, the management of which they might supervise themselves or, more commonly, devolve by annual contract to dairymen, herdsmen and others, while maintaining a small home farm for their own households. Even where large farmers were directly engaged in tillage operations, much of their labour needs were drawn from smallholding subtenants who paid part of their rent in duty labour. Indeed it was the existence of this captive reservoir of cheap labour that prompted landlords to pass the job of enclosure and reclamation onto their big-farmer tenants. The relationship between such tenants and those under them remains somewhat mysterious; the subtenants were not true labourers in that they also farmed on their own account, produced a saleable surplus and often held leases for terms of years (although rarely for longer than twenty-one years). In districts where grain cultivation expanded after the 1750s or where subtenants' own cattle herds had grown, the chief tenantry released more and more land to smallholders until eventually they themselves became dependent on rent rather than agricultural sales for the greater part of their income. In this way, such chief tenants earned the new label that Arthur Young ungraciously popularised in the 1770s: middlemen.

Small or labouring tenants who held directly from landowners, and subtenants who held from big farmers, differed only in that the former tended to have longer leases, to enjoy greater prospects of lease renewal, and to pay a somewhat lower rent per acre (and one exclusively in cash). All small tenants, whatever their contractual status, can be considered up to the 1750s as a single cottager class, consuming little that was not produced at home beyond tobacco, salt and alcohol, and employing none outside the family. They were generally tenants in partnership on a townland (the group rarely consisting of more than eight families) who came together or were brought together as joint lessees – to reduce the landlord's financial risk (they were collectively responsible for defaulters) and as a reflection of the cottager mode of agricultural organisation. At the beginning of a tenancy, 'infield' land suitable for tillage was divided up into family plots or fields, but all the pasture ground was left open, with each lessee entitled to graze a specific number of cattle at any time. More complex communal arrangements may have operated in parts of the west (e.g. the periodic redivision of the infield). Such micro-tenants were the principal victims both of short-term economic fluctuations and of the more insidious long-term pressures when they had to compete with graziers, master-dairymen and other capitalised speculators at times of rising cattle prices. Pamphlet literature from the 1720s to the 1760s is full of references to displaced villages or cottagers – from Sligo to north Cork – wherever extensive cattle farming prevailed. Those uprooted often seem to have gone literally up the hill, so that by the later decades of the century 'rich' counties like Tipperary, Meath, Waterford and Roscommon contained sharply contrasting neighbourhoods: clusters of large grazing farms, with modest numbers of permanent labourers living on the boundaries, adjacent to upland townlands which were now carrying an expanding population of smallholders of varying agricultural skills. This inverse correlation between population density and soil quality was a complete reversal of pre-1641 patterns, and was to remain a feature long beyond our period; market forces, not just landlord policy, created this new quirk in the Irish landscape.

* * *

As they became a distinct cultural element within the island, the new Irish gentry attempted to model themselves on their English counterparts. With some time lag, English-style country house architecture, upper-class leisure pursuits, consumption habits and intellectual fashions were adopted enthusiastically, sometimes uncritically, and usually with some Hibernian modification. The interest in stricter estate management and in agricultural innovation that developed in the south of England during the Restoration period was visible among quite a few of the Irish gentry by George II's reign. Meanwhile the passion for hunting, universal among Ireland's wealthier classes by the later seventeenth century, and for the newer sport of horse racing, fostered an interest in the art of controlled animal breeding, which soon had wider application. The direct involvement of many landowners in cattle importation in the seventeenth century was to continue in a more discerning way and created an abiding upper-class interest in 'improving' the quality of animal stock.

From the 1730s gentry interest in agricultural improvement was reinforced by the founding of the Dublin Society, a voluntary association designed to promote economic activities across the country that would improve the national balance of trade, re-establish the self-sufficiency in grain lost in the 1720s, and create employment for the poor. The society initially recruited over 300 members, and despite fluctuating fortunes it was to remain the major medium for transmitting new farming ideas; it published many agricultural works for gentry consumption and began to fund an experimental model farm in 1765. And from around the time of the society's foundation, commercial publishers in Dublin were reprinting foreign agricultural writings, and at the same time the first indigenous essays on farming were seeing the light of day.

It is more difficult to establish how far tenants were responsive to technical change, and to assess whether the failures of 'improving' landlords arose from the conservatism of the 'lower orders' or from the inappropriateness of the innovations they urged their tenants to adopt. Many landlords thought they knew the answer:

> I visited many of their wretched hovels, and endeavoured to convince them how easy it was to better their station. I explained the whole system of agriculture to them, and promised that their landlord would give them a long lease; I stated to them the comfort of warm clothing and comfortable houses; no answer, but that if such things had been possible, their fathers would have done so. The inhabitants of 'Otaheiti' are intelligent beings and industrious people when compared to those wretches.[15]

These uncomprehending sentiments of the Dubliner Sir Edward Newenham, on a visit to east Galway in the 1780s, were a late echo of very deep gentry frustrations. But so often 'the whole system of agriculture' of the enthusiasts had been either too costly to introduce or simply not profitable in the context of small partnership farming. However, definite productivity improvements did occur, and to locate them we must explore further how the component sectors of agriculture fared over the period up to 1775.

Cattle farming may have been the commercial centrepiece, but Irish agriculture always remained a mix of cereal cultivation and animal husbandry: shifts in the balance while important were never as extreme as contemporaries implied. The swing to dairying and sheepwalks in the Restoration period was geographically restricted; only in the early eighteenth century were many grain-growing areas of Leinster, Munster and east Connacht becoming permanently greener, and even then it was mainly a lowland phenomenon; in Ulster during the 1720s and 1730s the tilled area seems to have been actually expanding. And as Cullen has suggested, 'there was much greater substitution within livestock production and tillage respectively than between them'.[16]

The business of cattle production, as its volume grew and commercial arrangements became more complex, actually involved most inland farmers across the country. The big stock-owners, dealing in the buying in of two- or three-year old bullocks and maturing them for two or three years prior to final fattening, made their original purchases from those specialising in rearing the yearling stock, which in turn they had acquired from local petty cow-owners and from the dairying areas where the majority of the male progeny was sold for this purpose. The rearing areas – districts of low quality pasture, inaccessible regions in the west (most of Clare, Sligo and Leitrim for instance), and upland farms generally – came into their own in the 1750s with the sharp rise in cattle prices, and on balance this increased the opportunities for smallholders to increase their own cattle herds. The business of the 3,000 fairs held across Ireland in 1775 now becomes easier to comprehend: with the growth of small-scale cattle ownership and the advance of specialisation in cattle rearing and dairying, such a constellation of transaction centres became essential.

The production of butter and soured milk for domestic and local consumption had been universal in seventeenth-century Ireland: per capita consumption of dairy products must have been among the highest in Europe. However, with butter (although not its by-products) becoming an increasingly traded commodity, rural butter consumption contracted very considerably, with buttermilk taking the place of butter in the diets of the majority. In the 1670s and 1680s commercial dairying spread through the hinterlands of the south Munster ports and of Belfast as well as in parts of Leinster, and in the eighteenth century the greatest butter-producing zone embraced Counties Cork, Waterford and Kerry. There it displaced other types of farming as townland tenants built up large herds of milch cows and contracted them out in groups of twenty to forty to poorer dairymen, together with a specific allocation of land; the extra head of cattle that dairymen could squeeze onto this land plus the dairy by-products (and sometimes the calves) were the dairyman's only profit; his 'rent' usually consisted of a hundredweight of butter per cow. The new dairying districts gave more employment than did the sheep and store bullock areas, but by 1750 they also were singularly denuded of intensive agriculture: on twelve small townlands in Castle-magner parish (north County Cork) surveyed in 1744, there was no cereal cultivation recorded in five of them, and on the remaining seven town-lands there was an average of only two acres (statute) of cereals and 1.4 acres of potatoes per house.[17] It was a landscape almost bereft of farm buildings and other improvements, apart from large fields and massive ditches.

Dairymen had some prospect of becoming cattle-owning small-holders, but for most of those too poor to possess their own cattle, rural commercialisation meant no material advance: many of the descendants of the partnership tenants of the early eighteenth century made up the growing army of agricultural labourers, the so-called 'cottiers' of the later eighteenth century. Families holding half a dozen acres of land or less proliferated, the rent for which was frequently paid in agricultural labour on the lessor's farm. Labourers on annual contracts handled little cash – only when a farmer advanced money for food or implement purchases – and by the late eighteenth century this huge servile substratum needed to work upwards of 250 days a year to pay off the annual rent on 'cabin and conacre' (i.e. house and potato-ground). A growing number of those hiring conacre ground were unable to secure a regular work contract when taking the land, and had to seek casual wage employment or take to begging on the roads for the summer in order to maintain a toehold on the land. But the incomes of labourers and indeed of the somewhat less precariously placed partnership tenants could be shored up by newer, largely female, economic activities: the rearing of fowl and, increasingly important, of pigs, the spinning of flax and of wool. For rural male labourers themselves, money wages hardly rose at all before the 1760s, despite the upward drift in all land rents, including conacre, and in the case of families without ancillary earnings, real income was falling from about mid-century, at a time when the incomes of *bona fide* farmers, even those owning only half a dozen head of cattle, were beginning to rise. The old partnership-tenant class was splitting in two.

A proliferation of minute labourers' holdings, first in the main stock-raising and sheep-farming districts, later more generally, was contingent on a fundamental development in subsistence: the eclipse of both dairy-centred and of cereal-centred diets in the countryside and their replacement by the potato. The potato spread quite quickly in seventeenth-century Munster, especially in areas where dairy diets had prevailed, but it long remained a garden crop, worked by the spade, complementing oats or pulses in the diet and in certain seasons substituting for them. Potatoes required much less land than cereals to give the same calorific values, and were a welcome innovation in a backward pastoral society. They responded well to particular features of Irish ecology such as mild winters and the abundance of animal manure. By the 1720s potato cultivation in small plots for domestic subsistence seems to have become commonplace on the poorer soils of south and west Leinster, Connacht and west Ulster, but even in the areas of earliest propagation it was still the winter food only. Roughly between March and the first digging of the new potatoes, oats and, to a declining extent, dried peas and beans, augmented irregularly by fish and mutton, were the food of labourers and small farmers until the last third of the eighteenth century. The development by then of hardy varieties of potato such as the 'apple' that would remain wholesome for nine to twelve months was critical in extending the complete dominance of the potato diet. The declining earning power of labourers and the falling acreage they could afford to rent further strengthened the status of the land-saving potato. In addition, the revival in the commercial value of oats and other cereals from the 1760s accelerated the drift out of rural grain consumption in the more southern counties, first by the poor who could no longer afford it, later by farmers because of the profit forgone should they withhold grain from ready markets.

One- to two-acre gardens of potatoes (often in conjunction with cabbages and flax, and usually adjacent to the cabins of herdsmen, dairymen, shepherds, agricultural labourers and small independent farmers) became a universal element of the landscape as the economy expanded; without the potato, the organisation of the rural labour force would necessarily have been very different. Once the potato itself became a commercial crop, once it became acceptable to urban consumers, it started to be cultivated on a larger scale – in the corn field and as the initial crop in a rotation. Indeed this innovation had in the long run a profound effect on the maintenance of soil fertility and thereby on productivity, allowing the modification or elimination of the fallow period as well as improving cereal yields.[18] The potato was also an excellent pioneer crop on marginal land, and countless labourers received conacre lettings located beyond the existing boundary of permanent pasture, their sweat in cultivating a virgin potato crop being an integral part of the great reclamation process.

The international recovery in grain prices, evident in the Dublin wholesale markets from the first years of George III's reign, the boost to inland markets following the 1758 inauguration of the transport subsidy on grain and flour consigned to Dublin, and the widening impact of east Ulster's food deficit, all began to tip the balance between plough and livestock once again. Land values in districts where commercial grain production had never quite disappeared rose sharply, notably in coastal and south-west Leinster and along the navigable river valleys of east Munster – areas that seemed 'the richest … best improved, most populous and [where] the people wear a face of more content'.[19] Commercial tillage farms were often large by Irish standards, some encompassing most of a townland, but they were individually tenanted and managed. The regular enclosure of tillage land marked them off from the older type of grain farming, although innovations such as long, mixed rotations and green crops were almost unknown until the last years of the century.

Whether large or small they generated, acre for acre, at least five times more employment than grassland farms; despite the overall stickiness of agricultural wages, Arthur Young noted in several of the districts where tillage was expanding that earnings for labourers had risen sharply in the recent past.[20]

We can now give a tentative answer to the question of how far tenants were able or willing to engage in technical change leading to more productive farming. The introduction of various English breeds of cattle in quite large numbers during the seventeenth century seems to have sharply increased the mean size and milk output of dairy stock in Munster and Ulster, but this trend does not seem to have been maintained in the eighteenth century when nearly all attempts at selective breeding were directed towards increasing carcase weight for the slaughter-houses. There was no specialisation between the breeding of dairy and of beef cattle, and the improvements which did occur were in boosting the finished weight of five-year-old bullocks, which may have risen from somewhat under 5 cwt. to around 7 cwt.,[21] a consequence of occasional cattle imports and the gradual intermixing of old Irish and new English stocks as the networks of inter-regional cattle-dealing multiplied. The identity of the active agents in this process, whether landlords, large stock farmers, or the bull-owning farmers in the breeding counties, remains something of a mystery.[22]

As for pasture management, here there was less change. 'Artificial' seeding of clovers and grasses was still an exotic activity in the late eighteenth century – the natural abundance of wild white clover made such innovations less important than in England – and Young could find little sign of 'convertible husbandry' on the Dutch or Norfolk models outside the demesnes of the gentry. Meadow cultivation seems to have altered little (although the scythe was becoming more popular), and winter supply shortages of hay and of other fodder recurred in grazing districts every few years. However, the enormous expansion of lowland enclosure improved the drainage and thereby the yield of pasture, and insofar as scrub and rock clearance accompanied field-making, enclosure can be seen as part of the wider reclamation process. One specific novelty which spread after the middle of the century was the laying of lime on to permanent grass; when one clan of north Cork master-dairymen started to do this,

> the good fortunes [which] these people have made influences the crowd to follow them vainly imagining that everything they do leads to the happy ultimatum, getting money ... it is astonishing to see how the little people are copying them in this inactive method of improvement ...[23]

Tillage farming was also improved by the greater availability of lime – the proliferation of excellent limekilns struck Young on his travels – and of other organic and inorganic fertilising and neutralising agents; here the development of the minor road system, the spread of small wheeled carts and of cheaper beasts of burden (e.g. the mule) helped. However the incorporation of the potato into tillage farming remains the outstanding new element.

These advances, modest perhaps by English standards, were not, for the most part, articulated by the owners of the land. They created some of the necessary framework of supports and incentives (although by no means an optimal one), but the lasting agrarian changes, commercial and technical, were primarily instigated and supervised by the leaseholding farming classes – in their own self-interest.

MERCHANTS, TRADE AND CAPITAL

The extraordinary expansion of what had been the miniature ports of Dublin, Cork, Waterford, Limerick and Belfast was roughly of the same order as the expansion of foreign trade in this period (Limerick city actually grew faster than its trade, Belfast less dramatically than its commerce). The momentum of urban growth, exclusively a feature of the major ports, was dependent on their bustling quays – processing and service industries directly linked to overseas trade, educational, medical, legal and leisure facilities serving the expanding merchant class. 'Merchants' in this context were the men at the interface between inland, regional trade and long-distance maritime exchanges where external connections, a fairly large working capital, and personal reputation were the necessary ingredients for survival. Although there was a definite tendency towards specialisation as to routes traded and products handled, the classic wholesale import/export firm had diverse trading interests. Its strength rested literally on its credit and on its superior access to market information, internally and internationally, not on specific technical know-how except in bookkeeping and in the mysteries of remitting and exchanging monies.

One of the major issues here is the extent to which Irish merchants were venturers or dependent agents, active exploiters of the opportunities of international trade or passive beneficiaries of foreign demand and rural initiative. On the face of it, Irish merchants were not a major force in economic development, for much of both the export and import trades was conducted on the account of external principals, British, Dutch and

French, and on non-Irish shipping – in contrast to mercantile practices across the Irish Sea. The commission system, by which Irish port merchants executed orders to purchase, prepare and lade beef, butter, tallow, wool or whatever, prevailed in most branches of export trade in most ports; imports were similarly handled. Merchants in this situation bore far less risk than those trading on their own account overseas, and received modest and predictable profits (based on a 2.5 per cent commission on goods invoiced). Admittedly as the system matured many merchants in the commission business played an important role in shaping inland trade (and thereby made extra profits). By providing or guaranteeing seasonal advances to butchers, butter dealers or linen drapers, as was normal practice in Cork and Dublin through the eighteenth century, merchants enabled country producers and dealers to respond more quickly to a rising market and to have more financial flexibility in adverse times; and by delaying the time that they drew on their overseas principals, wealthy commission merchants could tie down their clients and charge for the service. Furthermore, there were certain non-commission branches of overseas trade, financed and organised at the Irish end; with Britain, the export of linen and worsted yarn and the import of sugar was generally on Irish account; much of the general trade with France and nearly all the quite substantial trade with Spain and Portugal remained in Irish control.

Anglo-Irish commerce remained the largest component of Irish maritime trade. Apart from the coal trade, it was conducted between the leading Irish ports and a small series of very powerful British centres, the merchant communities of which possessed greater capital and credit resources, serviced a larger and more affluent domestic market, and profited from their privileged role in British colonisation and seapower expansion. The commission character of Irish foreign trade therefore reflected the development contrasts between Ireland and England. Merchants from many Irish ports – old communities such as those of Galway and Kinsale, and emerging trading centres such as Belfast and Derry – had been alive to new opportunities, financing small transatlantic voyages between the 1620s and 1680s. However, even without the Navigation Acts most Irish ports would have shared the fate of English early starters such as Falmouth and Lancaster: gradual exclusion from long-distance trade as it became more specialised, more complex and subject to scale economies. Perhaps the only major Irish loser in the long run was Cork where before 1685 nearly half of Ireland's sugar imports and a third of its tobacco was being landed direct from the New World. A small number of Irish ship-owning merchants continued to trade with the West Indies after the tightening up of the Navigation Acts and to bring back plantation goods after making the obligatory entry at a British port, but this can rarely have brought attractive returns.

The total ban on reciprocal trade between Ireland and English America lasted only a generation, ending with the removal of the prohibition on imports from America in 1731 (a sign of the particular effectiveness of the Irish lobby in Westminster at that stage). The fact that an independent if secondary branch of trade did spring up – notably between Cork, the Ulster ports and the middle American colonies trading linen, butter and servants in return for flaxseed, timber products and raw materials for bleaching – demonstrates that the previous legislation had indeed somewhat restrained trade. Tobacco and sugar were not covered by the 1731 relaxation, and the right to import them directly to Ireland was the material issue behind the great political agitation of 1778–79. But, Cork's case apart, it is doubtful whether the Navigation Acts significantly distorted Irish capital formation; Irish consumers *may* have had to pay slightly more for tobacco and sugar, and the trajectory of growth of Belfast and Galway might have been rather different. However the centripetal pattern of British commercial development would not have been greatly disturbed by unrestricted Irish competition. The really profitable niche for Irish merchants as the north Atlantic economy opened up was in the provisions trades, and here there was no legislative interference. Long-term trends in provisions exports, particularly those of beef and pork, were tied to the cycles of British and French colonial expansion; but given the heterogeneous character of the demand for Irish foodstuffs – supplies for merchant vessels and naval craft, armies in America and military bases in the Mediterranean, best 'beefsteak' for white sugar planters and 'French beef' for the slaves – the development of the commission form of trade was quite logical.

The contrast between the predominantly commission character of the Atlantic trades and the 'Irish' character of trade with southern Europe was not as might seem between new and old lines of commerce, for the momentum behind the trade with Nantes, Bordeaux, Lisbon and Cadiz was also tied in with Atlantic developments. Most of the beef and butter sent there was re-exported to the Americas or used for naval victualling. In traffic with France – provisions in exchange primarily for wine, brandy and salt – trade was usually on joint account of consigner and consignee, both of whom were often Irish. There was generally a healthy surplus in Ireland's trade with southern Europe from the 1720s (in contrast to Anglo-Irish trade) and this imbalance in Ireland's favour was one factor drawing Irish merchants into an active overseas role in the Continental ports.

External circumstances go far in explaining the limited and uneven involvement of Irish merchants in international trade. The conventional view was that Irish merchants, after accumulating a small capital, abandoned trade and productive economic activity to become landowners and men of leisure. Even outsiders considered the Irish situation distinctive, with the ports resembling colonies 'where men go to make money but where they would have no desire to live out their lives'.[24] There does indeed seem to have been an unusually high turnover of wholesale houses by the standards of the larger British ports, and the numbers of principal partners was usually small, averaging only one or two. The turnover was probably greatest in Dublin and Cork and among Church of Ireland merchants. A model of horizontal social mobility can be applied to at least the big commission merchants, a process beginning with the younger sons of country gentry and wealthy tenants being apprenticed at high fees to leading merchant houses, serving their time there and possibly overseas, then with a capital portion charged on the family property setting up as an independent commission house or joining an existing one, and for two or three decades engaging in the highly competitive battle for overseas orders; the retreat of such a merchant or of his heir to rural *rentier* status completed the benign circle. An analogous movement was that between strong farming families and the less capitalised inland-oriented urban dealers, processors and higher-status retailers.

The prevalence of such patterns varied very much between the ports, although in all cases the links between rural landed wealth and foreign trade were strong; in other words, big merchants were drawn from families with some assets to begin with (the New Protestant elites of the 1650s and 1660s that included some of humble origin being the exception); as a rule, upward social movement in the port cities was relatively difficult. A capital fund of a few hundred pounds, a good social network in the supply hinterland, introductions to a small number of reliable correspondents in perhaps half a dozen overseas ports, and moderate intelligence were necessary requirements for the prospective commission merchant and ones that were not too difficult for those with a propertied background to meet. As for the return to the land, this can perhaps be overstated; there were, it is true, few merchants without some rural property, in fee or leasehold, inherited, acquired as a speculation, or brought in as part of a marriage settlement. But major land acquisitions with the intention of establishing a new 'county interest' only became a feature in the 1780s and 1790s. Nevertheless, the suspicion remains that the profits – or the anticipated profits – from rural land ownership and from large-scale lease speculation were sufficiently close to the return on capital employed in low-risk branches of commerce as to give solid reasons for the restless pattern of capital movement.

Irish merchants of the period were not however all of a kind. Anglican traders with strong landed connections may have dominated town government and civic institutions in the ports, but the role of Catholic and dissenter merchants was important in other respects. Catholic merchants had held a controlling interest in the centres of trade – other than Dublin and the Ulster ports – until the 1640s, but by 1660 in Waterford, Cork and the lesser towns on the east and south coasts their influence was reduced or annihilated, many individuals having emigrated or at least lost much of their real property. In Limerick and Galway, Catholic merchants remained more powerful, even after 1690, but both cities were in commercial decline from the 1680s until Limerick's revival in the 1750s. The ports that thrived most in the intervening period, Dublin, Cork and Waterford in particular, had a residual Catholic merchant element, but one which tended to be exaggerated for political reasons. These Catholic merchants, like their anglican counterparts, usually had landed connections, and thus those areas of the country where significant Catholic landownership continued into the eighteenth century – the old Pale and County Galway – were disproportionately well represented among Dublin's big merchants. Most of the surviving Catholic gentry had a network of relatives in Dublin business. Catholic merchants had a disproportionate (though not predominant) share of trade with France and southern Europe, although Protestant houses had the lion's share of the prestigious wine import trade. The *relative* importance of Catholic merchants probably increased during the decades of rapid economic growth after 1747, but even by 1775 less than a third of Dublin's wholesale merchants were Catholic, less than a quarter of Cork's. However, the business durability of many of these Catholic families, with their strong kinship links in the southern Netherlands, France, Spain and the Caribbean, was on average greater than in the case of anglican merchants, although their level of capital accumulation was not remarkable.

The other merchant minority consisted of the Protestant dissenters, Presbyterians and Quakers for the most part. Presbyterian merchants completely outnumbered rivals in Belfast and were strong in Derry and Newry; to a surprising extent they were also evident in Dublin. With the capital city becoming the financial and commercial centre of the linen trade, the province of Ulster remained part of Dublin's wholesale hinterland, and there was a profitable niche for northern merchants there.

Presbyterian merchant capital was grounded less on prior landed assets than on the wealth created in linen-dealing. In the late seventeenth century the small Quaker communities had been heavily involved in inland trade, particularly wool dealing and the woollen industry (in the south) and linen (in Ulster); despite the collapse of the woollen cloth export trade after 1699, Quakers consolidated their position in the wool trade, and through most of the eighteenth century maintained a remarkable hold on the valuable worsted yarn trade with England. Wool-related dealing laid the economic foundations for the great Quaker houses that had emerged by mid-century in Cork, Waterford and, less strikingly, in Dublin. These Quaker clans, part of a small closely-knit subgroup of Protestant Ireland with a distinctive business ethic, had probably the longest survival rate in trade: where anglican merchants might place male children in the professions, the army or the Church of Ireland ministry, Quakers kept their sons at one remove from the establishment social culture and for the most part kept succeeding generations in trade at home or abroad.

Within the port communities, merchants were of course a small part of the total skilled workforce: in the early Dublin trade directories, merchants associated with overseas trade formed only about one-tenth of the several thousand names of business and crafts people.[25] But although in Dublin the direct patronage of the gentry and institutions was a crucial element in the business of retailers and manufacturers, elsewhere it was merchants who created the orders for tradesmen and often controlled their credit. However, the economic power of the merchants was in part an extension of that of the banks: all such institutions were in this period private partnerships engaged in the business of remitting large sums of money around the country and between Ireland and England for merchants, landlords and state agencies; ancillary to this, they provided wholesale traders with short-term credit, issuing their own bank notes for bills of exchange prior to maturity or, less frequently, for other forms of collateral. As Cullen has pointed out, the banking businesses of Dublin, Cork and half a dozen other towns in the first half of the eighteenth century were innovative and versatile, embodying both merchant and landlord interests to mutual benefit; particularly striking then was the enormous expansion in paper money in the form of large-denomination notes, which possibly equalled the total value of specie in circulation by the 1720s and doubled again in line with specie by the mid-1750s.[26] Both the older surviving private banks and the small number of new banks founded in the second half of the century were conservative money-moving agencies first, reluctant creators of merchant credit second. The supply of specie improved markedly in the 1760s and the role of bank paper receded; in addition, many purely merchant houses had by then greater internal financial resources to meet seasonal pressures on credit without recourse to the bankers. Some of the 'landed' banks were anything but prudent in their own investment behaviour, channelling capital into rural property, mortgages, more speculative financial ventures, and even electoral funding.

Moneylending and credit arrangements were developing far outside the port towns in what remained a poor and occasionally cash-starved society. The acceptability of title deeds to land as collateral for fixed-interest loans (i.e. mortgages), and the additional opportunities for running up debts guaranteed by court bond meant that for the gentry deficit financing of major capital expenditures and marriage settlements, and even of ongoing consumption, was a straightforward process – if highly dangerous when done without restraint. Some landowners were themselves sources of long-term loans, but merchants, lawyers and wealthy farmers were usually the largest local lenders. Persons in the countryside holding surplus funds often faced acute difficulties in finding matching borrowers who could offer good securities and were willing to take money at the current level of legal interest.

In dealings among the lower levels of society, access to credit was on far less favourable terms. Rent payments which customarily ran six months in arrears were frequently dragged out especially in bad years, the penalty not being an interest charge but landlord displeasure, for such delays were rarely by agreement. Local retail transactions might not be settled for months after an initial 'earnest' had been paid, and although interest as such was not charged, the initial price was often adjusted to allow for the delay and perceived risk. Writing of the north Midlands, Charles Varley claimed in the 1760s that

> the poor generally sow a little flax-seed which they buy from a sort of petty merchant, at extravagant price ... for which they get a year's credit, till they spin it into thread, in consideration of which they pay about 200 per cent. If they run into debt ... they give a note payable before the summer assizes in the ensuing year; if they miss a payment, they are sure to be processed at the assizes ...[27]

Overt petty moneylending at interest and pawnbroking were rare outside the towns before the late eighteenth century; this was at least in part because of a rumbling controversy inside the Catholic church as to the morality of lending money at *any* rate of interest. Stricter interpretation of the church's usury laws would certainly have given the Catholic merchant a moral dilemma: not only was receiving interest at any rate forbidden, but even the sale of goods on credit, on time, where there was to be any consequent adjustment to the final price could be deemed usurious. In the more rural dioceses of the country the issue of moral trading was still causing friction even in the 1780s, yet the equivalent of Varley's petty seed dealers were to be encountered in every market town of the country by that stage.

The Irish port cities were industrial as well as trading centres, and merchant credit was extended to processors and manufacturers in the same way as to country merchants. Nearly all craft and industrial activities were small-scale workshop or domestic enterprises where human skills and working capital were the scarce resources. The new industries of the early seventeenth century – iron-smelting, fish- and timber-processing – had been developed away from the larger towns, and at the Restoration even Dublin had little manufacture beyond the myriad of paltry bakers, brewers, tailors, shoemakers and other retailing craftsmen. But over the next half century luxury goods were produced there on a growing scale: jewellery, gold and silver ware, silk and fine woollens, cut glass, paper, coaches and livery ware, were fashioned for the upper end of the home market. Dublin was of course a special case, being now the unchallenged distribution centre for the country's imports, the winter showground for the gentry, and the largest consumer market in its own right. Its silk and woollen industries, which grew rapidly up to the 1720s and more erratically thereafter, controlled the Irish market for fashion fabrics until large-scale English imports and high domestic costs began to spell permanent trouble in the 1760s. At their peak, master weavers, dyers, throwsters and other employers may collectively have given work to as many as 15,000 to 20,000 men and women in the neighbourhood of Dublin. Wages were high by rural standards, but living conditions were precarious; years of high food prices had devastating effects on the Liberties, the manufacturing heart of the city; years of very low farm prices which depressed consumer demand and hit landlord cash-flow led to industrial unemployment, which in turn sent the artisans out begging at the doorsteps of the wealthy.

Construction and food processing were the dominant branches of craft and industrial employment in the various ports. Both sectors were in theory organised along guild lines, with strict controls over apprenticeship and work practices, but the economic independence of most craft masters was gradually undermined in the course of economic expansion, with a successful minority of families in each trade establishing a controlling interest; from bricklaying to brewing the number of employers contracted as their scale of operations grew, and in some activities considerable family fortunes were made. This shift in the nature of industrial employment and the level of capitalisation, already evident by the 1770s, was to proceed much further before the end of the century. In industries linked to foreign trade – animal slaughtering, coopering, chandlery, salt-making, and sugar-making – which attracted merchant investment (sometimes even direct control), change came earliest. In Dublin and Cork there emerged under the wholesale merchants, and heavily involved with them, a tier of fairly wealthy manufacturers; some merchants doubled up as processors themselves (particularly on the import side – sugar, salt, timber), but until the late eighteenth century the scale of fixed capital tied up in non-textile urban industries was modest by comparison with other sectors of the economy, and merchants in this era were more inclined to diversify their investments into urban and rural land speculation than to sink capital into urban industry.

Industrial activity was of course not restricted to the ports. Brewing, distilling and tanning for example were widely dispersed through the market towns. A large volume of woollen cloth was produced in several west Leinster and Munster towns where the industry had first taken root in the seventeenth century, generally with proprietorial sponsorship. Kilkenny city blankets, Carrick-on-Suir ratteens, Athlone felt hats, Bandon camblets were known nationally, and – despite the 1699 prohibition – a substantial export trade to Portugal in various types of south Munster woollens had developed by the 1720s and lingered on until the 1760s. This was dwarfed by the great cross-channel trade in woollen and worsted yarn, initially very much a Munster phenomenon: Cork-based traders purchased Tipperary and Connacht wool, employed skilled sorters and combers, and then put it out directly or through small-town agents to many thousands of poorer women who were paid a piece rate. At its peak in the 1760s when Cork- and west Leinster-based Quakers controlled the yarn trade, perhaps thirty thousand rural women were regularly employed in spinning wool for the English market; yarn-making for Irish weavers would have fully employed at least the same number again.

These developments in the woollen trade seemed modest beside the transformation of linen-making from a dispersed country craft to the single most valuable sector of the Irish economy. Linen cloth exports at the beginning of the eighteenth century were still less than a million yards p.a. – the output of little more than 1,000 or 2,000 weavers – but by the early 1770s around 20 million yards were leaving the country, and possibly as much again was purchased on the home market.

Several distinct factors help explain its take-off: first, there was an indigenous Irish tradition of flax growing and 'bandle' linen manufacture for domestic purposes since at least Tudor times; even at that stage Ulster and the north midlands were the chief source. Flax fitted well into Ulster's small-scale cropping patterns, and some very old traditions of flax cultivation survived the industrial take-off.

The second element helping to propel the linen trade was the difficulties seventeenth-century Ulster landlords had had in turning their lands to profit: poorer soil quality and bad communications put them at a disadvantage vis-à-vis the south, where estates were nearer the established ports, urban markets and new lines of Atlantic commerce. Encouragement of the linen trade in this context meant giving especially favoured treatment to new tenants with weaving skills, subsidising the purchase of plant, and even buying the whole output of weavers until the manufacture took root locally. And as commercial weaving spread unevenly through much of lowland Ulster, the strong support of a few landlords in each district at the infant-industry stage seems to have hastened its success, although landlord sponsorship in unpropitious circumstances was not a sufficient condition for growth. Historians used to emphasise the dramatic effects of the Huguenot settlement in the Lagan valley in 1698, but while the French refuge at Lisburn may have widened the range of finer linens woven in east Ulster, the other claims for them were propaganda; County Down linens, were already 'well made and bleach'd, and little inferior to French cloth'.[28] Even the supposed technology transfer in the seventeenth century from Scotland and the north of England, i.e. the inflow of migrants with pre-existing textile skills, has probably been exaggerated.

The third element in linen's success was international and fiscal. Despite having a long established and widely dispersed linen manufacture, England still depended in 1660 for its finer linen on French and Dutch cloth. Linens were the only major industrial import into an increasingly self-sufficient economy. This situation was changed by the erection of what were at first temporary retaliatory tariffs against France in 1678. Over the following three-quarters of a century most British import duties were for fiscal reasons raised higher and higher, and this included Continental linens. This tariff wall was erected at a time when domestic and colonial demands were greatly expanding. English, Scottish and Irish linen producers therefore all benefited in a growing and increasingly protected market. London gave tacit support to the

Dublin government's encouragement of linen manufacturing; since at least the 1660s linen's expansion had promised to strengthen the Protestant interest and to increase Irish customs revenue. State policy reflected the aim of many private landowners in seeking to extend the industry, and the Irish parliament's benevolence was in fact far more potent than the supposed English goodwill towards the Irish industry; even the 1696 removal of customs duties on Irish linens entering England, an undoubtedly advantageous measure, was achieved only through viceregal lobbying from Dublin.

The emergence of a forceful class of entrepreneurial middleman was a further element in the dynamism of eighteenth-century linen. Many of the early drapers and experimental bleachers were Quakers who financed their trade and investment by borrowing from landowners and Dublin merchants. These men made rapid advances in cloth-finishing methods, improving the quality and lowering the cost of the long-drawn-out rubbing and washing processes which whitened the weavers' dirty webs; by the 1730s Irish bleaching methods were actually being transferred to the Scottish linen industry.[29] Bleach greens increased in capacity and sophistication, dozens clustering along the easily harnessed minor rivers of Armagh, Down, south Antrim and east Derry; their owners worked on contract for dealers or, increasingly, bought the cloth themselves in monthly fairs or the more frequent 'brown' linen markets which were spreading across much of Ulster. Drapers and bleachers dealt directly in cash with the thousands of small rural weavers; the vitality of these markets in Armagh, Antrim, Down and Tyrone, where sales worth £1 million p.a. were being transacted in the early 1780s,[30] had no parallel. The bleachers were by then more Presbyterian than Quaker, with a minority of anglicans and hardly any Catholics among their ranks. They kept very close commercial links with Dublin, where the huge northside Linen Hall remained by far the most important sales and despatch centre until Napoleonic times. But by the 1780s the Dublin linen merchants and factors were playing a less strategic role in providing financial and marketing services as the scale and self-confidence of Ulster capital increased. By that decade at least one-fifth of the adult male workforce of the nine counties of Ulster, drawn from all the religious denominations, was directly involved in linen weaving, earning a wage double that of agricultural labourers – and far more in the case of the fine cloth makers of the Lagan valley. Employment in ancillary processes and services gave lowland Ulster that 'air of improvement' that so deeply impressed eighteenth-century visitors.

Coarse linen making had been implanted in many dozens of landlord villages outside Ulster before the 1770s crisis in the industry, but it had only spread beyond landlord patronage in parts of Leinster (Louth, Longford and King's County), north Connacht (Sligo, Mayo and parts of Galway), west Cork and west Kerry. By the 'seventies the most important development outside the weaving zone was the expansion in domestic yarn spinning; just as in the southern half of the country wool spinning offered a vital if small cash income for poorer women, so from the Boyne valley to Clew Bay and northwards the regular sales of linen yarn to 'huxters', at home, at fairs or at specific yarn markets, helped ensure the viability of the small-farm economy. When west Ulster and north Connacht had initially diversified from their dependence on cattle rearing to flax in the early eighteenth century, much of the yarn was exported via Drogheda and Derry to England. But after the 1760s the growing yarn and food deficit of east Ulster was drawing these western areas into a stronger and essentially benign economic relationship; even the remotest coastal communities of Donegal and Mayo were benefiting by the demand from the east for kelp as a substitute raw material for bleaching.

The rise of the Irish linen industry as a whole was in international terms an exceptional phenomenon. A fortunate conjuncture of circumstances, external and internal, changed the face of the northern third of the island. What made this development so distinctive was the fact that not alone were the drapers, bleachers and merchants greatly enriched, but the economic benefits were suffused through rural society. Where more southerly developments were producing a stratified, unequal rural society with a labouring poor hardly improving at all in circumstances, linen deflected the development of a huge agricultural proletariat and produced a more even distribution of the land into small but prosperous farms. However it was work within the home, not on the farm, that generated most of the cash income and the material rewards. And therein lay the linen economy's vulnerability.

Edmund Burke (1729–97) became the most famous Irishman in the contemporary English-speaking world. He was of Munster Catholic background, his father conforming to the Church of Ireland. His fame was the result both of his philosophical writings and of his role as leading intellectual voice of the English Whigs for a generation, both inside and outside Westminster. From the time that he sat for this miniature in the early 1760s until his death, he played a quiet but fundamentally important role in repositioning relations between the British state and Catholic Ireland, recognising the leaders of the latter as a potentially conservative force. (Watercolour on ivory by Nathaniel Hone the elder: N.G.I.)

5

Coalition under Stress, 1760–89

OLD ELITES AND NEW OPPOSITIONS

THE ACCESSION of the youthful George III in 1760 released a general expectation of change, of less corrupt politics and of a larger and more robust British empire, a mood which immediately infected Ireland. Among the many loyal declarations, one signed by 600 Catholic laymen was notable for its obsequious optimism. The new reign meant the first general election for thirty-four years, and public comment on the election predicted a radical change in the personnel of Irish politics. The reality was somewhat different. In most constituencies, even in some counties, there was no contest. Only a third of the successful MPs were newcomers, and a majority of these had close family connections with existing members. Yet it was the first election in which newspapers played an important part. The Irish press had come a long way since 1727 in terms of the coverage of domestic politics; the Lucas affair and the money bill dispute had changed the political horizons of many literate freeholders in Dublin, Cork, Limerick and Belfast, where local newspapers and booksellers were now well-established. Through the early months of 1761 the press was full of political advertisements, declarations and addresses by candidates and their support groups; much of this emanated from candidates who were critical of the *status quo*, both in government and in the house of commons itself. Many candidates pledged themselves to support a septennial bill (to bring about general elections at least every seven years) and articulated a new suspicion and hostility towards the dominant factions. The grandees were beginning to pay the price for their exploitation of public and patriotic sentiment in 1753–54 and for their subsequent 'betrayal'. And although the election results only gave a very muffled echo of independent freeholder opinion, a new cynicism towards the big power-broking families was there to stay.

There was, however, an exceptional result from Dublin city, for

Charles Lucas in a remarkable political resurrection had returned from his English exile and taken one of the city seats. In spite of his modest social background and the limitations of his parliamentary rhetoric he quickly became accepted as one of the leaders of a loose group of 'patriot' MPs and peers who, over the next two decades, made up for smallness of numbers by the strength and persistence of their critique of the administration, and by the support they received in the opposition press, not least in the *Freeman's Journal* which Lucas helped to establish in 1763.

The commons' patriots of the 1760s were a motley group, led by Henry Flood, lawyer, Kilkenny landlord, and electrifying orator; Sir Lucius O'Brien, enthusiast for economic improvement and archetypical independent 'country' MP (for Co. Clare), and Charles Lucas, all in permanent opposition to government. Their strength lay in their intellectual ability and persistent demand for specific reforms, the intention of which was to curb the power of the executive. Their ideas owed much to English 'country' Whig ideology of the previous generation, but elements of a distinctive 'hiberno-patriotism' were becoming evident in press, pamphlet and parliamentary performance: the legal and political strengthening of College Green vis-à-vis ministerial power and influence was central to their thinking. From a cleansed parliament would flow constitutional and economic benefits for the political nation. As to who constituted the political nation was to be another day's business. A much wider band of gentry and MPs supported their policies privately – and sometimes publicly when the government was in weak hands or when their leaders encouraged them to criticise the Castle.

Early in the first parliamentary session the commons voted in favour of a septennial bill, a measure which the patriot group particularly wanted in order to increase the responsiveness of the house and to give MPs greater leverage vis-à-vis the government and faction leaders. And because support for this measure had become the touch stone by which a candidate's 'independence' had been measured in the 1761 election, Speaker Ponsonby and his predecessor found themselves with many of their supporters formally committed to this reform (whatever their private preferences). Even in the Irish privy council a majority did not wish to earn out-of-doors unpopularity by refusing to forward such a bill, secure in the knowledge that it would be blocked by the British privy council. The patriot tail, therefore, was beginning to wag the dog, even if the dog was not as yet being forced to move.

At the more rarefied level of relations between the faction leaders – the parliamentary managers – and the government, the first years of the new reign were not entirely harmonious. The current British interpretation of Poynings's law held that, before a new Irish parliament could be licensed, the Irish privy council had to draft two pieces of legislation as 'proper causes' for parliament's assembly, and that one of these had to be a money bill. The formal presentation to the commons of legislation over which they had only the power of veto had been the ostensible reason for the 1692 'sole right' conflict, and had offended the commons' sensibilities on the rare occasions when a new parliament had met. In 1727, after strong speeches defending sole right, the symbolic bill had been grudgingly accepted. But on the next occasion, 1761, the lords justices (the battle-scarred trio of Shannon, Ponsonby and Stone) were anxious to avoid an embarrassing showdown and privately sought the submission of two non-financial bills to inaugurate parliamentary business. But the importance of denying the Irish commons sole right in money bills was an equally important principle to the legal advisers of the British privy council, and the faction leaders did not resist. They co-operated with the new viceroy, the amenable and easy-going earl of Halifax, in supporting a money bill in the commons, and their control of the house was demonstrated by the 4:1 majority in favour of the imposed bill. (The monies voted for the wartime military establishment allowed for a temporary doubling of manpower, a third of whom were to serve overseas.) From the beginning, however, the patriot minority seem to have had disproportionate power on the committees, to judge by several early resolutions critical of the government. Throughout the 1760s they compensated for their small numbers by superior parliamentary skills and legal knowledge.

Halifax and his immediate viceregal successors were birds of passage, each overseeing a single biennial parliamentary session. Government in their absence remained in the hands of the lords justices. But there was a new and deep-rooted sense of dissatisfaction shared by nearly all the handful of English ministers who gave Irish affairs any thought in the 'sixties, a belief that the government of Ireland was out of balance and that the managers, the parliamentary undertakers, had too great a control of patronage. As we have seen, there was already a determination to strengthen the discretionary powers of the lord lieutenancy in Chesterfield's time, to re-establish 'English government' when Lord George Sackville was chief secretary, and to clip the power of the great ones during Hartington's and Bedford's administrations. For a variety of reasons each failed to alter the system – not least because they did not stay in Ireland long enough – and most of their immediate successors in the 1760s came to the job with similar intentions. Speaker Ponsonby's power was, in fact, at its zenith at this period; he had at his disposal a large slice of government patronage, a strong say in the conduct of the commons and in the composition of committees, and a dominant influence in the now thoroughly politicised revenue service; his elder brother, the earl of Bessborough, was a leading figure in one of the Whig factions at Westminster and held ministerial office in the short-lived first Rockingham government. Yet Ponsonby and the now semi-retired earl of Shannon were aware of their political vulnerability; there was always the danger of an aggressive viceroy, backed by an unsympathetic ministry, and they also realised that the political nation outside the landlord constituency which they and their forerunners had usually been able to represent, control and depend upon, was now stirring.

In 1764 the old enemies Shannon and Stone both died, leaving as in 1729 something of a vacuum. The absence of any major Castle attempt to seize the initiative before 1767 was a direct result of government instability in London, which also led to a succession of short-term viceroys. But behind this appearance of discontinuity, a tiny administrative machine in Dublin Castle and in London continued to provide an essential professional back-up for lords lieutenants and lords justices in their still narrow range of functions. Two long-serving bureaucrats were in fact pivotal: Thomas Waite and Sir Robert Wilmot. Waite was the viceregal under-secretary at the Castle from 1747 to 1780 (his military functions were hived off in 1777). The convention since 1701 had been that when Dublin Castle was in the care of lords justices, the under-secretary became their permanent secretary while the chief secretary stayed with the viceroy on his Anglo-Irish peregrinations. Waite, a lawyer by training, was by the 1760s an indispensable adviser to governors on both technical and political questions; he also acted as *chef d'équipe* in the Castle (his wife was the Castle housekeeper). He became a MP in 1761 and, more remarkably, a privy councillor in 1771; he retained throughout his career a low public profile. His opposite number and intimate correspondent was the 'resident secretary' in London, Sir Robert Wilmot; he was private secretary to the lord lieutenant and the main channel of communication between him, the chief secretary and the lords justices during viceregal absences from Dublin, and a crucial link between the Castle and Whitehall during parliamentary sessions. Wilmot had been appointed by Devonshire in 1740 and remained in control until 1772; his services were vital in speeding Irish legislation through the British privy council (when timing could be all important), and in handling the practical aspects of relations between the Irish treasury and revenue commissioners, and the Whitehall treasury. As

Malcomson has suggested, without a Wilmot 'the ramshackle system of governing Ireland through largely absentee lords lieutenants and chief secretaries'[1] could not have survived as long and as successfully as it did.

Outside the hothouse of high politics in Dublin there were signs of rather different tensions in the 1760s. The Seven Years War (1756–63) had stirred the old fears of the gentry: suspicions of their Catholic neighbours were, as in 1744–45, strongest in Protestant Munster, and sectarian antagonisms were sharpened there by the 1760–61 election. Quite apart from the dredging up of obsolescent penal laws, parliamentary elections revealed the survival of Catholic gentry influence at county level, albeit expressed by proxy. There were several constituencies in 1760–61 where landed candidates were identified, fairly or unfairly, with 'the Catholic interest'; such men were often recent converts themselves or had many Catholic relatives. Tipperary was a case in point where one of the three candidates was the wealthy Thomas Mathew, of convert background and closely associated with surviving Catholic members of the Ormond clan. The election was closely fought and Mathew's opponents made much of the danger of a powerful 'popish interest' in the county. Mathew was elected, then unseated after an election petition. The fight had bitter local consequences.

It was probably a coincidence that on the southern margins of Co. Tipperary agitation by small partnership tenants against the enclosure of common pasture began to spread, and this was exploited by Protestant politicians in the county as evidence of a Catholic conspiracy and a French plot. The war made such talk faintly plausible in Dublin, and the war was indeed the catalyst of the anti-enclosure movement. High prices for pastoral goods in the years after 1760 were reflected in a boom in land values, especially in Munster cattle country; the losers were the marginal mixed farmers and smallholders, and their collective protest launched a remarkable agrarian movement. There was the distant precedent of the Connacht disturbances in 1710–11, when large numbers of cattle had been killed or maimed as a protest against the spread of ranching tenants. Since that time, violent incidents in the countryside and collective agitation had been small in scale, uncoordinated, and directed towards very specific ends. The tories had disappeared by the 1720s, and incidents involving more than a dozen people had been confined to communal 'rescues' of cattle impounded by the rent receiver or sheriff, to coastal smuggling mafias, to fair-day brawls and to urban food riots. The slow growth of the economy and the very effective if informal means of law enforcement that had evolved since the beginning of the century – a

Protestant gentry/magistracy backed up by a large and widely dispersed standing army, manned by non-locals – had given five decades of unprecedented rural passivity. Stories of highwaymen and bandits were given colourful prominence in the Dublin press – but precisely the same was the case in England, which may indeed have become by 1760 a more violent society than was Ireland.[2]

The Tipperary trouble spread far from the first parishes where it occurred. Alarmed magistrates used the metaphors of pathology to describe the extraordinary spread of the social epidemic. To their opponents, one of the more sinister characteristics of the agitators was the way sizeable groups would rendezvous and march or ride (on stolen horses) around the countryside at night, identifying themselves by wearing the cheapest country fabric at hand, coarse white linen, and by blowing horns. They went to work imitating sometimes the fox hunt, sometimes the army, borrowing symbols from both. The 'Whiteboys', as they were soon called, resorted to small amounts of personal violence and a great deal of blood-curdling intimidation. The trigger for the first outbreak of agitation seems to have been quite specific, the unilateral restriction of access to 'upland' pasture imposed by large grazier tenants on their subtenants, probably with landlord collusion; but the example of these unprecedented events in south Tipperary and the absence of swift retribution emboldened many others. As the agitation fanned out through Tipperary and into west Waterford, north Cork and Limerick, the bundle of grievances became larger: resentment by ex-tenants who had been denied lease renewals, resentment by the poor at the way tithe was levied by intermediaries, resentment by most at the level of tithe on potatoes. The participants, even the leaders, were nearly all of low social rank, although they seem to have received support from above, some of it for reasons of private vengeance, some on grounds of compassion. Among the compassionate were several Catholic priests.

The organic appearance and large scale of this outbreak of rural disorder frightened the local elite. Several Ulster-recruited regiments were moved in to reinforce local garrisons and strengthen the nerve of the magistracy in April 1762. Army behaviour seems to have terrified the smallholder population through many baronies, although there was no large-scale military encounter. Both the north Munster magistracy and the army general who was called in to pacify the region subscribed to a conspiracy theory that a popish insurrection was in the offing. A special commission composed of two leading judges asserted the opposite; they discounted the existence of any political disaffection and took the economic grievances at face value. Halifax accepted their more sober view. By eighteenth-century standards the resulting trials were mild affairs; only twelve persons were sentenced to death.[3]

Later in 1762 the agitation welled up again in Tipperary and in parts of Kilkenny, and survived intermittently for three years. The issue of enclosures slipped into the background, and tithe remained the common denominator. The objection to tithe was not primarily a sectarian one – landholders of all denominations grumbled about it – nor was it because tithe was the greatest financial burden on tenants (land rent was always several times greater). But tithe was hated by the poor because it was levied in an arbitrary and uneven manner – between parishes, between different types of farmer, between different years – and the bigger farmers who undertook to collect it had more discretionary power and were less supervised in their petty harassment than the agents and rent receivers of the gentry. In addition, tithe by the 1760s was, like the hearth-money tax, one of the transactions that had always to be settled in cash, and this for the poor increased its inconvenience.

The aim of the agitation was not the elimination of tithe, but its reduction and regulation. Various attempts by the Whiteboys to enforce a schedule of 'fair' tithe charges formed an important precedent for future rural redresser movements. Another innovation was the fairly general use of an initiation oath, probably borrowed from contemporary urban artisan combinations, to enforce a bond of secrecy. In the official culture where oath-taking was a profoundly serious act, the introduction of the Whiteboy oath could be interpreted as a means of demonstrating and enforcing an alternative authority (however it might be derived); certainly in later secret societies the oath had such functions, but in this case it was more likely a colourfully packaged means of deterring participants from ever becoming prosecution witnesses.

The connection between the Whiteboy disturbances and the intra-gentry religious tensions in Tipperary lay in the way many of the hotter Protestant families sought to use the conspiracy theory to attack both the local Catholic gentry and the Catholic clergy. Prior to the first special commission five priests and a number of Catholic gentlemen had been arrested for technical breaches of the penal laws or for fomenting the supposed insurrection. In 1762 every wealthy landed Catholic throughout the affected counties seems to have felt the threat of being dragged down by a new regional popish plot. And the victim at Tipperary's Tyburn in 1766 was a young parish priest from Clogheen, Nicholas Sheehy. Socially well-connected, he was already known in the region for his strength of character before 1761, in which year it seems he had given moral support to the original levellers of ditches. Sheehy became the victim of the 'conspiracy' lobby, led by Shannon's brother-in-law, the earl of Carrick, who in the early 'sixties became incensed at the failure of the law to inflict 'exemplary' punishments. Sheehy was indicted by the Tipperary grand jury in 1764 'for high treason and rebellion', and was tried in Dublin in 1766. The case was thrown out because of the non-appearance of a key witness. However this only led to a further trial in Tipperary at which the priest was accused of complicity in the murder of the missing witness. The evidence against him was weak – as indeed was the proof that the witness was in fact dead – but the Tipperary grand jury was dominated by a group determined to destroy the supposed Catholic challenge at all levels by means of this and similar 'show trials'. Sheehy was tried and executed at Clonmel in March 1766, together with four less notable victims, and the incident did indeed have 'exemplary' effects: Whiteboys almost vanished for several years, 'to Newfoundland and to the mountains ...'.[4] Not the least remarkable feature of this affair was the conflict between the dominant local gentry and the Castle, both as to what had caused Whiteboyism and as to how far the conventional norms of evidence should be relaxed to secure convictions. Outside the cockpit of Tipperary, many Protestants, especially in Munster, supported the harsh measures: a pointer to their mental state was the fact that during 1766 over 700 subscribed to a new Cork edition of Sir John Temple's *History of the general rebellion of 1641*, and nearly 200 to a Cork edition of William King's *State of the Protestants of Ireland under ... James*. Ancestral myths were being refurbished. Meanwhile Sheehy became a folk martyr.

It was no coincidence that at the other end of the country the first case of large-scale social protest occurred during the summer of 1763 in seven Ulster counties. In contrast to the Whiteboy movement it only lasted one season and was more public and self-confident in its display, labelling itself the Hearts of Oak. It gathered its supporters together in far larger numbers than did the nocturnal Whiteboys; there was little physical violence; and it was more successful in its objectives. It was primarily a tax revolt – against the anglican clergy for excessive tithe charges and the indiscriminate levying of church fees, and against the gentry whose enthusiasm for large-scale spending on roads and bridges was pushing up the county rates (still a modest burden compared with rent). Resentment over county 'cess' was compounded by strong objections to the duty labour that every family had to provide the parish overseers for the upkeep of roads. This mass demonstration of annoyance led to meetings and marches several thousand strong (contemporaries talked of tens of thousands), and to menacing visits to the gentry's houses where mounted Oakboy leaders would instruct gentlemen to swear that they would support a drastic reduction of the road budget. As Magennis has suggested, the precedent of the parish-based militia mobilisations in 1745, 1756, and after the seizure of Carrickfergus in 1760 was vital in this, the first great display of the Ulster protest march. And a tantalising connection has been hinted at between the spread of the Seceders and other breakaway Presbyterian congregations in south Ulster, and local leadership of the Oakboy movement in some districts.[5]

The repression was swifter and sharper than in Munster: there was a series of bloody encounters between the army, directed by local JPs, and Oakboy groups, as a result of which about twenty redressers were killed. But in the subsequent criminal proceedings the prosecutions nearly all failed, not because of the non-appearance of witnesses as often was the case in Munster, but because juries refused to regard Oakboy actions as constituting treason. The 'middling orders', Presbyterian and anglican, who dominated the petty juries were not unsympathetic to their less respectable crusading neighbours, for those indicted were mainly Protestants.

One of the minor ironies of the Oakboy affair was the prominent role of the governor of County Armagh, Viscount Charlemont, art connoisseur and patriot politician in Westminster and College Green. His success in suppressing the Oakboys earned him an earldom, but this in no way compromised his token leadership of the Irish patriots. Their newspaper, the *Freeman's Journal*, while ambivalent on the Oakboy movement, sang a distinctly Protestant tune through the 'sixties and was an unsympathetic witness to the Whiteboys' tribulations. A major reason for the sectarian hostility of the paper and of Dublin-based radicals was a long drawn-out clash between the trade guilds of Dublin and of most southern cities, and local Catholic traders over the legality of 'quarterage'.

The exclusions of Catholics from civic freedom in Irish boroughs had been fairly complete since the 1690s, but this practice rested not on parliamentary statute, which only closed civic office to Catholics, but on local corporation by-laws or simply on the regulations of individual guilds. Actual freedom for Catholics to trade in the larger towns was not in itself an issue any more (indeed by the 1760s, Catholic businesses probably predominated in number if not in turnover in most urban centres outside Ulster). Many trade guilds in the later seventeenth century had allowed Catholics to become quarter-brothers, a form of membership which gave no civic or political privileges but which provided Catholic masters some economic protection and support from the guild plus some share of fraternal conviviality, in return for regular payments. The big guilds in Dublin and Cork tried to compel all Catholic master craftsmen and traders to become quarter-brothers of the appropriate guild, but they were never completely successful in this. Catholic resistance was based on the belief that such compulsion had no legal basis. As early as the 1730s Cork Catholics were threatening to test quarterage in the courts, but it was not until 1758 that they took a case to the court of king's bench where its legal status was declared non-existent; subsequent appeals confirmed this landmark decision against the guilds. It was a remarkable victory for 'popish tradesmen' over a Protestant corporation. The response by the Cork and Dublin guilds was to seek support in parliament for a quarterage statute that would set aside the legal judgment. Backed by the *Freeman's Journal*, the campaign widened to an attack on Catholic encroachments on municipal power. Lucas introduced heads of a bill restoring quarterage in 1767; it passed the commons in 1768. However there was a discreet but well-organised Catholic lobby against it, and it was rejected by the privy council. Over the following ten years there were six further attempts to get a quarterage act.

This failure of an articulate Protestant vested interest to get partisan legislation enacted is revealing: it highlights the sophisticated organisation of Catholic merchant committees in the ten towns which had petitioned parliament and raised funds to fight the political battle against the reimposition of quarterage. Their efforts were co-ordinated by a small group of Dublin Catholic merchants and professionals who had organised a more representative Catholic 'General Committee'; this had first met in 1760 to draw up petitions of loyalty in the aftermath of the token French landing at Carrickfergus, and had co-ordinated the address to George III in 1761. Through the late 1760s and early 1770s the Catholic Committee shadow-boxed with Dublin corporation until the guilds abandoned their hopes of reimposing quarterage. The issue had originally been merely a financial one, but by the 1770s it had become a struggle of principle. Quarterage bills always secured commons majorities, but their subsequent suppression never created much of a row; the issue was not one that the gentry felt very strongly about. The repeated defeats of the urban Protestant lobby was another demonstration of just how far rural and proprietorial interests dominated the house of commons. But the most important reason behind the Catholic traders' victory was the attitude of successive lords lieutenants. All accepted the arguments of Catholic lobbyists, and this was yet further evidence of a more even-handed approach by the Castle and of a willingness to look beyond the Protestant political community, first hinted at in the viceroyalties of Chesterfield and Bedford.

The lord lieutenant who stopped Lucas's quarterage bill was Viscount Townshend, the sixth viceroy since George III's accession. He had arrived in 1767, and with English ministerial politics still unstable, it was assumed that his stay in Dublin Castle would be as brief as the rest. Townshend defied such expectations and remained in Dublin for five years, the first fully resident lord lieutenant of the eighteenth century.[6]

Townshend came from one of the great Hanoverian Whig families and was a veteran army commander, as concerned with imperial defence as his more famous brother was with imperial finance. His remit from the cabinet in London was to secure permanent funding for an additional 3,000 soldiers on top of the 12,000 that had been kept on the Irish establishment since 1699. In 1767 'augmentation' of the Irish army was treated as an imperial priority – and a task that Townshend's English colleagues assumed would be politically straightforward. The recent rise in Irish revenue yield removed the excuse of Irish poverty, and the gains Ireland was now deriving from colonial trade suggested that Ireland should contribute more to imperial defence.

The Shannon and Ponsonby clans sought increased patronage and pensions in return for helping to push such unpopular legislation through parliament. London refused to sanction the extra patronage, and so they withdrew from co-operating with the Castle in the management of parliament. As an alternative Townshend sought to build up support among the more independent MPs and encouraged them to pass another septennial bill. This proposal was cleared in London (the duration of parliaments was actually set at eight years) and after its successful passage a general election was arranged for 1768. But with a poll so close, few independent MPs were prepared to ally themselves publicly with the government in support of army augmentation and the necessary higher taxes. The commons not surprisingly postponed a decision on augmentation until after the election.

It was from this time of frustration that Townshend showed his singularity. In common with his brother and the king's much abused adviser, the earl of Bute, he had a strong sense of the corrupt state of contemporary politics and of the enormous cost of systems of government where factional interplay heavily influenced policy-making. His austere public service ideology, imperial perspectives, and tough single-mindedness of purpose set him apart from most viceroys, although his recurring manic depression led many to underestimate him. After the temporary defeat on army augmentation he sought permission from Whitehall to change the *modus operandi* of his office. Like his immediate predecessor the earl of Bristol (who never reached Dublin), Townshend wanted to be allowed to remain continuously in Dublin; he linked this to a comprehensive plan to obviate the need for lords justices; to re-establish Castle control over much of the patronage then in the control of individual office-holders; to make the revenue commissioners accountable to the lord lieutenant; and to have several of the overmighty office-holders dismissed. The British cabinet at this stage agreed only to his request to be permanently resident. But he succeeded in implementing the other measures over the following four years.

The new parliament met in 1769, its membership fairly similar to that of 1761; the 'undertakers' were still in limbo, neither directing government business in the house as heretofore nor directly opposing. A revised augmentation bill was easily passed (the Irish parliament thereby establishing a legal authority over the 'Irish' regiments for the first time). But the rudderless state of the commons was revealed a few days later when the old chestnut of an imposed money bill at the beginning of a parliament cropped up. The patriots seized their opportunity and brought a majority of MPs with them in throwing the bill out. The commons' own money bills were subsequently passed, but Townshend nevertheless repeated Sydney's 1692 gesture after an identical challenge to the official interpretation of Poynings's law, and he prorogued parliament for fourteen months with most of its business still undone.

Speaker Ponsonby and the second earl of Shannon were naturally blamed for this constitutional challenge though they had only been passively involved in opposition. Both were counting on the collapse of the Grafton ministry and Townshend's recall. But although Grafton was indeed replaced by Lord North early in 1770, the new government kept Townshend in Ireland. It turned out to be a much more robust administration than the shaky coalitions of the 'sixties and was to survive in power for a dozen years. Its support for Townshend and its hostility towards the Irish undertakers for their obstructionism in 1768–69 transformed the viceroy's position during 1770. In the spring the principal faction leaders and their allies were removed from the privy council, Shannon was dismissed from a lucrative sinecure and, most critically, Ponsonby's twenty-year reign as chief revenue commissioner ended abruptly. Their close supporters were similarly purged. Their vast influence over the disposal of general government patronage was suddenly gone.

The temporary closure of parliament and the dismissal of the undertakers did not create the public reaction that some expected. But those opposed to Townshend's broom were themselves deeply divided, the patriots having little sympathy for the undertakers, and Shannon anxious to act responsibly in order to ensure that the government would soon woo him back. Townshend's offensive showed just how narrow Ponsonby's public support had been: anti-government feeling did not build up around 'John Bull's pimp' in the way it had so spectacularly done sixteen years previously around Henry Boyle. Ponsonby's English connections were themselves in disarray, and he lacked the political intelligence to outmanoeuvre Townshend. Neither he nor Shannon wanted to force another general election at which they might be squeezed between government-backed candidates and more extravagantly patriot ones. In any case Townshend's aristocratic opponents did not attempt to whip up popular antagonisms, preferring to wait for another ministerial change in England – which never came.

The viceroy and his able Ulster-born chief secretary, Sir George Macartney, spent the year forwarding three interlocked policies to strengthen Castle power: the cultivation of support from among the lesser parliamentary factions – notably those led by the earl of Tyrone (the Beresfords) and Lord Loftus – their support being won by the usual techniques, office, patronage and the promise of peerages; secondly, the government sought to win over public opinion by blackening the undertakers in a series of commissioned (and anonymous) pamphlets; and thirdly, the Castle sought to gain direct control over appointments in the revenue service. The strategic aim was to build up a solid group of MPs who would be as tightly controlled by the chief secretary as Ponsonby's acolytes had been by him. Greater control over patronage, especially in the revenue area, was the essential prerequisite to constructing such a party.

The fruits of the Castle's endeavours were evident in two very well attended sessions of parliament in 1771. The undertakers were unable to prevent the passage of resolutions of support for Townshend, and Ponsonby resigned the speakership, having lost his dominant position in the house. Townshend supported the candidacy of the senior Limerick politician, Edmond Sexton Pery, who had not been a government supporter. A lawyer closely associated with the patriots in the 'sixties, he displayed a patriotism richer and more complex in its ideology than most; he was completely out of sympathy with the constitutional imperialism of Townshend or Macartney. His great virtue in government eyes was his independence from factional interests and the respect in which he was held in the commons. Pery's election also underlined the limited extent of Townshend's victory; the new Castle 'party' was smaller and unsteadier than had been expected, and shortly before his recall, Townshend wooed Shannon back into supporting the government.

Townshend's qualified success in the direct management of parliament implied some modification in the 'ruling coalition', some strengthening of London's power over that of the Irish gentry. But this should not be exaggerated; the real sufferers were the Ponsonby faction and, to a much lesser extent, that of Shannon. Their interests since the mid-fifties had become separated from the Protestant gentry as a whole; the more representative lesser interests and independent MPs were probably on balance more powerful and better served in terms of their class interests after the fall of Ponsonby; they certainly had greater access to the Castle than before. Furthermore, as events at the end of the decade were to show, the Castle could still completely lose its influence in parliament. And the government's new need for patronage to sustain their commons following had a very positive result for the gentry: the old pattern of appointing Englishmen to the highest (and most lucrative) offices in the courts and the church began to be reversed; such plums were politically too valuable to be wasted on any but Irishmen.

The precedent of a resident viceroy was not abandoned. Lord Harcourt relieved Townshend in 1772 and profited from the stronger government control over parliament. Harcourt was a more relaxed and diplomatic figure and was supported by a chief secretary, John Blaquière, who was only too ready to be a full-time parliamentary manager and vote-broker in the commons. Until the American crisis intruded into Irish parliamentary politics in 1775, the Castle's discreet deployment of its power allowed a period of calm in public affairs. However the financial costs of Townshend's policies were only now apparent; the increase in the army payroll and patronage accelerated the growth of a budget deficit. Some remedial measures were quite successful financially, notably a lottery scheme and a stamp tax on newspapers, pamphlets and legal documents. The most radical proposal which initially had Irish government backing was for a tax of 10 per cent on all rents remitted to absentees. The continuing damage to the economy incurred by the haemorrhage of money to absentees was an article of faith for most Irish economic commentators since the 1720s, but the issue only attracted public attention when specie was scarce, or when the economy was depressed and credit tight. Through the 'sixties the patriots had been more concerned with ministerial corruption and the inflation of pensions and places than with strictly economic issues. However, the financial crisis in Dublin in 1770 and the much wider commercial slump which spread from England in 1772 made the taxing of what constituted about an eighth of Irish head rents topical and attractive to patriot and independent MPs, and to Harcourt it seemed a valuable means of tapping the otherwise untaxed income of the wealthy. However, as soon as Blaquière had floated the idea in 1773, a politically powerful absentee lobby in England arose to kill the proposal. They were helped by the Irish undertakers who exploited the fear that an absentee tax would be the prelude to a general Irish land tax, and the measure was narrowly defeated in the Irish commons. Harcourt emerged unscathed from an embarrassing affair which illustrated both the complexities of interest-group politics and the constraints on radical fiscal change.

THE AMERICAN WAR

There were ominous signs in 1774 that the political resistance of Americans to British imperial legislation, specifically in the area of taxation, could soon be extended to armed confrontation. By the time the first shots were fired at Lexington in April 1775, several distinct perspectives on the imperial crisis had emerged in Ireland. First, the Dublin government which, of course, had no independent influence in the formation of colonial policy, concerned itself with the political and military implications on Ireland if war broke out. The advantages for the Castle of a loyal core of MPs in the commons were now more evident than ever, and Harcourt continued to buy over individual opposition leaders. But the principal concerns of the Castle in 1775 were military and financial: how to respond to the likely demands on the army then garrisoned in Ireland without further straining state finances and without threatening law and order at a time when soldiers were being used 'to aid the civil power' more frequently than at any time since the 1690s. When parliament assembled in October 1775 a strongly loyal address to the king was passed, and attempts by the opposition to insert more conciliatory references to the 'rebels' were voted down by nearly two-to-one; however, more than half the commons' members were absent for these votes. A more practical victory for the administration was the agreement by parliament to release a third of the 12,000 troops for American service.

These parliamentary votes did not provide an accurate reflection of Protestant Irish attitudes towards America. The anglican gentry had been generally sympathetic towards the colonists, not least because of the veiled threat that the explicitly imperial powers exercised by the Westminster parliament since 1763 could equally well be used to diminish the competence of the Irish parliament. Many read in the local press the impassioned American constitutional arguments which themselves made reference to Irish constitutional issues and owed a debt to several writers from an Irish Protestant background – Molyneux, Robert Molesworth, John Trenchard and Charles Lucas. With a slighter constitutional history than Ireland's, colonial Americans were forced to wrestle with universalist concepts of political and natural rights while Irish political thinking was still log-jammed in the old issue of the constitutional status of the Irish parliament. The full impact of American ideas would only be felt in the following decade.

Apologists for American resistance were received sympathetically by the Irish gentry up to 1775. Many shared the Americans' suspicions of the tyrannical tendencies of North's administration and echoed their hostility to the 1774 Westminster act which had conceded full religious freedom to the Catholic church in the colony of Quebec (ceded by the French in 1763). Of the fifty-odd Irish MPs who supported compromise with the thirteen colonies in 1775, some were patriots, some the members of the shrunken Ponsonby and Leinster factions. The latter were opposing government in step with their English Whig connections who denounced North's American policy throughout the crisis. The more strident opposition of the patriot rump, led by Barry Yelverton, a lawyer from Cork, was consistent with the libertarian arguments they had been putting forward since the early 'sixties; the warnings which had reverberated through many issues of the *Freeman's Journal* seemed proven as a corrupted ministry prepared to trample down the liberties of free-born Anglo-Americans.

Several pro-American public meetings were organised in Dublin, and resolutions were passed by the lower chamber of the corporation against the government's American policy. In November 1775 an address to the crown urging a conciliatory policy was signed by some 3,000 freemen and other prominent citizens. One of the organisers was James Napper Tandy, a minor merchant and guild politician in the Lucas mould. Tandy's politics at this stage were very similar to the old apothecary (who had died in 1771), but Tandy was less of the autodidactic scribbler than Lucas, more of the demagogic street politician, and as his later career showed, his radicalism deepened with age. The other prominent organiser in Dublin was Sir Edward Newenham, a senior revenue officer with a Cork gentry background. He was extravagantly pro-American through the 1770s, but his admiration for the American cause was in part informed by his fervent anti-Catholicism (his attempts to implicate a Jesuit in the launching of the Oakboy movement in Ulster must have seemed faintly ridiculous even at the time).

Closely aligned to the Dublin-centred world of the patriots were the 'middling orders' of Ulster. The exceptional coverage of American affairs in the *Belfast Newsletter* and the *Londonderry Journal* is an indication of the immediacy of events in America to literate Ulster people. The early 1770s had been a troubled time throughout most of the province. Harvest losses in 1769 and 1770 had been particularly severe, cattle prices depressed, and on top of this an unprecedented decline in the external demand for linen in 1772–73 had led to a drop in living standards. Between 1770 and 1772 the eastern half of the province had been disturbed by a new agrarian redresser movement, the Hearts of Steel, which had begun on the huge Donegall estate in south Antrim as a tenant combination against Belfast land speculators. It then extended into four neighbouring counties as an agitation against the new rents being demanded at the re-leasing of farms, against intermediate gentlemen tenants as a group, and against county cess. Quite large gangs of Steelboys intimidated landowners, agents and newly-established tenants, using arson and verbal threats. Farmers rather than rural weavers seem to have provided the main impetus behind what was for the eighteenth century an unusual protest: it was explicitly directed against the landowners themselves. The steep rise in recent land values in east Ulster made the renegotiation of tenancies a difficult process, and at a time of falling incomes after 1769 old tenants, used to better times, resented having to adjust again to an 'economic' rent. Not until 1772 were army reinforcements introduced into Ulster, but house searches and mass arrests that year caused a panic through much of the north-east – although the later trials were something of a farce as juries once again declined to co-operate.

The tough repression of the Steelboys enlarged an outflow of emigrants to colonial America which had resumed in 1769. Ulster migration across the Atlantic was half a century old, but in these years before the American war it was running at an average four times that of previous decades, with over 20,000 leaving the province between 1769 and 1774. The economic recession, coming at the end of a generation of linen-centred prosperity and of rapid rural population growth, had precipitated this exodus, and the close shipping links between the northern ports and the middle colonies provided the opportunity for such a sudden surge; emigration in this context was truly a safety valve.

The economic, cultural and family links between Ulster and the middle colonies were therefore particularly strong in the 1770s. How far Ulster's Presbyterian complexion reinforced the region's pro-American sympathies is debatable; the strongest attacks on British policy published in Ulster came from Presbyterian pens, but it is not clear whether Ulster anglicans of similar status were demonstrably different in their attitudes.

Sentiment in Ulster was avowedly so hostile to the government that army recruitment in the province in 1775–76 was avoided. Most Ulster people, however, had only a garbled understanding of the conflict: 'all busy in enquiring about America, anxious to go there, and wishing an end to the war'.[7]

Attitudes to the American conflict among Irish Catholics were, on the surface, the complete reverse: repeated expressions of loyalty and condemnation of the king's new enemies. South of Ireland migration to colonial America (which in the previous half century had been perhaps a quarter of that from Ulster) had been a disproportionately Protestant affair, yet Munster Catholics as well as Ulster presbyterians were to have family connections with some of the military leaders of the revolution. But there was a consensus among literate Catholics that their interests would not be advanced by support for the Americans, whereas explicit endorsement of British policy at a time when the government was desperately trying to marshal public opinion behind it might be rewarding. The evidence of Irish-language poetry points to a rather different attitude among some unpropertied Catholics; Tomás O Míodhcháin, the Ennis schoolmaster who penned a celebration of Washington's first victories in 1776, was hardly unique in his unreconstructed hostility to all things British.[8]

For the first time since 1714 a distinct Catholic interest was now present within Irish politics and in the calculations of government. Catholic gentry, merchants and professionals on the eve of the American war had at last some bargaining power and the prospect of influence. A growing minority of anglican gentry was convinced that modification of the penal laws was desirable. For some the case rested on a new religious broad-mindedness, inspired ultimately by the Europe-wide debate on religious toleration, for others on a recognition that the supposed grand plan behind the penal laws had failed. But for most reformers it was the belief that a relaxation of the tight property and inheritance laws would benefit not just Catholics but landlords (especially those seeking to borrow money), and indeed the whole economy. Thus in the 1760s and early 1770s there was much talk around parliament of legislative changes. An act of 1772, allowing Catholics to take sixty-one-year reclamation leases, was however the only positive result. As Bedford had found in 1757 with the registration bill, the great strength of conservative support for the penal *status quo* cut across other political divisions.

Catholics were however buoyed up by external political developments: the Quebec concordat in 1774, following similar minor Caribbean arrangements, established the precedent for *de jure* recognition of

Catholic institutions in selected parts of the king's dominions. The death in Roman isolation of James III in 1766, followed by the Vatican recognition of George III as legitimate British sovereign, had removed the ancient question-mark against Catholic loyalty. The earl of Bristol – Church of Ireland bishop of Cloyne (1767) and then of Derry (1768) – took the lead in a new search for a legal formula by which Catholics could swear allegiance to the Hanoverian line. He won the cautious support of Catholic ecclesiastics in 1767 and then tried to get government support. It was not until 1774, when he acted as intermediary between the government and the Catholic Committee, that an acceptable oath was devised which included an abjuration of the pope's temporal powers; it had an easy passage through parliament. Like Ormond a century before, Bristol saw one desirable result of such an oath being available: it would sharpen divisions and tensions within the Catholic church. And indeed controversy sprang up, most Munster bishops stoutly encouraging laymen to take the oath, whereas the new Catholic archbishop of Dublin, John Carpenter, came out in opposition. In counties where the Catholic gentry were still present (parts of east Leinster, north Munster, and County Galway) and in the leading port cities, the loyalty oath was quite popular: in the following two years over 1,500 took it. Its comparative success contrasted with the failure of the abjuration oath of 1709, and thereby robbed the opponents of Catholic relief of one argument.[9]

The strongest change of circumstance favouring Catholics was in the matter of army recruitment. Until the 1750s few Irish Protestants and virtually no Catholics had been recruited into any British regiment. But in the early stages of the Seven Years War, unauthorised recruiting by English regiments began in the southern counties and formal government permission was given for the enlistment of Catholics as marines. In 1770 Townshend was overruled in his plans for the more extensive recruitment of Catholics within Ireland, but nevertheless in the following years large-scale recruitment took place in the provinces. Prior to 1774 Catholic enlistment was covert and religious oaths were simply waived, but the new oath of allegiance changed that. Irishmen of whatever religion had formed only about 6 per cent of all non-commissioned ranks of the British army in the mid-fifties, whereas it has been suggested that on the eve of the American war the proportion may have been over 20 per cent.[10] There were considerable recruiting problems in much of Britain by that stage and so it was to the metropolitan periphery, to the Scottish Highlands and to parts of Catholic Ireland, that the army was being forced to go to augment its numbers.

The recruitment of a wholly Catholic regiment was first attempted in Kerry in 1775, but this was abandoned because of the small numbers coming forward and the parliamentary row that the scheme gave rise to. Nevertheless over the next three years the recurrence of army manpower problems kept alive the Whitehall interest in expanding Catholic recruitment.

* * *

The American war lasted for eight years, becoming after 1778 a European conflict as well. In Ireland it impinged on political and economic life in a quite central way. Despite parliamentary victories in 1775, the government was justifiably nervous about being able to retain its dominant position. Therefore it became quite as immersed in the 1776 general election as Phipps's regime had been in 1713. The aim was to help in the re-election of less wealthy government supporters by increasing their pensions or salaries, and to reinforce the loyalty of wavering borough-owners by grants of new peerages. An unprecedented eighteen new Irish peerages were created during 1776 and more than two-thirds of these controlled votes in the commons.

Harcourt retired willingly that year and was replaced by the somewhat pedestrian earl of Buckinghamshire, whose one asset was his wife, one of the Conolly clan; her brother, MP for County Derry, and her brother-in-law, the young duke of Leinster, were opposition leaders and the 'conciliators' of the previous year. But this political connection outside the Castle party was somewhat unsettling for those within it, and the ambiguity of Buckinghamshire's power base contributed to his future difficulties.

The next session of parliament, in 1777–78, was dominated by economic questions, specifically the malign effect of the war on Irish trade. Even office-holders were openly critical of the way that Irish commerce had been hit by the decisions of the British treasury lords. In February 1776 they had imposed a prohibition on the export of Irish beef, butter, pork and other provisions to all places except Britain and the colonies still under British control. There was a number of wartime precedents for this, but until now embargoes had been of short duration. The 1776 ban imposed from London remained in force for three years. Its object was to ensure that the strategic larder for the war – Ireland – remained capable of supplying the requirements of British army and navy contractors. From 1778 an additional motive for such an embargo was Britain's desire to deny French access to Ireland's secret weapon, salted provisions. The opponents of the embargo claimed that its perpetuation could only do long-term damage to Irish trade with the Continent and would cause a sharp economic depression within the country, and that the only reason for its existence was to boost the profits of London military contractors. In fact, much of the political anger was misdirected; the scale of official purchases more than compensated for the loss of French trade and Cork, the centre of the provisions trade, was a prosperous place for most of the war.

By 1778 the wider economy was however in severe recession. This had almost nothing to do with the embargo but was caused, indirectly, by the war. A commercial depression had spread from Britain; credit lines shortened, most farm prices collapsed, and linen demand for the second time in a decade dropped back. The wave of bankruptcies in 1778 was probably greater than five years previously, and government finances were now far worse. The military budget in the first two years of the war had been at unprecedented levels and government revenues plummeted. Emergency short-term arrangements with Dublin bankers and the British treasury had to be made. And with the collapse of the disposable income of both landlord and tenant, urban industry was severely affected.

The unprecedented crisis in the Irish exchequer and the forceful if empirically faulty diagnoses of Irish poverty by leading parliamentarians led the viceroy to back calls for a substantial revision of the British Navigation Acts in so far as they restricted Irish overseas trade. North and some of the British cabinet were quite open to these arguments at a moment of imperial crisis, and they backed a bill at Westminster (which MPs of Irish background had introduced) to remove all restrictions on Irish colonial trade – excluding wool and woollen exports and tobacco imports. But hostile lobbying by English manufacturers in the provinces emaciated the bill, although the final act of 1778 still contained significant concessions. However the antecedent mutilation of the original measure overshadowed the final reforms.

1778 was also the year of the first major act modifying the penal laws. The initiative for this came (covertly) from the London government; a group within the British cabinet had become convinced that Catholic relief in Scotland and Ireland would assist the climate for Catholic recruitment, and that by giving substantial concessions to the Catholic gentry and church, their co-operation in promoting enlistment would be all the greater. The plan was to begin by dismantling *English* penal legislation, and to arrange for a similar Irish bill immediately in its wake, followed finally by relief for Scottish Catholics. But just as with the Irish commercial concessions, the government underestimated domestic

English and Scottish antipathy to religious toleration: the Scottish legislation had to be abandoned because of popular disturbances, and the English relief acts led to a delayed backlash on the streets of London with the bloody Gordon riots in 1780; the Irish proposal had survived but was much modified in its passage through the Dublin parliament in 1778. Without the superintending eye of Edmund Burke in Westminster, the Irish legislation might indeed have been lost.[11] In its final form the relief act reopened the rural and urban land market to Catholics after their exclusion for 74 years, permitting oath-takers to take leases for terms of up to 999 years.

The collapse of hopes for an American peace, the entry of France into the war, and the threat of domestic disorder because of the new depression created a sense of vulnerability among the propertied classes during 1778. The regular army was now much depleted and there was an attempt in parliament to secure a government-funded militia. The earlier militia arrays of 1715, 1719, 1745 and 1756 had been badly organised, under-equipped and uncoordinated demonstrations – momentary statements of Protestant alarm at the threat of invasion; outside the towns the initiative had always rested with the gentry. It seems unlikely that more than 50,000 Protestant males had ever been drilled. A new bill, modelled on the English act, proposed a county-based militia and provided for more rational and standardised arrangements; all the act lacked was funding and the Irish government was in no mood in the summer of 1778 to allocate even the £17,000 p.a. estimated as running costs for the new militia.

The other response to the 1778 malaise was the creation of local paramilitary groups. These had a double lineage, one located in the south-east of the country, in Wexford and in Kilkenny, where another agrarian agitation had broken out in the early 1770s that could not be contained by local JPs. The resentments of farmers over tithe valuations, and of labourers at the inflow of seasonal workers from Munster, had deteriorated into violent local vendettas and to another judicial counter-terror instigated by the county gentry in 1775–76. Only the formation of a large number of independent armed companies of Protestant gentry and their chief tenants in the south-east and south midlands had returned the region to tranquillity.

A second type of paramilitary body was set up in the spring of 1778 in Belfast: a Volunteer group, democratic in its structure (officers determined by election) and committed to remaining outside government control. Its aim was to train its members in local defence in the event of invasion. The great *esprit* of the first Belfast corps set an instant fashion for such enterprises, some demonstrably town-based and Presbyterian, others gentry-led. Outside Ulster, military associations and societies were also set up that year, ostensibly for national defence; these were closer to older militia corps and to the south-east independent companies than to the Ulster Volunteers – and could easily have been integrated into an official militia. However, even they exhibited the northern tendency for special uniforms and distinctive company emblemata. The very real danger of French invasion in 1779 swelled the number of corps and blurred their different origins. Membership rose to about 15,000 that spring and soared to around 40,000 by December.[12] By then a somewhat bemused Buckinghamshire had moved from open hostility to a grudging recognition of their utility; in July he had authorised the release of large amounts of light arms for their use.

Most families involved in early 'volunteering' had previously served in local militia troops; thus the spatial distribution of Volunteer corps reflected Protestant demography across the country. Yet the Volunteers differed sharply from former militia corps in several respects: their non-legal status, the length of time they remained active, their faltering efforts to develop a regimental structure and a national command, and their independent political life. Admittedly their non-legal status was little more than a technicality by the end of 1779, for at the beginning of the 1779–80 parliamentary session votes of thanks to the Volunteers were easily carried in both houses. The agents behind this parliamentary gesture were Conolly and Leinster, and it was a political move designed both to strengthen their personal authority within the new Volunteers and to associate their parliamentary tactics with the armed force out of doors.

* * *

The urban depression carried over into 1779 and was acute in Dublin and Cork; as a result of this non-importation resolutions against the import of British consumer goods were passed at grand jury and county freeholder meetings in the spring. Most Ulster counties stayed aloof, for the linen trade was reviving and non-importation was seen as a two-edged sword by the linen interest. In Dublin, a group of guild politicians organised the trade boycott. This group, which included Napper Tandy, ran a highly successful campaign publicising the names of those not co-operating and they had the support of several newspapers; imports of fine woollen cloth fell dramatically. American inspiration for their tactics was obvious.

The non-importation movement, coming on top of the general

economic malaise in the major cities and political posturing by the Volunteers, frightened the lord lieutenant into repeatedly pleading with London for greater economic concessions. A cross-party group of MPs at Westminster, most with Irish links, initiated a series of debates and reports on the Irish economy, and as a concession North removed the charge of the 'Irish' troops serving in America from the Irish exchequer, a saving of £70,000. Buckinghamshire meanwhile solicited detailed analyses on the causes of economic difficulty from a dozen leading Irish politicians. Nearly all of them identified British legislative restrictions on Irish trade as the major problem. They were making a false diagnosis. The economic crisis was in fact a cyclical one, made worse by the war. The apocalyptic talk of national bankruptcy was informed by political not economic reasoning. There was a distinct political crisis which arose from a crucial weakening in the authority of both the London and the Dublin governments vis-à-vis the Irish gentry class, and from an uncharacteristic willingness of the Westminster opposition to use 'Irish poverty' for party advantage. It was hardly surprising that some, including Lord North, were privately convinced that an Anglo-Irish union could be the only secure political arrangement.

As the parliamentary session of 1779–80 approached, the Castle administration was in disarray. Even level-headed office-holders like John Beresford warned that unless Whitehall pursued a clear policy, conciliatory or otherwise, 'the consequences will go further than you may possibly imagine'.[13] Parallels with the thirteen colonies on the eve of the war were in many English minds. The personal failure of North to devise a practical political strategy for Ireland created exceptional difficulties for Buckinghamshire when he had no concessions to offer the Irish parliament. An extraordinary rhetorical offensive by the young Henry Grattan, violent in its criticism of British policy towards Ireland and populist to a degree that only Lucas could have equalled, set the tone for two months of political suspense. Office-holders backed a commons resolution demanding 'free trade alone', i.e. the repeal of British commercial restrictions.

To reinforce the link between a parliament in which the administration had temporarily lost control and 'the people', several large demonstrations of Volunteers were organised outside parliament including one around King William's statue on his birthday, an old city ritual but one which had never before been so powerful a piece of political theatre. The extravagant slogans on this occasion (*parati pro patria mori* etc.) were not lost on the administration. Where in earlier times the proroguing of parliament would have seemed an instant remedy, the political arousal out of doors made such a course of action now too dangerous for the government. Buckinghamshire had neither the personality nor the politics of a Townshend, and his assessments of the Irish political storm never erred on the side of understatement. No effective attempt was made to rally government support in the commons: the fault for this must lie with his ineffectual chief secretary, Richard Heron.

The opposition forces decided to agitate for a 'short' money bill as a means of extracting concessions. Grand juries and county meetings echoed this call. Three distinct political groups were by then in temporary coalition: elements of the old parliamentary opposition who had close connections with the Westminster Whigs; a large but amorphous grouping of patriot and independent MPs committed to major reform, now joined by some of the very able office-holders who had defected to Harcourt's 'broad-bottomed' administration before the war; and, thirdly, outside parliament there was a more radical group, mainly located in Dublin, who were extreme patriots in their ideology and were distinguished by their willingness to use extra-parliamentary means – the city mob – to secure economic and constitutional changes; Grattan came nearest to being their parliamentary spokesman. The potential for tensions within such a coalition was obvious, but the government failed to exploit these or to regain the initiative. The opposition had no difficulty in pushing the short money bill through the commons.

By the time the British parliament reassembled in late November, North's administration had decided to repeal all British commercial legislation that discriminated against Ireland. This was presented by North's allies as an act of great magnanimity when Irish finances were faltering, although one junior minister, Henry Dundas, echoed his mentor Adam Smith by asserting that such restrictions were archaic and only clogged the flow of commerce; Hely-Hutchinson, on the Irish side of the argument, had also used Smithian free-trade arguments. The Westminster legislation was passed quickly before another flood of English protests could well up.

The political crisis in Dublin subsided with confirmation of the British measures in December 1779. The majority of MPs saw the *volte-face* in British policy as a great political victory over entrenched English vested interests. The patriots praised the role of the Volunteers extravagantly, but among the city radicals there was a more guarded reaction: 'no illuminations, no rejoicings … until our constitution [is] made free'.[14]

In the heat of the free-trade agitation when the rhetoric of unity from parliament and county meetings implied a widening of the political nation, a proposal in the commons to remove the 1697 ban on Catholics possessing arms without licence found very little support, despite the fact that Catholic gentry in several southern counties had been offering material support to the Volunteers; some had actually joined up during 1779. The commons' refusal to waive the arms prohibition discouraged such tendencies, and MPs turned instead to the more congenial business of a repeal of the 1704 test which in theory kept dissenters as second-class citizens. Unlike the situation two generations previously, this was now totally uncontroversial in the commons; only a few anglican bishops and the government itself were reluctant to move on Presbyterian relief, but the legislation was secured in 1780. Presbyterian 'emancipation' caused surprisingly little stir, despite the symbolic importance of repeal. The spotlight was now on other things.

Even before 1780 there were signs that some of the patriots regarded 'constitutional freedom' as a realisable political goal. The warnings by the English Whig opposition that Irish constitutional independence would be the price to be paid for the current mismanagement of Ireland had the unintended result of stimulating such talk within Ireland itself. A coalition of patriots and independent MPs agreed in the spring of 1780 to try and build up support for three basic constitutional changes: a new declaratory act which would assert that the crown and the parliament of Ireland were alone 'competent to make laws to bind this kingdom'; a modification of Poynings's law so as to remove from the Irish privy council (and, indirectly, the viceroy) any role in framing Irish legislation; and an Irish mutiny act to establish the army's accountability to the Irish parliament on terms identical to those in Britain.

None of the three proposals in their original form made much headway, for the government had won back the initiative in the commons and, more importantly, many of the peers and larger gentry made it clear that they wanted no part in further constitutional agitation. Even Leinster, whose use of the Dublin Volunteers had been so effective in 1779, opposed plans for Volunteer resolutions endorsing the new constitutional proposals.

Buckinghamshire was replaced by the young earl of Carlisle at the end of 1780. Despite taking over after the return of political calm, the new viceroy sensed that 'the aristocratic part of the government has lost its balance; ... there is an evident necessity of regaining from the people that power, which if suffered to continue in their hands, must end in the general ruin of the whole ...'.[15] Grattan and his allies had persisted in appealing to public opinion outside parliament and in making menacing threats against those within who did not respect the will of the people.

Such American-sounding phrases were echoed at Volunteer parades and at some county assizes. However by early 1781 the momentum was slackening and even among the Dublin Volunteers only a minority of corps continued a radical posture.

Carlisle's administration concerned itself in 1781 with reconstructing the Castle's parliamentary majority. The patriot press reacted to the government strategy by debating for the first time the need for electoral reform in order to make parliament less vulnerable to the corrupt influence of the executive. The newspaper debate was also inspired by a powerful reform movement in England.

Meanwhile a new threat of French invasion in 1781 expanded Volunteer numbers to their maximum: by the end of the year there may have been as many as 80,000 involved in the military craze, two-fifths of them in Ulster. It was still an overwhelmingly decentralised, heterogeneous organisation, and despite its 130 pieces of artillery it was a fighting force of little value if invasion had actually occurred. Military discipline was often lax and there were no arrangements for long marches or distant campaigns. Even the spectacular annual displays in Belfast, when up to 5,000 Ulster Volunteers mounted mock battles, masked the reality that actually sustained Volunteering: its fundamental virtue (in the eyes of the gentry) was as an agency of local law enforcement, in which magistrates were often Volunteer officers and their associates in arms their leading tenants. The policing function of the Volunteers, whether against Whiteboys, smugglers, illicit distillers or urban rioters, was crucial during the war years. In social terms the Volunteer corps were convivial clubs where a limited degree of class interaction between gentry and Protestant freeholders was able to develop. Regimental and county reviews provided tempting opportunities for these overwhelmingly Protestant fraternities to debate public issues and to pass political resolutions, and to develop a sense of civic identity. The concept of the citizen-in-arms as the fullest expression of public-spiritedness and of the free citizen's protection of liberty in a corrupt world was the common theme running through Volunteer speeches and sermons. Such discourse drew much of its strength from its essentially Presbyterian frame of reference.

The fundamental changes in the status of the Irish parliament made in the spring of 1782 were in a sense the culmination of the patriot agenda, but their coming was sudden. The early months of the 1781–82 parliamentary session had been fairly sedate, dominated by the fateful news from America. The patriots, joined once again by Henry Flood, had brought forward a series of reform measures, some old favourites (an Irish habeas corpus bill and the proposal that judges' appointments should be made more secure from executive review), and others which were carried over from the previous year's defeats. The government tactically conceded habeas corpus but had sound majorities to defeat or defer the rest.

The political climate then began to change rapidly. Through the winter Volunteer corps in increasing numbers declared support once again for the patriots' proposals; more important, North's long-serving government was beginning to fall apart. The Volunteers had been deliberately stirred up by patriot MPs frustrated at the government's parliamentary strength. At a large meeting of south Ulster corps in Armagh at the end of 1781 a call was issued for a non-military convention of delegates from every corps in Ulster to consider 'vigorous and effectual methods ... to root corruption and court influence out of the legislative body'.[16] The architects of this initiative were second-rank south Ulster gentry including Francis Dobbs, a patriot MP of advanced if fluctuating views. This meeting of some 140 Volunteer delegates produced a concrete but radical manifesto for constitutional change which mirrored the main patriot demands; it was in effect a call for legislative and judicial independence. The two slightly controversial parts of the convention's business were resolutions that only parliamentary candidates at the next year's elections who subscribed to the Dungannon programme should be supported, and that the recent measures relaxing the penal code were welcome. A national convention of Volunteers was envisaged to sustain the political momentum, but this was hardly necessary as the manifesto was endorsed (although not always in its entirety) at county meetings and municipal 'aggregate' meetings across the whole country over the next two months.

This political current would not have been irresistible in normal political circumstances. But it coincided with the fall of Lord North's government in London in March 1782 and its replacement by a Whig ministry headed by the marquis of Rockingham. The Whigs had been happy to exploit Irish political and economic grievances in Westminster over the previous three years and this left them in a weak position to resist the new patriot/Volunteer groundswell in Ireland. Carlisle was withdrawn from Dublin with unprecedented haste and replaced as viceroy by a Whig magnate, the duke of Portland; the initial government intention was to play for time. Grattan however refused to respond to private Whig pleas for a postponement of his plan to propose a fiery declaratory resolution when parliament reopened in April. The viceroy's opening address referred ambiguously to 'a final adjustment as may give mutual satisfaction', but a moderately worded resolution in reply (proposed by Speaker Ponsonby's son) was swept aside by Grattan who called for a formal declaration of Ireland's status as a distinct kingdom, that the 1720 Declaratory Act be repealed, and that Poynings's law be rewritten. His well-rehearsed speech was one of the great set-pieces of the eighteenth-century Irish parliament, rich in allegory and historical allusion and enormously seductive to his audience and its subsequent readers, although rather thin in hard constitutional argument. His resolution was carried *nem. con.*

Over the next two and a half months the British government – with considerable misgivings – repealed the Declaratory Act and allowed the patriot proposals on Poynings's law, the Mutiny Act, and the revised status of judicial appointments to reach the statute book. A second major Catholic relief bill also passed through fairly uncontroversially – extending the terms of the 1778 act, and removing many of the ecclesiastical restrictions on the clergy and religious worship. But significantly the patriots did not press for the removal of the British privy council's veto powers over Irish legislation nor for the replacement of the great seal of Britain by that of Ireland at the point when Irish legislation was receiving the royal assent. And the whole question of the accountability of the Dublin Castle executive to the Irish parliament was not even posed at this point. Yet in a formal sense, the Irish parliament had at last achieved equal status with Westminster and for the patriots, with their strongly legalistic mentality, that was what mattered. They had won.

THE LEGACY OF '82

The Rockingham government which had been forced to make the constitutional concessions in 1782 was only in existence for a few months before the sudden death of its leader. It was left to successor administrations to develop an Irish policy now that formal British control over the Dublin legislature was diminished. The residual power of privy council veto over Irish legislation was a very blunt instrument (used in fact only once) and the political authority of the lord lieutenant and his executive had now to rest on their holding the support of a majority of Irish MPs and peers. This in turn could only be brought about through judicious government patronage, but even pensions, places and peerage promotions could not guarantee loyalty in the lobby: Irish MPs from open constituencies were now less willing to be seen as clients of the

Castle when many of them had to pay at least cosmetic attention to constituency public opinion. The exploitation of out-of-doors politics by the patriots since 1778 had created, both in Dublin and in counties where the electorate extended beyond a few hundred, a heightened interest in national politics and a critical new attitude towards MPs' behaviour.

The early months of the new constitutional order left many of the implications of parliamentary independence unclear: was the British legislation repealing former restraints sufficient to withstand legal scrutiny and political counter-pressure? Which parliament was responsible for Ireland's external relations? Could the Irish parliament establish its own armed services? Who was to define Ireland's trading rights within the empire? Portland had hoped to halt any further constitutional challenge by changing the political composition of the Irish executive; he anticipated that the appointment of several of the Irish politicians who had old links with English Whig grandees – notably the Ponsonbys – would secure an Irish declaration recognising 'the superintending power' of Westminster in external affairs and in international commerce. But Portland's stay was so short that his optimism was not tested. His successor in the Castle, the young and zealous Earl Temple, was resolutely against such a partisan method of gaining a parliamentary majority – on the familiar grounds that royal government could only be weakened by fostering English party loyalties in College Green. Temple and his brother, chief secretary William Grenville, wrestled hard to remove the ambiguities of the 'settlement'. In external commerce Temple envisaged an arrangement whereby all duties and restrictions would be standardised between Britain and Ireland, and that in external diplomatic negotiations Britain would simply act on behalf of Ireland. Despite their ingenious aspects, Temple's proposals were something of a fudge: Ireland would in effect be the passive rider on a tandem.

At the time of Rockingham's concessions, the British cabinet had privately wished to do nothing that would imply that the British parliament was ceding control over external affairs. Attempts to make this clear at Westminster, some coded, some unguarded, provoked the first stirrings of a campaign in Ireland led by Henry Flood to press for a further Westminster statute that would explicitly renounce all controls over the Irish parliament. Flood threw his weight behind this agitation for private reasons, being understandably bitter at the popular adulation of Grattan; the latter, befriended by Portland, vigorously defended the sufficiency of Rockingham's concessions. Flood's campaign was strengthened in November 1782 when a judgment was given in the English court of king's bench on an Irish case that had been transferred to London before the repeal of the Declaratory Act. In the immediate publicity given to this apparent violation of the restored Irish appellate jurisdiction, the timing of the transfer of the case was ignored. It helped make 'renunciation' the new popular issue, taken up by the Volunteers and supported at many county meetings. Rockingham's successor as prime minister, Petty's great-grandson the earl of Shelburne, was determined to ride out the new agitation. When and if the international peace negotiations were successful he intended to adopt a much tougher policy against Irish opposition, within and outside parliament. Temple and Grenville actually supported the idea of a clarifying act, but one which would still leave open the question of external and imperial responsibility; Grenville managed to persuade Shelburne into sponsoring a bill that declared the British parliament's recognition of 'the right claimed by the people of Ireland to be bound only by laws enacted by his majesty and the parliament of that kingdom in all cases whatever ...'.[17] Again a skilful fudge, which left the definition of those rights for another day. This English bill of 'recognition' reached the statute book despite the fall of Shelburne's government and the formation of a third British ministry in just over a year (the Fox-North coalition). The act satisfied those campaigning for renunciation and completely restored Flood's prestige in Ireland.

The most sustained and controversial British effort to tidy up the 1782 settlement was the elaborate legislation debated in both parliaments during 1785 and usually referred to as the Commercial Propositions. The first year of peace had been very difficult economically in Ireland, and the Irish parliament was buffeted by conflicting demands for action; John Foster, then chancellor of the Irish exchequer, devised a plan to harmonise Irish customs duties with those in Britain, to reduce duties in both countries on commodities exchanged between them, and to remove the legal obstacles preventing the development of an Irish re-export trade in colonial goods. Foster and other Irish office-holders found the British government highly responsive to this rescue plan, the new prime minister, William Pitt, in particular.

Pitt's interest in Irish affairs had begun in 1782 during his meteoric rise to power, and he was anxious to follow up Temple's abortive commercial proposals and extend them to the constitutional sphere. Pitt insisted on linking a commercial treaty with a financial one on the grounds that Ireland should make a fixed contribution to the imperial defence budget. Irish office-holders strongly advised against coupling the two issues for tactical reasons, but Pitt's enthusiasm for the plan only intensified. The two sets of proposals were presented to the Irish commons in February 1785; the imperial contribution was amended so as to operate only in years when the Irish budget had a surplus and in years of war (a compromise later overruled by Pitt), but otherwise the arrangements were accepted. However an even more comprehensive set of proposals on Anglo-Irish relations was placed before the British parliament, and these stirred up trouble. There were vociferous protests from English manufacturers at the prospect of greater Irish access to the British domestic market, protests which were fanned by Pitt's parliamentary opponents. Pitt stood firm. However the scope of the proposed commercial treaty was widened; it was now proposed that the Irish parliament should enact without modification all existing British legislation relating to colonial trade, shipping and other branches of external trade, and should do so automatically in future. Temple's tandem was back.

The revised resolutions were presented to the Irish commons in August 1785, prior to their formal drafting as legislation. But at this point the whole scheme was bitterly attacked by many MPs and the Castle barely managed to secure a majority. The constitutional implications – the implicit recognition of the overarching function of Westminster in external trade – were so unpopular that MPs were prepared to jettison what most conceded were substantial economic concessions in defence of a political principle. At this point the whole initiative was abandoned.

For Pitt it was his Irish apprenticeship; he had misjudged the mentality and the malleability of Irish MPs and had underestimated their respect for constitutional form over economic substance – as exemplified by Grattan's fine rhetoric and his apparent inability to understand the complexities of the actual proposals. Almost a year of tedious preparation was therefore wasted. But the incident remains a major political landmark in Anglo-Irish politics. Temple had set the precedent for an English commercial initiative that was intended to be an equitable settlement as seen from London. Pitt had invested both time and political capital in the scheme, which he defended vigorously against British vested interests in the hope that what he saw as a comprehensive framework for coping with the external and bilateral ambiguities of 1782 could be firmly established. The bitter saga taught Pitt a lesson.

The failure of the Commercial Propositions was not however total: over the next eight years the tandem moved forward when the Irish parliament – by careful government management – passed navigation and trade legislation identical to new Westminster measures. There were moves in the early 1790s which went some way towards establishing the Anglo-Irish grain trade on a reciprocal 'most favoured nation' basis, along the lines of 1785. And in 1793 Irish traders were finally allowed to re-export colonial produce.

The Irish office-holders who had helped Pitt to draft the original Commercial Propositions in 1784 were part of a small group whose rise to power in the Castle was on the face of it a new expression of the old coalition. John Beresford, John Foster and John Fitzgibbon formed the core of an informal cabinet from about 1784 until 1798. During that period they had at least as much influence over Irish policy as the old undertakers and lords justices had ever had. Yet they neither exercised nor sought to exercise great private claims over government patronage. Indeed they did not need such patronage because their power rested not on large parliamentary followings nor on specific numbers of clients who had to be cultivated, but simply on their indispensability to the British government as repositories of administrative and political experience and as men of sharp judgment. In this way they were far more than mere backstage bureaucrats in the Thomas Waite mould. The three of them were by any standards exceptionally able; they held strong political beliefs that were generally in harmony with those of Pitt and his circle. They were politically united among themselves in their jaundiced view of the 1782 compact, in their opposition to any scheme of parliamentary reform (although Beresford after 1793 is a partial exception here) or to any political concessions to Catholics, and in their fundamental commitment to the preservation of the existing gentry-dominated social order. Their views helped to break the opposition momentum for reform, and their stern approach to law and order heavily influenced both legislation and enforcement. Their barely-concealed opposition to Pitt's new departure on Catholic policy in 1791–93 won over the then viceroy, Westmoreland, but not his London masters. Yet the troika survived this episode intact. Their continuance in power, serving altogether six viceroys, did not therefore depend on a precise identity of interest or attitude between themselves and Pitt, but resulted from Pitt's own retention of office for nearly two decades and the administrative continuity of which they were a part. The one thing that threatened their position before 1798 was political change in London: the inclusion of the Portlandite Whigs in Pitt's wartime coalition of 1794 led to a Whig viceroy, Fitzwilliam, and the dismissal of Beresford and two lesser office-holders in the early weeks of 1795. But Fitzwilliam's blizzard melted before spring and Beresford was reinstated.

The need for a group of Irish 'men of business' in the full confidence of the viceroy was directly related to the changed constitutional position after 1782. There was now a far greater volume of political business requiring the attention of the executive thanks to the institution of annual parliamentary sessions in 1783. And with Poynings's law gone, the Castle had to pay far greater attention to the management of the commons and, specifically, to the drafting of legislation. Neither the political energy nor the intellectual quality of the lords lieutenants during the 1780s and 1790s was the highest, and the chief secretaries – the parliamentary managers since Townshend's day – were a mixed bag. Without men of the calibre of Beresford, Foster and Fitzgibbon, the Castle's capacity to control College Green would have been much weaker.

Beresford was the eldest of the troika, and in background and outlook shared much with the old undertakers. He had risen to favour when Townshend had wooed the Beresford faction as one of the second-rank powers to fill the void left by Speaker Ponsonby's fall. A revenue commissioner since 1770, he became chief commissioner in 1780. He was a good administrator in the traditional sense, but as younger brother of a wealthy peer and father of seventeen children he was anxious to use his bureaucratic power for the advancement of his family and his immediate connections. This he did with far greater finesse than John Ponsonby. His long reign over the revenue was at a time of great manpower expansion (there were about 3,000 in the service by 1800), but this was not another case of political job-creation; it came at a time when indirect taxes were mounting and administrative costs rising in proportion. And to a modest extent Beresford was an agent of administrative reform. His greatest triumph came early with the realisation of the controversial new Dublin Custom House/revenue headquarters – the most important Irish public building project of the century and an extravagant statement of the pre-eminence of the revenue service within the state apparatus. His wider influence within the government and public bodies was pervasive yet covert and relatively restrained. Above all, he was Pitt's man in Ireland: personal loyalty to Pitt and contempt for Ponsonbys and patriots remained Beresford's articles of political faith.

John Foster's family background was professional rather than aristocratic. His father had been a very successful barrister, ending up as senior judge in the court of exchequer under Townshend. Foster followed his father into parliament when still under age in 1761, and pursued both politics and the law until his administrative and parliamentary skills brought him into the limelight under Buckinghamshire. From 1777 he had had responsibility for the direction of the Irish exchequer, although he only became chancellor in 1784. At this period he first displayed his distinctive grasp of economic issues and his views on how the state could and should promote trade and agriculture. Like Beresford, he had not been swept along by the patriot tide, but he was quick to see the potential of the new discretionary powers of the Irish parliament in promoting development; 'Foster's Corn Law' of 1784 seemed at the time a politically bold measure to stimulate Irish grain exports. Foster had a passionate interest in the range of industrial and agricultural activities present in his native county and constituency, Louth: linen manufacture, tillage farming, new proto-factory enterprises. From this developed his distinctive ideology – highly conservative on religious and political questions, balanced by a paternalistic economic patriotism. Foster's belief was that prosperity would divert communal energies from faction, subversion and politically divisive reform.

Foster switched from government office to speakership of the commons in 1785 on Pery's resignation. A Ponsonby challenge failed to materialise and the government's candidate was unopposed. Although never as close to the centre of power as the other great counsellors (and often on bad personal terms with them), Foster remained part of the charmed circle after 1785 and was almost consistently loyal to the government of the day. Foster combined this with continuing parliamentary (if not public) popularity; as Malcomson has put it, 'his influence in the house derived … from his ability to rationalise what in other members of his class was prejudice, and give articulation to what in them was instinct'.[18] Like Speaker Boyle he cultivated the image of an accessible, independent country gentleman, and his conservative politics were more congenial to most rural gentry than were the advanced views of the reformers and of the capital's politicians. As Speaker of the commons he took his responsibilities very seriously, helping to draft the legislative programme, determining the order of business and reforming practical aspects of its procedures. Indeed if any politician had a proprietorial association with the post-1782 parliament it was not Grattan but Foster. Grattan shunned office and responsibility after a brief moment of power in 1783; Foster loved power – not for its own end nor for personal financial gain – but as a means of directing state policy towards economic development and away from political compromise.

John Fitzgibbon, the youngest of the three, came like Foster from a wealthy legal family which had acquired landed property. But Foster's ancestry was anglican whereas Fitzgibbon's father was a convert. Since the 1690s most of those with a *converso* background in public life had sought the relaxation of the penal laws, but a minority became more Protestant than the Protestants; John Fitzgibbon was one such case. Throughout his parliamentary career he was bitterly opposed to concessions to Catholics and displayed what in the 1780s was an unfashionable contempt for the Catholic clergy. Yet his enmity was based less on a desire to maintain the existing religio-social balance within Ireland than to protect English control: 'the British connection ... was Fitzgibbon's God'.[19] He was a brilliant court performer and a wealthy barrister before becoming attorney-general in 1783. His skills in parliament derived from his mental agility, the sharpness of his tongue and his personal courage. His speeches and personal correspondence displayed an almost Swiftian indignation against the folly and political short-sightedness of those around him. He had an eye for the uncomfortable truth and even in the 1780s saw the end of the Irish parliament as a likely and desirable consequence of the compact of 1782. His constant opposition to reform reflected his strongly authoritarian nature and his belief that any widening of the political nation would endanger the connection. In the 1790s he liked to appear as the prophet whose time had come.

Despite his own legal environment he despised the legalistic and constitutional obsessions of those in the patriot tradition. And in a wider sense he regarded legal processes as necessarily subservient to *raison d'état*. His elevation to the lord chancellorship in 1789 (for which he had had to lobby hard) allowed him to dominate the whole Dublin legal establishment. His command of the court of chancery, the main forum for litigation over property, transformed its sleepy procedures. His hot-blooded temperament and lack of English political connections weakened his influence in London, and the violence of his opposition to Irish political change made him exceptionally unpopular within the country. 'Black Jack' to reformers and radicals became the symbol of Castle power and of obdurate inflexibility. But he was no English puppet.

The troika emerged as a distinct group during the winter of 1783–84, after Northington's heterogeneous group of office-holders – including Grattan – had proved unable for the task of parliamentary management. Indeed Castle leadership had been weak during the general election in the summer of 1783 when reform of parliament had become the great public issue, reflecting a similar debate in England. The object of the Irish reform campaign had at first been to copper-fasten the independence of the legislature. With the majority of borough constituencies and of MPs under the influence of a few dozen wealthy landowners, the house of commons was always at the mercy of those who controlled patronage, namely the government, until such time as the representation of the counties in parliament was increased. However the great debate of 1783 centred on the excessive power of the borough-owners within the boroughs, and the imbalance in the constitution between 'the aristocracy' and 'the people'. To some extent it was a case of old players wearing new costumes, for the champions of parliamentary reform at the local level were generally out-groups within the elite, 'independent' gentry families who were seeking to challenge those already holding parliamentary seats, especially the ones clearly identified as supporters of the Castle. The new costume in 1783 was a Volunteer uniform, for the reform debate gave a fresh political role to many Volunteer corps as the reviewing season approached.[20]

First in Munster, then more strongly in Ulster, Volunteer corps associated with independent gentry met and passed general declarations in favour of parliamentary reform. The campaign in Ulster was organised from Lisburn, a borough sufficiently open for a genuine electoral battle between proprietorial candidates and those running on a reform ticket. Lisburn was in fact the only borough in 1783 where 'reformers' won, although many of the new county MPs were committed to reform, and every electoral contest within Ulster and many outside it were touched by the reform debate. And despite the failure of Pitt's reform bill in Westminster, Irish enthusiasm for reform outlived this general election.

In September, with the election virtually over but before parliament assembled, nearly 400 Volunteer representatives met at Dungannon to decide on a specific reform programme. This colourful assembly, drawn largely from the province's gentry, revealed for the first time the fundamental ambiguities within the reform movement: was the object of reform to weaken Castle influence over parliament and to create a representation that reflected more accurately the will of the propertied classes within Ireland? Or was it to widen the constitution, to weaken the political power of the greater landowners and to strengthen the 'middling orders'? And was the political nation to remain exclusively Protestant? The blueprint approved by the assembly was in fact quite radical: annual parliaments and elections; a secret ballot (on the existing franchise in the counties); the abolition of some small boroughs; and the opening up of the borough franchise. It was decided to hold a national convention in Dublin to collate this with the programmes from other provinces. The issue of the Catholic vote was left to the Dublin convention to decide. The aristocratic bishop of Derry, the earl of Bristol, had led a radical minority consisting of mainly east Ulster Presbyterians who advocated Catholic political rights. The majority however fought shy of new concessions to Catholics.

The other provincial conventions were subdued affairs but the national convention, held for three weeks in November 1783, was potentially explosive. The radicals sought to present it as a shadow parliament, a truly representative assembly of the propertied class backed by a gentry-controlled armed force, meeting to proclaim the limitations of the house of commons. However the 'Rotunda parliament' spoke with many voices as to the extent of reform and the appropriate way to approach College Green with its plans. Despite the fighting talk of the earl bishop a majority of the delegates were extremely reluctant to mount any constitutional or paramilitary challenge against parliament, and many active participants, including the chairman Lord Charlemont, sought bland resolutions and no more. The convention managed to avoid a debate on the embarrassing issue of the Catholic franchise by convincing itself (wrongly) that Catholic gentry and the Catholic Committee were giving contradictory signals as to their wishes. After a few days of confusion Henry Flood was co-opted onto the drafting committee. The veteran patriot hammered out a solid reform bill, much less sweeping than the Dungannon proposals and silent on the Catholic issue. He was delegated to introduce it into parliament. He did this, but it was rejected by more than two-to-one, with solid support coming only from the MPs sitting for 'open' county constituencies. After this slap the convention broke up in disarray, resolving only on an innocuous course of action, the gathering of petitions to MPs in favour of reform.

These Irish developments had given the Fox-North government in London a bad fright. However the Castle administration had kept its head; the policy of giving quiet hints to its 'friends' in the convention that they should divert and side-track the proceedings, and to its supporters in the commons that they should proclaim parliament's rights against the undue influence and pretensions of armed associations, was almost completely successful. The near humiliation of the reformers was the first instance of government victory over a strong popular movement since before the American war.

The prospects for electoral reform in Ireland were now fading. With the old faction leaders and borough-owning families united with the Castle in opposition to constitutional change, there was little chance of a parliamentary majority for reform. Flood, for all his set-piece brilliance, lacked the political commitment to wear down his opponents. And a winter of well-organised petitioning by freeholders from twenty-two counties and eleven cities in favour of reform had hardly any impact on the voting behaviour of MPs when another reform bill was introduced in March 1784. Yet at this point, the reform movement, instead of dying, underwent a transformation.

In this, Dublin city played a strategic role. Since the general election in 1783 there had been a growing agitation in the capital for selective import tariffs as a means of relieving what was an intense industrial recession; this had been orchestrated by several radical guild-politicians. After a long parliamentary investigation, protectionist proposals were thrown out by the house of commons at the end of March 1784. City politicians, led by Napper Tandy and backed by a sympathetic press, immediately exploited the genuine sense of popular betrayal felt by the artisan population that MPs, corrupted by English influence, had chosen to ignore their plight, and that Foster, 'Jacky Finance', was the arch-villain of the piece. After a huge public meeting the commons chamber was forcibly occupied and had to be cleared by troops. The *Volunteer Journal*, a new city paper edited by a young Catholic, Mathew Carey, passed far beyond the normal bounds of opposition journalism in its verbal assassination of Foster and its advocacy of political separation as the only path to prosperity. Foster reacted by statutory counter-attack, drafting and rushing through parliament a libel bill which for the first time exposed newspaper publishers to legal challenge. The passing of the act deepened the unpopularity of government in the press, but it formed the starting point for a generation of Castle control over the city's editors.

In the late spring of 1784 the protectionist campaign was taken up again in the form of non-importation resolutions against English textiles by meetings of freeholders, guilds and Volunteer corps in Dublin and in the larger towns. The focal point remained Dublin where the boycott gave rise to much greater violence than in the similar campaign of 1779, and the non-gentry Volunteer corps, some at this stage openly recruiting Catholics, noisily declared their support. The campaign was economically effective in that English cloth imports shrank back, but politically it was probably counterproductive.

The new governing circle perceived a direct challenge to its authority and placed a sinister interpretation on events. Indeed the authorities had reason to feel alarmed: the campaign for industrial protection by urban interests was being coupled to a new type of agitation for parliamentary reform. For the first time a non-gentry, urban, part-Catholic, part-dissenter group was leading a national political movement. It was this novel alliance that made the second reform movement seem far more insidious than the gentry-led Volunteers of 1783. The new reform movement was launched by the guild politicians with several prominent east Ulster reformers lending their support. An 'aggregate meeting' of Dublin citizens (not just freeholders) was held, from which invitations were sent to all county sheriffs to convene freeholder meetings for the purpose of sending delegates to a reform 'congress'. A vague resolution in favour of a limited Catholic franchise was passed, and this gave a handle to the new movement's enemies.

Through the summer of 1784 the earl of Charlemont used all his considerable influence with the Ulster Volunteers to have the Dublin reform initiative rejected and the 'Catholic' Volunteer corps repudiated. Meanwhile the Castle deployed the newspapers under its control to publicise extraordinary rumours concerning Catholic intentions – puritan/papist alliances, military conspiracies and French agents. Dublin reformers were also discredited by being linked with the violent intimidation of cloth importers who had not co-operated. The new viceroy, the duke of Rutland, although not all of his Irish cabinet, actually believed for a time that there was a grand conspiracy involving France.

The involvement of individual Catholics in the reform and non-importation campaigns acutely embarrassed the majority of the gentry and merchant members of the shadowy Catholic Committee. It had studiously avoided all official contact with the parliamentary reformers. But, stung by the anti-papist tone of the government press, it resisted efforts by 'friends' of the Castle to extract from it another declaration of loyalty. It adhered to a policy of neutrality between the administration and the reformers even though the short-term cost in so doing was considerable: Catholic silence lent some credibility to the scaremongering of Castle hacks.

The Catholic issue fatally weakened the provincial response to the non-gentry reformers. When their congress met in October 1784, only ninety-five delegates (out of a planned 300) had been selected by the counties, and a mere forty men appeared, east Ulster, Dublin and the province of Connacht alone being well represented; the rural delegates were drawn from all levels of the gentry, whereas the Dublin and east Ulster ones were mainly mercantile. It was an intriguing but not yet formidable alliance. The congress quickly adjourned after agreeing to concentrate on a purely Protestant reform policy drafted in order to shore up provincial support. A further session three months later actually attracted around 100 delegates. But by this stage the momentum had been lost and reformers pinned all their hopes on Pitt's revived interest in electoral reform. In the autumn of 1784 he had privately intimated his commitment to limited Irish reform in order to strengthen the representativeness of parliament, but Rutland and Thomas Orde, the chief secretary, were totally opposed: they believed reform would weaken the Castle's ability to manage parliament. Yet despite the hostile attitude of Dublin Castle, Pitt only gradually abandoned his ideas for constructing an alternative foundation for 'the British connection' other than executive domination. However in 1785 his proposals for British reform were defeated at Westminster, and this closed the door on the possibility of a London-sponsored Irish reform process.

The formal redefinition of Anglo-Irish relations in the early 1780s had occurred at a time when the Irish economy was in considerable difficulty. The failure of either 'free trade' or parliamentary independence to usher in a rapid recovery of employment and incomes created the discontent on which the various popular movements between 1782 and 1785 capitalised. Recurrent economic adversity also affected parliamentary and government behaviour: after the concession of 'free trade' there was a noticeable expansion of public efforts to stimulate and to regulate the economy. The years between 1780 and 1786 were remarkable for the series of apparently unrelated projects and initiatives which enhanced the role of the state.

In parliament, the house of commons' committee system became much more active. Since the 1750s investigative committees, usually established in response to petitions from outside the house, had become more and more common: in the mid-1760s there were about thirty per session, by 1785 over fifty. The four 'grand committees' met weekly throughout every session, and the most consistently active was that on trade, which channelled the parliamentary energies released by the 'free trade' victory to other economic issues; Sir Lucius O'Brien and Foster among others sought to develop economic policy and initiate economic legislation. The first fruit was a swingeing Combinations Act in 1780, outlawing all forms of journeyman club or association; guild-masters and manufacturers were given new protection against their employees both for economic reasons – that wage costs were damaging competitiveness – and for social reasons – that journeymen, particularly in Dublin, were increasingly turbulent. The danger posed by the Dublin 'mob' became something of an *idée fixe* in parliament, and the evident inadequacy of the Combinations Act led parliamentarians to turn to a policy of industrial relocation; projects offering textile employment outside the capital were seized upon as a means of thinning the city's volatile weaving population. Venturers in the infant cotton (or cotton-linen) industry, especially those setting up outside a ten-mile radius of Dublin, were given aid in the form of subsidies on cloth sales, while direct parliamentary grants were given to twenty petitioners who claimed to be investing in manufacturing plant. A quite disproportionate amount of support (over £50,000) was given to the well-connected Robert Brooke for his colony of displaced Dubliners at 'Prosperous', County Kildare; its short-lived prosperity collapsed with Brooke's bankruptcy in 1786, and with it the policy of direct industrial aid. Nevertheless, that policy had given a critical thrust to the take-off of cotton, a technologically advanced industry which was to become an important employer in several regions during the next forty years.

The much older parliamentary policy of import substitution had contributed to the enthusiasm for cotton: the inflow of 'Manchester manufactures' had soared between 1780 and 1782, coinciding with a temporary crisis in the Irish linen trade. Import substitution also lay behind public support for the fishing industry in the early 'eighties. A general subsidy on commercial fishing vessels and a small export bounty on Irish fish had been introduced in 1763, and this was much extended and amended in 1781 and 1785. The architect of the new legislation was William Burton Conyngham, heir to a huge Donegal property and a government office-holder since Harcourt's time; in 1785 he secured £20,000 from parliament towards the development of the Donegal herring fishery, specifically for the new island fishing town of 'Rutland' on which he expended a further £30,000, and he also persuaded parliament to impose much higher duties on herring imports. 'Rutland' turned out to be an even starker disaster than Prosperous: north-west herring catches were falling by the late 1780s and sand overwhelmed the town itself.[21] This and other white elephants, where huge commitments of public funds were made without preliminary evaluation, revealed the limitation of parliamentary committees when they were confronted by influential projectors and the uncritical enthusiasm of the powerful.

A more positive sphere of parliamentary action related to the physical development of the capital: the Dublin Wide Streets Commissioners, a statutory body established in 1757, greatly expanded its activities from 1779 as various local tax revenues were assigned to it by legislation. It took on the spectacular redevelopment of the central street system of the metropolis and became a planning authority in a fuller sense from 1790, when all private street proposals in the city had to be vetted by the commissioners. The lord lieutenant appointed them, but they were mainly MPs with Dublin property interests. They were in fact an extension of the executive – dominated by the Ponsonby faction in the 1760s and by Beresford in the 1780s and 1790s.

Two major public bodies established by parliament in the early 1780s were also very close to government: the Bank of Ireland and the Post Office. The old proposal for a national bank resurfaced as a patriot measure in 1780, but the idea was only taken up by Carlisle's administration in late 1781 in response, it seems, to a new financial crisis. Government financial arrangements were still affected by the disappearance of three leading Dublin private banks in the 1778 crisis, and there were strong administrative as well as political attractions for the Castle in encouraging the establishment of a public bank modelled on the Bank of England. The justification for the move was that it would lower interest rates, but Dublin's merchant community was divided on the idea. However, in contrast to the 1720 bank scheme, the gentry supported it, and they were equally represented with merchants on the original subscription list.[22] A capital stock of nearly £500,000 was raised by 1783, and although the government had no formal involvement, the Bank of Ireland had very close ties with the Castle and was headed then and for long thereafter by politically conservative men of business.

An autonomous Irish Post Office was established by statute in 1784, with its own secretariat, answerable to the lord lieutenant. It remained very much a wing of government. Its first secretary, John Lees, former Castle under-secretary, kept the post for life, and it evolved in many respects as a true *ancien regime* institution: Lees' relatives and friends filled the lucrative positions and received contracts, and his own income far exceeded his salary. Yet under him the mail-coach service was inaugurated (in 1790), general efficiency improved and business greatly increased: postal revenue in 1702 had been £16,000, was £40,000 in 1786 and well exceeded £100,000 before his death in 1811. The proliferation of post offices created another bureaucratic network across the country, rising from 145 in 1784 to 266 in 1800. And a direct consequence of Lees' transformed postal system was the government's success in building up an intelligence-gathering capacity during the 1790s.

Police reform was politically a far more sensitive issue, first tackled in the 1780s. Civil law enforcement in the countryside had over the previous century rested on the JPs and the locally-nominated county sheriffs, and in the towns on the parish vestries, the mayor and aldermen. The inadequacy of existing arrangements had been revealed by the success of the Volunteers in reducing, even temporarily eliminating, various forms of illegal collective activity, specifically agrarian disorders and trade combinations. However, the waning number of active Volunteers and the upsurge of urban trouble in 1783–84 forced a new policy. The street politics and intimidation campaign in Dublin were the immediate catalyst, and in 1786 Fitzgibbon introduced legislation to centralise and transform the watch system in the capital. The proposal caused enormous controversy, and not just in Dublin. Independent MPs saw the measure as a dangerous extension of executive control since the new constabulary was to be supervised by aldermanic commissioners appointed by, answerable to, and paid by the lord lieutenant. The bill was passed, but the new system remained unpopular, for although the streets of Dublin were better policed, the price – higher local taxes and the loss of parish accountability – was deemed too high. Whiggish MPs later made the reversal of the Dublin police act one of their major objects. The huge 1786–88 anti-tithe campaign in Munster led to a wider police act in 1787: county police establishments, in effect salaried constables answerable to the governor of each county (by definition an aristocratic friend of the Castle), were permitted. They were set up in only a few of the disturbed Munster counties and were of limited utility. They too were resented on grounds of cost and accountability. But in each case precedents for the next generation were being set.

The 1780s therefore mark a time of innovation in the concerns of the state. Some initiatives came from parliament, some from the Castle, and most involved those who operated in both spheres. There was however no advance in several areas that were to be of critical importance in the nineteenth-century widening of the state, notably primary education and a national poor law. Rutland's chief secretary, Thomas Orde, started a public debate on state educational policy in 1787, but this bore no immediate fruit. As for poor relief the harvest failures of 1782–84 had little impact on policy apart from Foster's corn law. The inadequacies of the Woodward Act of 1772, which had allowed grand juries to establish 'houses of industry' for infirm and able-bodied beggars, were fully apparent by the 1780s (only five such houses had been established), but no re-examination of first principles occurred despite the self-evident need for an expansion of publicly-funded welfare institutions. The example of the English poor law, with its seemingly over-generous and costly parochial provision, was taken to be a dangerous warning by the Irish gentry. And the success of voluntary charity in keeping down excess mortality in the hungry years at the end of the American war helped to postpone the day of reckoning.

The Dublin newspaper press had since the 1720s helped to open up the world of politics to a slowly widening circle outside parliament. The American Revolution and the local victories of 'patriot' politics emboldened some to engage in more explicit attacks on the political establishment. The young Catholic editor of the *Volunteer Journal*, Mathew Carey (1760–1839), went too far in April 1784, printing an image of John Foster hanging from the gallows in front of parliament. Carey had to flee to America to avoid imprisonment, but became one of the early United States' most famous publishers.

6

Vortex

To most Irish people who lived through the 1790s, they were extraordinary years. The political drama in France which had been unfolding since 1789 began to have major domestic consequences in Ireland by 1791, and two years later a European war broke out which involved Ireland more directly than had any conflict since 1691. The 'French wars' spanned more than twenty years, but even in its earliest phase the international crisis helped to bring about a profound polarisation of Irish public life, a process which culminated in the insurrections of 1798.

The polarisation of Irish politics and the pursuit of quite irreconcilable objects by the politically active groups within the country did not of course begin in 1793, nor with the spread of democratic, French-inspired ideas. We have to look back into the 1780s. Signs of the inflexibility of the Castle in response to calls for reform had been evident in 1784, and this became more pronounced with the consolidation of the troika. In the short run this caused little reaction. After the reform agitation and the excitement over the Commercial Propositions, parliamentary politics quietened down for several years, midway between elections and at a time of sharp economic recovery. No sustained opposition to Rutland's administration emerged, and his successor in 1787, the earl of Buckingham (formerly Lord Temple) had an easy time until the sudden emergence of a threat to the stability of Pitt's government in London: late in 1788 George III became mentally ill and the prospective regency of the prince of Wales, whose relations with Pitt were frosty, threatened the ministry's future. The crucial issue was in what form the royal prerogative should pass to the regent. Pitt's Whig opponents led by Charles James Fox were anxious to give full powers to the prince in the expectation that this would precipitate a Whig ministry, but Pitt resisted this and the debate still raged in Westminster when the Irish parliament met in January 1789.

With encouragement from London, College Green Whigs, notably old Speaker Ponsonby's sons William and George, were determined to exploit the ambiguity of the 1782 settlement and to assert the right of the Irish parliament to determine the powers of the regent in relation to Ireland. The Whig bandwagon began to roll, and many with no previous links but who bore resentments against the golden circle in the Castle joined them. Even as venerable a faction-leader as the earl of Shannon supported the opposition, and in February both houses passed an address to the prince, asking him to assume the regency. Buckingham, with strong support from Fitzgibbon, refused to forward it to London; therefore parliamentary commissioners were appointed to present the address directly. However George's mental health recovered by March to the mortification and discomfiture of the many lesser office-holders and Castle MPs who had mistakenly deserted the government. Aside from starkly revealing the loopholes in the imperial relationship established in 1782, the regency crisis and the alliances it threw up led to the creation of a formal Whig party in the Irish parliament, composed of erstwhile patriots, the Ponsonby and Leinster connections, and others who had now wrong-footed themselves. Not all of the veteran patriots were comfortable at the direction of events. Flood, now based in England, saw the synchronised behaviour of Westminster and College Green Whig factions as subverting the Irish constitutional gains of 1782–83, and he got mischievous pleasure at the humiliation of Grattan's ambitions in March 1789.

The Whig group by the summer of 1789 could still count on the support of nearly one-third of MPs, but their common programme was a limited one: to reduce the encroachment of the executive on parliament specifically by securing a 'place bill' (to outlaw office-holders from being MPs), a pension bill (to freeze the amount of crown pensions charged to the Irish exchequer), and – the greatest innovation – a responsibility bill (to establish an Irish Treasury Board that would monitor and sanction the issue of all public monies). To strengthen the group and to prepare for the 1790 election, 'Whig clubs' were established in Dublin, Belfast and several other towns. The Dublin club, organised by the earl of Charlemont, set the tone for the provinces, but because of Charlemont's extreme caution on religious policy, advocates of additional Catholic relief were silenced.

The political audience for the Irish Whigs was in fact small. Even in the hotly contested constituencies in the 1790 election such as County Down (where 6,000 voters came out during the sixty-eight-day poll and an incredible £36,000 was spent by the warring Hill and Stewart clans) political debate as such was minimal; nearly 90 per cent of the Down freeholders voted in line with their landlords' wishes.[1] Whig catch-cries in most constituencies replaced the Volunteer uniforms of 1783, but the 'independent' or Whig interest had few great victories to celebrate outside Dublin, and the government's parliamentary position was in fact enhanced.

Over the following two years the Whigs failed to build on the promise of 1789. National politics were dominated by the shadows of Jacobin triumph in France and the new assertiveness of the Irish Catholic Committee. Whig parliamentarians were profoundly divided on both issues, but the Irish government itself was in greatest difficulty over the Catholic question. By the time the Castle finally surrendered to pressure from London for the re-enfranchisement of Catholics in 1793, its authority was considerably weakened. To re-establish its parliamentary position and to broaden Irish support for the new war, it stole some of the Whigs' clothes: a Place Act of sorts was passed which prevented certain categories of government office-holder and crown pensioner from in future sitting in parliament, a new hearth-tax act which exempted many thousands of one-hearth families from the tax; substantial tariffs on cotton textiles were at last imposed; and trade to India was opened for the first time (thanks in this case to Westminster legislation). But the most notable constitutional development was the government-sponsored Consolidated Fund Act which revolutionised the formal structure of Irish state revenue by ending the crown's nominal control over 'hereditary revenue' and by setting a fixed budget from which all royal pensions were to be paid; all other state revenue was to be allocated in whatever way the Irish parliament voted. The concept of an annual budget, presented by the chancellor of the exchequer, was thus introduced. The discretionary power of the lord lieutenant over state expenditure (by means of king's letter or royal warrant) and the veto powers of the British treasury were ended and an Irish treasury board was established, accountable only to parliament. The Irish Whig demand for a 'responsible' parliament with complete control over public expenditure was realised – or was it?

The irony of this adoption of Whiggish measures by the Castle during 1793, the apparent result of which was to strengthen the Irish parliament, can only be fully explained by reference again to English politics: over the previous year there had been the strong possibility of the broadening of Pitt's ministry and the entry of some of the English Whigs into power. Pitt's espousal of certain Irish policies championed by the local Whig interest had distinct dividends for him in any domestic English negotiations during the winter of 1792–93, and indeed there were attempts from Whitehall to woo the Irish Whigs directly.[2] Such covert negotiations came to nothing, but some of the legislative programme set in motion by these political developments was taken over by the Irish executive: these measures were popular in that they posed little real threat to the government's management of the commons. And with the onset of war and the prospect of much greater public spending on defence, new taxation was going to be required; the new revenue arrangements promised to make the task of securing parliament's compliance much easier. The new treasury board did of course create the *possibility* that Irish cabinet government based on the will of parliament would emerge, but that possibility was denied from the start by the real cabinet in the Castle, for it was they in large measure who formed the new board.[3]

These deft moves by the Irish administration came at the end of a period of great political uncertainty when the question of Catholic political rights had muddied Anglo-Irish relations and forced a return to first principles. The dismantling of the penal laws was turning out to be at least as drawn out and as fraught as their introduction. Whitehall had as we have seen prompted the first major relief in 1778, but the initiative for the 1782 acts, the measures which had allowed Catholics almost complete freedom to purchase freehold property and to teach, came from within the Irish parliament. Carlisle's administration had indeed given strong backing to the proposals, but the commons majority for them was large. It was the high noon of patriot unity. The role of the Castle was very different in 1784 when it helped – through intermediaries – to break the impetus of parliamentary reform by raising the Catholic bogey, but the tensions of that year, at least between government and leading Catholic spokesmen, quickly eased as the reform challenge passed.

At national level, the Catholic issue had then receded into the background, but in the later 1780s religion was a factor in two waves of local communal disturbance. In County Armagh an intermittent rash of incidents had begun in 1784 involving Catholic and Protestant weaver/farmers. The improving relative status of Catholics in this prosperous, populous and religiously mixed county may have raised Protestant fears, and the involvement of small numbers of Catholics in local volunteering in 1783–84 caused a stir. But as Miller has suggested, it was the existence of large numbers of young, financially independent weavers of all denominations which may have undermined traditional family discipline and made the fine linen zone a uniquely volatile rural society.[4] Sparks from the 1783 election, from the extension of Volunteering in 1784, and from Charlemont's campaign against Catholic relief started a slow-burning fire: groups of Protestants, soon to be known as

Armagh

Peep-of-day-boys, raided many Catholic houses, searching ostensibly for firearms. Initially there was considerable gentry hostility towards these Protestant 'banditti', but the appearance of Catholic counter-groups, styling themselves Defenders, weakened magistrates' sympathy for the Catholics. There was a growing series of fairly harmless sectarian faction fights at fairs and horse races, and by the late 1780s there were occasional public displays of strength – daylight processions – by the two parties. Some gentry then openly recruited Peep-of-day-boys into Volunteer corps, while Defenderism spread southwards and eastwards into Down and Louth. By 1790 Defenderism became a secret society, organised around Masonic-style lodges, with essentially defensive objectives. The weaver/farmer founders had no great political objects any more than the Peep-of-day-boys had, but the Defender mode of organisation was put to new uses and was to be diffused across a dozen counties over the next few years.

In the far south, agitation against the tithe system had surfaced again in 1785–87. The 'Rightboy' movement of those years was quite distinctive in the sophisticated coherence of its demands for tithe reduction, the scale of the regional tithe boycott, and the discipline of what was predominantly a non-violent campaign. Covert gentry support in Cork helped in this (disappointed protagonists of the 1783 election had sought to discomfort the earl of Shannon and his clerical allies). The attack on tithe was not in essence sectarian, and this was strikingly borne out by the extension of the agitation to the highlighting of the abuses of certain Catholic clergy who were accused of levying excessive dues. Such unprecedented multi-denominational anti-clericalism helped gain limited parliamentary sympathy for the campaign.

The division of gentry attitudes towards what was an essentially illegal conspiracy stirred up a remarkable pamphlet war. The most widely read contribution was one by the anglican bishop of Cloyne, Richard Woodward, which adopted an unfashionably sectarian tone. He presented the tithe campaign as the beginning of a general attack on the established church, and his elaborate defence of the church's privileges and practices attracted criticism from both Presbyterian and Catholic apologists. The Church of Ireland was indeed being challenged from two directions by then, but Woodward's diagnosis was off the mark. On one side, enlightenment-inspired deism had begun to have some impact, on the other the mainly anglican followers of John Wesley were now disengaging from the established church. Methodism and the other stirrings of evangelical Protestantism posed a real threat to episcopal authority. Dire warnings of Protestantism under siege helped to disguise these tensions.

Such warnings became far more common after 1790, for by then the Catholic Committee had come to life again, stirred by the political awakening of English Catholics and the arrival of complete religious toleration in France in the early months of the Revolution. The Committee, with its combination of gentry members and urban middle-class delegates, was still a Dublin-run phenomenon. New elections in 1790–91, involving the capital and fifty-two towns, brought in Munster for the first time (although the leading gentry spokesman for the Committee since the early 1780s had been the ever prudent Lord Kenmare, the largest resident Kerry landlord). Both the general committee and the inner committee maintained a gentry/delegate balance, but the spokesmen for the non-gentry interest after 1790 were far less deferential or cautious than those of a decade previously. The chief activists were veterans of the 1784 reform campaign – John Keogh and the new secretary, Richard MacCormick; both were wealthy middle-aged Dublin merchants who had been on the radical edge of the Committee in 1784. Outside Dublin a new assertiveness was evident in the resolutions passed by Catholic electoral meetings in the provinces.[5] This self-confidence can perhaps be seen as the political manifestation of a more fundamental process, the tightening up of parish and diocesan structures of Catholicism and the intensification of pastoral activity; this had been visible to all with the appearance of the first solid post-Reformation chapels in many rural parishes, notably in Ulster and the west, in the course of the 1780s.

The Catholic Committee's strategy at the start of 1791 was to win government support for an end to Catholic exclusion from the law, the magistracy, grand and petty juries, and for limited access to the county parliamentary franchise. But the Castle was not interested (nor at that moment was Whitehall); there was no Irish parliamentary pressure for Catholic relief, and the Committee itself appeared to be divided as to whether to run a public campaign, or to petition parliament and rely on government favour. Throughout 1791 the cracks within the Committee widened, with most of the gentry, led by Kenmare and the Catholic bishops who had participated in the Committee's proceedings, pinning their hopes on private diplomacy, and nearly all the delegate-members opposing the old politics of caution. There was also internal division over the question as to how the Committee should respond to overtures from the Dublin and Belfast radical politicians, the Francophiles who were wooing Catholic support for constitutional reform. When a number of leading Committee members joined a new radical club, the Dublin Society of United Irishmen, at the end of 1791, the Committee conservatives were outraged.

The political chimera of 1784 – a Catholic middle-class/Protestant radical alliance – was suddenly a real possibility. The case for an alliance was set out persuasively in *An argument on behalf of the Catholics of Ireland*, written by a young Dublin Protestant lawyer and former Whig Club pamphleteer, Theobald Wolfe Tone; it achieved wide circulation, notably in Ulster. Tone's stated object was a thoroughly reformed parliament involving Catholics, an object obtainable only through the joint endeavours of Catholic and Protestant opponents of 'the present despotism'; his argument was primarily for Presbyterian eyes, but it made a strong impact on southern Catholic opinion too. The prospect of such an alliance frightened Westmoreland, but the prevailing Castle view was more sceptical and remained hostile to concessions to Catholics – some government members opposing on principle, others in the belief that it would be impossible to get new Catholic reform measures through the commons. In London, however, government attitudes were changing – under the influence of Edmund Burke and his son Richard, who from September 1791 acted as the Committee's English agent. Burke senior held by then a unique position of influence within English governing circles as the author of much the most convincing and profound intellectual assault on the French political experiment and on the insidious menace of French ideas. Burke junior therefore had easy access to Pitt and his ministers and, closely briefed by Keogh, he helped to alter the attitude of Grenville, Dundas and possibly Pitt towards the status of the Catholic Committee and the danger of a Catholic/dissenter alliance.

Meanwhile a group of forty Dublin Catholic radicals, mainly Committee men, formed a new Catholic Society to agitate openly for complete Catholic relief; the extremity of the language used in their public declaration and the unequivocal demand for political equality gave Westmoreland's chief secretary, Hobart, the chance to try and divide the Catholic Committee by demanding from them a disavowal of the declaration – in return for a promise of government support for limited new relief. But although the declaration was strong stuff for most of the Committee, the majority refused to repudiate it. The minority withdrew, and published a more traditional loyal address, petitioning for relief not by right but on the old grounds of good behaviour. The last weeks of 1791 saw a furious rearguard campaign by Kenmare and his allies, aristocratic and episcopal, to secure Catholic signatures for the 'loyal address', but among the sixty-seven signatures that they drummed up there were very few merchants or delegate members. Final victory for the advanced party on the Catholic Committee over Kenmare and the bishops came in January 1792: Kenmare was expelled from the inner committee and plans went ahead for a more forceful petition. It was not quite the classic 'democratic' victory over 'aristocratic' interest, but the dominance of the old gentry families in Catholic politics never completely recovered from Kenmare's forced secession.

Rumours of new Catholic measures abounded as parliament met in January 1792. Dundas had indeed instructed Westmoreland to frame a major relief act which would include the restoration to Catholics of the right to hold firearms and would hold out the prospect of the vote. But Westmoreland successfully represented the total opposition of the Castle to such a policy, using the Irish parliament's opposition as the main argument. The Dublin government did, however, agree to sponsor a bill which opened up the legal profession to Catholics – a concession to Kenmare and his party, and a move which was to transform the job opportunities for wealthy Catholic families.

The Irish commons, stung by Burke's apparent success in Whitehall, were in an unusually ugly mood towards the Catholic Committee. Thus the Committee's new petition to parliament, drafted by Burke, did not even find a seconder among MPs, and a further petition, more circumspect in its language, was thrown out in February – after an orgy of anti-Catholic rhetoric – by 205 votes to 27, Grattan and the duke of Leinster's supporters making up the isolated minority. The subsequent passing of the limited relief act did nothing to undo the bitter effects of the February debate. The Catholic activists who had hoped for 'emancipation' – the expression was new – now developed a deep contempt for the Irish parliament and its members. The cheap personal attacks made in the commons on Keogh and his wealthy ally Edward Byrne rallied provincial Catholic support for the Committee, and helped soften the rift between the city politicians and the seceders.

In the parliamentary attack on the Catholic Committee, many MPs had claimed that its members were now little more than a self-appointed clique of Dublin traders. The Committee devoted most of its energies during 1792 to challenging this: first a declaration of Catholic principles was drawn up in March rebutting much of the old anti-papist arguments that MPs had refurbished, and copies of the declaration were very widely circulated; in hundreds of parishes signatures endorsing the declaration were collected by the Committee's provincial contacts, including many parish priests.

The unprecedented success of this covenanting campaign encouraged the adoption of a new electoral arrangement for the Committee. This envisaged every Catholic parish selecting a representative to attend a county meeting where in turn delegates would be chosen for the General

Committee, some of whom would be Dublin-based, some resident locally. Gentry would no longer have a personal claim to be on the Committee. During the latter half of the year, delegate meetings were held in every county and city – despite some resistance in Galway and Mayo where the still entrenched Catholic gentry were divided over the new politics, and bitter condemnation of their initiative by grand juries in the majority of counties. The government had no legal machinery to defeat the Committee's grand design, and in December 1792 the newly elected body – the Catholic Convention as it was quickly dubbed – assembled 200 yards from the Castle in Back Lane. Dublin residents were still dominant in the 230-strong meeting, but Catholic gentlemen from the provinces were there in sufficient numbers to produce an entirely new atmosphere. Analogies with the 1688 parliament were not, it seems, lost on the participants, even though there was no attempt to mimic parliamentary procedures. The chairman of the proceedings was not one of the assembled gentry but the affable sugar-baker, Edward Byrne. The tentative plans of the inner committee that the convention should petition the king for specific concessions (the franchise and jury access) were lost sight of when a northern liner draper, Luke Teeling, called for 'nothing short of total emancipation', nothing which implied their acquiescence in 'one fragment of that unjust and abominable system, the penal code'.[6] Despite subterranean misgivings, the surface unanimity of the convention was maintained, and a petition for total equality was drafted. A more open dispute arose over the manner by which the petition should be presented: the cautious wished to follow precedent and hand it to the viceroy, but the hostility of the majority towards the Castle was quite explicit; as one of Kenmare's erstwhile seceders put it, 'we will not, like African slaves, petition our task-masters',[7] and so a small delegation was appointed to carry the petition directly to London.

Within a month of the convention's meeting, the delegates were presented to the king, and had long if inscrutable discussions with Dundas. Nothing specific was promised, but the Catholic initiative was rightly regarded as a great coup against Westmoreland and the Castle. Indeed the Irish government remained in the dark as to the delegates' negotiations until after the beginning of the 1793 parliamentary session. Yet the chief secretary Hobart began to regain Castle control over events in negotiations with the inner committee concerning their planned petition to parliament. He managed to divide them as he pressed for an undertaking that a compromise relief bill would give 'satisfaction' and peace. The proposed bill would concede the parliamentary franchise to all forty-shilling freeholders, a socially not religiously restricted right to hold firearms, a general right to apply for civic and corporate membership, and the end of the bar to jury membership. Catholic access to parliament itself was still being denied. But to Keogh and his cronies, Hobart's proposed bill seemed victory enough.

For the troika and their circle, the new concessions went dangerously far. They had been the steel behind Westmoreland's opposition to Dundas a year previously, and Fitzgibbon and his confidantes had fanned the flames of Protestant fury during 1792. An unapologetic and very public defence of the 'Protestant ascendancy' – another political term that took on a new specificity – was made by Dublin corporation in September 1792,[8] and later by most county grand juries, encouraged if not directed by Fitzgibbon with the intention both of demonstrating to London the strength of Protestant opposition to political equality, and of overawing the Catholic Committee. Fitzgibbon and Foster also orchestrated a house of lords inquiry into Defenderism early in 1793 which concluded by accusing leading Committee activists of intimate involvement with the Defenders. During the long debate on the new Catholic relief bill, Foster and Fitzgibbon made scathing attacks on the assumptions underlying relief – yet with the rest of the Irish office-holders they grudgingly supported the bill in the lobby, and the commons majority in favour of the final draft was large.

Yet the bad grace with which leading government politicians moved the bill through parliament robbed the measure of much of the political effects which Pitt and Dundas had anticipated. Because it was essentially a permissive measure rather than a coercive one, much depended on the attitude of the Protestant gentry and the Protestant corporations: would they admit their Catholic peers to grand juries and civic freedom, and would they give life leases to the Catholic tenantry thereby enabling them to vote? In the immediate aftermath of the act, corporate bodies were in general unwilling to open their doors, and although small numbers of wealthy Catholics gained guild membership in 1793, many more were blackballed. Catholic gentry fared slightly better and several dozen were appointed magistrates in the next year or two, and in some counties they were empanelled on the grand jury. But the governing circle's generally negative attitudes removed any sense of pressure on county gentry or on corporations to respond beyond their own inclinations to Catholic aspirations.

The marathon parliamentary debate over Hobart's bill had been complicated by a second proposal – complete political emancipation – which was put forward by George Knox, an Ulster MP and protégé of the absentee and immensely wealthy grandee, the duke of Abercorn. As one of the largest Ulster proprietors and an acquaintance of Pitt, Abercorn saw himself as a latter-day Ormond, a prospective lord lieutenant with an Irish power base drawn from a coalition of interests. Abercorn's conversion to total emancipation was opportunist, but the fact that Knox's amendment secured sixty-nine votes demonstrated that he was not alone in this. To many gentry it seemed that there was now a political prize worth competing for – the Catholic vote and the goodwill of the Committee. A sharp division among landed and middle-class Protestants now appeared in counties and corporations between the 'ultras', the rock-hard supporters of Protestant ascendancy and of the principle of the indissolubly Protestant character of all public institutions of the state, and the more agile Protestant politicians who canvassed for Catholic support and were publicly committed to complete emancipation; there was as always a substantial and more volatile middle group open to influence not least from the Castle. In those counties where the power-broking families were divided nearly equally – such as Wexford and Limerick – tensions within the gentry not seen for eighty years began to emerge, but in many counties the dominant orientation of the local gentry was fairly clear. The new alignments did not always reflect recent political divisions: although most Whig-related families supported Catholic relief there were some who vehemently did not, while some of the MPs who in 1793 held advanced Catholic views had been Castle supporters in 1790. But in a more subtle way, the new division reflected a much older history: landowners who had Catholic relatives, and this usually meant those with deep local roots, were rarely to be found among the ultras. The most prominent old family associated with the Catholic cause was the Leinster Fitzgeralds, and indeed the duke had kept in touch with the Catholic Committee through 1792. By contrast the Ponsonby brothers had kept their distance, being late (and opportunistic) converts to the desirability of Catholic political rights.

The twists and turns of the Ponsonbys were striking in other ways. During the 1793 session William Ponsonby reopened the question of parliamentary reform, and for a time received unlikely support from government allies. However the impetus behind Ponsonby's move was very different from that of the radicals; he sought a more 'rational' representation in parliament to end the situation in which some extensive property owners had too little parliamentary leverage and some impoverished borough-owners too much, the consequence of which had been to facilitate the Castle's management of parliament. 'Aristocratic reform' therefore meant a reassertion of the influence of leading Irish gentry in the old Anglo-Irish coalition and was an attractive agenda in the wake of London's show of strength over Catholic policy. There was a sense of anger and betrayal within Protestant Ireland, both because of the way the British government had bulldozed its policies so insensitively on the Irish parliament, and because of the deeper suspicion that London no longer recognised the Protestant interest as its natural ally in Ireland.

Commons' support for any form of constitutional change ebbed fairly quickly. Yet events in England gave the Ponsonbys quite a different avenue of opportunity. A long-threatened split in the British Whig party over France and reform finally occurred at the beginning of 1794, and opened the way for a wartime coalition between Pitt and the supporters of the duke of Portland, leaving the Foxites in opposition. The Portlandites joined the wartime government in July 1794, and Portland himself took over the home office from Dundas. The home office was now the Whitehall department of state handling Irish affairs, and it was part of the Pitt/Portland agreement that a senior Whig should also take over in Dublin from Westmoreland. Earl Fitzwilliam, a Whig aristocrat, was the obvious candidate having a large Irish property (in Wicklow) and an Irish wife (a Ponsonby). Middle-aged but without much political experience, Fitzwilliam was enthusiastic about the prospect of 'purifying' the Irish administration and calming the country before the war came any closer. His views were moulded by the Whigs' mentor Edmund Burke, and reinforced by fresh contact with Grattan and the Ponsonbys. The Castle administration seemed to him, as to them, an unedifying faction of self-seeking and bigoted men whose policies were dangerous and divisive.

Whig ambitions for new measures and new men for Ireland, and specifically for the dismissal of Fitzgibbon, were vetoed by Pitt, but a more modest policy brief for Fitzwilliam was finally agreed by the British cabinet in October 1794, although some ambiguities remained. Rumours of Fitzwilliam's reformist intentions had been circulating in Ireland for months, and despite the fact that the Catholic Committee had dissolved itself in 1793 (forced to do so by the Convention Act which made national representative assemblies illegal), the Committee veterans re-emerged and organised a flurry of local petitions praying for the completion of emancipation. On his New Year arrival in Dublin, Fitzwilliam did not disappoint his Irish friends. For despite instructions not to purge key office-holders, he immediately unseated Beresford from the revenue, the two long-serving and powerful under-secretaries at the Castle, Edward Cooke and Sackville Hamilton, and sought to secure the office of attorney-general for George Ponsonby. Fitzwilliam's display of viceregal independence was interpreted in several ways – that he had fallen under a Ponsonby/Grattan spell, that the despatch of Beresford was a symbolic gesture to establish his Irish popularity, that it was the prelude to government measures which the troika, left intact, would have sabotaged. Fitzwilliam himself explained the dismissals to London as resulting from the necessity to clear away the overmighty and corrupting influence of the Beresfords before the viceroy's authority could be established. Fitzgibbon was untouched; his dismissal from the chancellorship had been expressly ruled out by Pitt. Beresford's removal had neither been cleared nor discussed. Pitt's strongly negative reaction to the ousting of Beresford was Fitzwilliam's first warning of trouble.

His executive purge was not however the main cause of his undoing (despite later suspicions); it was his Catholic policy. Before coming over, Fitzwilliam had favoured the repeal of all remaining anti-Catholic legislation at the same time as the establishment of a locally-based auxiliary militia – or yeomanry – to be manned and officered largely by Catholics. However he had not got cabinet approval for official sponsorship of a Catholic relief bill such as would give Catholics the right to sit in parliament; it was not clarified as to what the Castle's role should be if pressure for such a bill came from other quarters. Fitzwilliam in Dublin became convinced that enormous pressure for emancipation existed, that Protestant opposition was not overwhelming and that the political price of disappointing Catholic hopes would be huge. Fitzwilliam misinterpreted the British cabinet's silent response to his policy of benign neutrality towards an emancipation bill as reluctant agreement. It was nothing of the sort; his colleagues in London were awaiting a detailed briefing of the proposal and the legislation, which he never supplied. Instead he proceeded to give informal support to Grattan and those promoting a Catholic bill, without committing the government as to its final form. This was the last straw for Portland who felt obliged to move for Fitzwilliam's recall at cabinet on 21 February. There was unanimity. Fitzwilliam was barely aware of the total opposition of his London colleagues when he got the shock news. The lobbying in London against his purge had already weakened him, but it was his Catholic policy which led even his Whig allies to disown him.

Why had the British government so obviously turned its back on further Catholic concessions in 1795 after the bold actions of 1793? First there was the king: he had become convinced that assenting to emancipation would violate his coronation oath; submissions from Fitzgibbon in 1793 had materially influenced the king in this quaint belief, and his disapproval of Fitzwilliam's activities was signalled to Pitt. In addition, some members of the British government were becoming aware of the danger of weakening the Protestant interest. Another factor may have been Pitt's wish to hold back on further Catholic relief until such time as there was something to trade it for – such as Catholic support for an Anglo-Irish parliamentary union. A final point is that, despite impressions to the contrary in Dublin, the Portlandite Whigs in general and the duke of Portland in particular were conservative on the religious question; Fitzwilliam (and his mentor Burke) were somewhat out on a limb in an increasingly reactionary London.

Fitzwilliam's sudden departure had traumatic effects on Irish politics. Camden, the new viceroy and a friend of Pitt, firmly opposed Grattan's Catholic emancipation bill (eighty-four MPs supported it) but he tried to soften Catholic disappointment by supporting a proposal to establish a state-funded Catholic seminary at Maynooth. This was also a victory for the Catholic bishops, now led by the shrewd but conservative Archbishop Troy of Dublin who enjoyed the full confidence of some in the Castle (notably Thomas Pelham); his visceral anti-revolutionary sentiments were shared by most but not all of his clergy.

Several other favourite Irish Whig measures were adopted by government to calm the situation in 1795. But the Fitzwilliam episode had a fundamentally souring effect on Catholic and radical attitudes, and suspicions of the partiality of government now seemed very well-founded; shortly after his arrival Camden assured a northern peer that 'provided the great body of the Protestants will exert themselves' in maintaining law and order, he was 'ready to make every exertion they can desire to prevent the admission of Catholics to seats in the legislature'.[9]

The threat to the existing order in 1795 came in two forms: rural collective violence associated mainly with the Defenders, and an east Ulster radical conspiracy, largely Presbyterian in composition, which was now considering the offer of military support from France to realize an Irish revolution. The province in which the fruits of economic development had been most widely distributed was now the most profoundly alienated.

Constitutional radicalism had flourished in the hothouse atmosphere of Dublin and Belfast since 1791. Disillusionment at the Whig Clubs' lack of interest in parliamentary reform and exhilaration at the events in France stirred the veterans of the 1784 movement and, with the help of a new generation of enthusiasts, political societies of 'United Irishmen' were established in the autumn of 1791 in Belfast and Dublin. Wolfe Tone's pamphlet, which had stressed the necessity of interweaving Catholic emancipation and parliamentary reform, was having precisely the results its author had hoped for, and Tone himself was midwife at the birth of both Belfast and Dublin societies. But despite the overlap in personnel and the common ideological starting point, the societies north and south evolved along different paths. The Dublin Society became much the most active and prolific political debating club the capital had seen; its aims were the drafting of a comprehensive plan of parliamentary reform and the mobilising of Irish public opinion behind the plan. Mobilisation was to be achieved by the production of persuasive pamphlets, press declarations and public meetings. Yet although the society flourished at the time when Jacobin democracy was in the ascendant in France, it operated very much within the tradition of Irish political opposition. Its indictment of the 1782 settlement was harsh ('our late revolution we declare to be fallacious and ideal – a thing much talked of, but neither felt nor seen'[10]), but little harsher than reformers' words in 1784. The Dublin Society's public rhetoric was filled with French allusion and libertarian symbolism, but the philosophical base for its reformism lay in Locke's contract theory and the English writers who had influenced the early patriots, not in the subversive democratic speculations of Burke's critic, Thomas Paine, whose *Rights of man* was first reprinted in Dublin nine months before the foundation of the society.

During its two-and-a-half-year history as an open organisation the Dublin Society attracted more than 400 members; a few were country gentry, many were professionals, and far more were city merchants or textile manufacturers. The lawyers and those with university links tended to dominate much of the proceedings, rather to the chagrin of Napper Tandy and the veterans of aggregate city meetings. Membership was predominantly Protestant in the early stages but this was cancelled out by a stronger Catholic influx latterly. On the religious question there was some diversity of opinion as to whether the right to vote should be restricted or not, and divisions within the Society along sectarian lines occasionally surfaced.[11] But more striking was the essentially secular character of such a society in a city where its middle classes were traditionally fractured by religion. Many of the advanced delegate-members of the Catholic Committee joined, and the Society was delighted by the adversarial posture of the Committee during 1792 (although Keogh with the scent of victory deliberately distanced the Catholic convention from the United Irishmen). Until 1793 there were also links with some of the Grattanite opposition in the commons, and the duke of Leinster's brother, Lord Edward Fitzgerald, MP for County Kildare, was far more of a true Jacobin than most of the Dublin United Irishmen. But in 1793 the near unanimous parliamentary support for war and the Whig opposition's acquiescence in the militia, convention and gunpowder bills opened a rift between them and the radicals who of course opposed the war.

The government became far more repressive towards radical dissent at the end of 1792. Richard MacCormick's (rather naive) plans to resuscitate Volunteering in the city, mimicking the French National Guard, led to the suppression of all city corps in December, and several leading members were put on trial for sedition. Despite this and after much agonising the Society eventually produced its reform plan early in 1794: constituencies of equal size, universal male suffrage, annual parliaments, payments for MPs – it was more radical than some desired but did not include the secret ballot. By now active membership had much declined; the taint of disloyalty frightened many, and the excesses of the Terror gave them their excuse. The society was formally suppressed in May 1794.

Dublin's radical example was not followed in the other southern cities. Thus the Society there remained a crucial intellectual bridge between Ulster radicalism and the emancipation movement in the south. The original Belfast United Irish Society was a smaller, tighter body than Dublin's but turned out to be only one of a number set up in east and central Ulster, linked in some cases to Masonic lodges, in others to 'independent' Volunteer corps. The Belfast societies attracted linen drapers, tanners, merchants, apothecaries – a good cross-section of the port's thriving middle class. Twelve of them subscribed £3,000 to launch a radical newspaper, the *Northern Star*, which turned out to be far better edited and managed than its Dublin equivalent. Commercially successful, it blended political comment, general news and a cultural interest in the Irish past, quite absent from earlier opposition papers.[12] The Belfast radical leaders were, like their fellow citizens, largely but not exclusively Presbyterians of the more tolerant, non-Calvinist, 'New Light' variety. They viewed Catholicism as an obsolescent, irrational system, its clergy as reactionary, but its people as fellow Irishmen and willing political allies against the monopolising establishment in Dublin and their English masters.

The Belfast radicals' success in popularising a French-derived radicalism throughout Ulster was a cumulative process that spanned five years. Initially the revival of Volunteering between 1791 and 1793 was turned to advantage; at a time when gentry-led corps were being mobilised in south Ulster against Defenderism, corps farther east were persuaded by the radicals to attend annual Bastille Day parades near Belfast in 1791 and 1792 at which, *inter alia*, pro-Catholic resolutions were passed. Subsequently, the United Irishmen co-operated with various county notables to organise a reform convention in Dungannon, which met at the beginning of 1793. County delegates were drawn from five eastern and northern Ulster counties, and after much horse-trading a fairly moderate reform programme was endorsed: borough abolition, rational parliamentary representation, frequent elections, and the Catholic franchise; separatism and republicanism were condemned, and a national convention called. This was the last act of Ulster constitutional reformism; the Belfast radicals were frustrated by such compromise and were soon to feel the rough side of government harassment, while liberal gentry were deterred from pursuing reform by the coming of war. Armagh, Cavan, Monaghan and Fermanagh went unrepresented at Dungannon; there the smell of powder was too strong.

Defenderism had gone far beyond south Ulster by 1793, but the border counties of Leinster and Ulster remained its heartland. It baffled authorities by its protean character, a 'traditional' agrarian conspiracy against tithe proctors in some districts, a smuggling or illicit distilling combine in others, a rash of journeymen's drinking clubs in the larger towns of north Leinster. Various initiation oaths were used by the Defenders, but the recurring tone was anti-Protestant, pro-French and proto-nationalist, and the recurring theme imminent deliverance from the world of monarchs, Protestants and rich men, and a total redistribution of property. Yet for all their burglaries of firearms, the Defenders were primarily a passive, 'horizontal' or federal conspiracy which reacted to external threats and opportunities; artisans and labourers seem to have played a much greater role than sedentary farmers.[13]

The first major blood-letting in this charged situation occurred in January 1793, when the army killed several dozen Defenders in Meath as they attempted to rescue their leader; there were perhaps as many fatalities here as were caused by all agrarian disturbances between 1760 and 1790.[14] The following summer was worse. The new county militia force of 18,000 men was for the first time to include Catholics; the legislation spelt out that recruits were to be chosen by a random system of balloting the names of all cess-payers. This proved profoundly unpopular, and anti-militia disturbances occurred in nearly every county. Clashes involving the army left about 230 dead and provoked a profound new hostility to the redcoat.[15] The raising of the militia seems to have been widely interpreted as an act of Protestant or Castle revenge after the concession of Catholic relief. This *grande peur* was not it seems organised by the Defenders, but the new severity of army behaviour hastened the process of social disintegration.

By 1795 Defender networks had spread through predominantly

Catholic districts in fourteen counties. In September of that year large numbers of Defenders converged on a part of north Armagh beyond their normal frontier, and were involved in a series of armed skirmishes with Protestant weaver-farmer groups, all stemming, it seems, from a fair-day brawl. The Defenders were worsted, and the Protestants in imitation of their Catholic opponents began to establish local oath-bound 'Orange' lodges. Indirectly linked to this was a campaign of arson and intimidation against Catholic smallholder weavers in north Armagh and down the Lagan valley; the victims were paying the price for the activities of their less vulnerable co-religionists farther south. These attacks led to an exodus of up to seven thousand Catholics in the winter of 1795–96, most of whom drifted west along the trade corridor to north Connacht – where flax was plentiful and Protestants few. The Armagh Orangemen were tamed by their magistracy in 1796, but by then news of Protestant excesses and rumours of government complicity were country-wide, and these gave greater legitimacy and meaning to the pungent sectarianism of Defender oaths.

Despite such events within twenty miles of Belfast, the United Irish movement remained a robust organisation there and thereabouts. In contrast to the situation in Dublin, most of its founding members were still politically active and were now unequivocally committed to revolutionary change and a republican constitution, to be obtained, it was generally accepted, with French military assistance. Even before the war Belfast radicals had been more interested in extreme solutions than had Dublin United Irish members, and late in 1794 plans were devised to transform the northern societies into an oath-bound, cellular and hierarchical system. After the Fitzwilliam episode, such plans were formally agreed, but it was only late in 1796 that a parallel military hierarchy was organised by the existing county committees in east Ulster. Only then was the government able to get hard evidence as to the precise lineaments of the Belfast-directed conspiracy. The Belfast United Irishmen had amassed considerable financial resources which were used for small arms purchase, publication, legal costs and inducements to new members, but the promise of a French invasion was the most powerful credit card. From east Donegal to mid-Down, United Irish cells were established, but there was markedly less success in the mainly anglican and Orange districts of south Ulster – although even Orange lodges could occasionally be won over. The greatly increased volume of firearms in circulation and the air of profound political uncertainty forced many Protestants to side with whichever informal armed association, Orange or United Irish, was locally in the ascendant.

In their dealings with the Catholics, the northern radicals followed what seemed a rational strategy: they used the few Catholic United Irishmen (notably the Lisburn Teelings) as intermediaries to establish a series of links with Defender 'captains' and lodges through south and west Ulster during 1795–96, gradually integrating them into the United Irish structure. To the radicals such collaboration was attractive, extending their influence into new districts and among Catholic militiamen, and greatly increasing the overall numbers they could muster. They expected to be able to mellow Defender sectarianism and instil a revolutionary republicanism in its place. By 1796 the Defenders were feeling the rough justice of the magistracy, the military and the Orangemen, and needed little convincing of the advantages of a link with the well-to-do urban revolutionaries who claimed to have the ear of the French Directory. The very success of this marriage was enough to frighten some Protestants out of the conspiracy. Nevertheless at its peak in the spring of 1797, the Ulster movement claimed to have 118,000 members (84 per cent of them in Down, Antrim and Derry) and 7,000 firearms.[16]

Farther south the development of revolutionary politics was slower. Before the war a second stratum of radicalism, consisting of reading clubs and societies dedicated to Paine's ideas and to 'levelling principles' had coexisted in the capital beneath the Dublin United Irish Society. Their shopkeeper and journeyman members were veterans of the street politics of 1779 and 1784 and their inchoate radicalism was more sweeping than that of the United Irish society. They attracted little attention from the Castle until 1795, by which time several of the clubs were incorporated into the Defender system. In addition a number of much older journeyman societies appear to have transformed themselves into Defender lodges.[17] When the still active rump of the Dublin United Irish radicals began to construct a cellular revolutionary organisation late in 1796, they made immediate use of these artisan networks, and within a few months the clubs were part of a fairly disciplined conspiracy, headed by a small circle of pre-war constitutional radicals and two young Jacobins of gentry background, Arthur O'Connor and Lord Edward Fitzgerald.

Long before radical Dublin resumed a national role in revolutionary politics, its finest author, Wolfe Tone, was proving to be a skilful diplomat in France. In 1794 he had dangerously compromised himself by associating with the Rev. William Jackson, an emissary from France, and had made only too clear his despair at the prospects for internal political reform; his observations quickly reached the Castle via an informer. He was lucky to be only deported for his treasonable remarks, and went to the United States in 1795. There, after some soul-searching, he began a personal diplomatic offensive to secure large-scale French military assistance for a United Irish-directed insurrection. Before his departure from Ireland his radical friends, Protestant and Catholic, in Dublin and in Belfast, had strongly endorsed such plans.

Sufficiently encouraged by the French minister in Philadelphia, Tone sailed back across the Atlantic in early 1796 and reached Paris in February. He managed, against the odds, to win powerful endorsement for his ideas within the new French Directory. A large invasion force of nearly 15,000 well-armed men was sanctioned and given orders to help establish a democratic convention and an Irish executive under United Irish and Catholic Committee leadership. Tone's case had been strengthened by the independent mission of O'Connor and Lord Edward to the French authorities late in the summer of 1796. After many delays, the armada sailed from the Breton port of Brest in December 1796, led by Tone's patron, Lazare Hoche. The military planning behind the expedition was seriously flawed. But this was never fully revealed, because exceptionally bad weather dispersed the fleet before it reached Bantry Bay. Vessels waited a week off south-west Cork for the easterly gales to subside; they continued to blow.

The Hoche expedition startled Ireland. The United Irish leadership at home had not been able to follow events in France closely, and the government had been let down by defective British intelligence. The sight of French squadrons in Bantry Bay did not lead to any sympathetic action on land, although what would have happened if the wind had changed is another matter. The prospects for large-scale surprise assistance from France were never to be so good again: Hoche died in 1797, the pro-Irish party in Paris declined in influence, and British intelligence and naval surveillance improved.

Irish-based radicals failed to appreciate this, and it was only in the twelve months following the Bantry Bay expedition that United Irish organisation spread in earnest outside Ulster and Dublin. County directories were established in all Leinster and in some Munster and Connacht counties by the end of 1797. The events at Bantry helped recruit the faint-hearted, and local United Irish cells sprang up involving not just lower-class Defenders or southern Whiteboy/Rightboy organisers but, more importantly, disaffected farmers, urban traders and minor professionals, many of whom had had no previous political involvement apart from perhaps organising signatures for the Catholic Committee in 1792 or Catholic emancipation petitions at the end of 1794.

The response of government to the gathering domestic crisis between 1793 and 1797 was for the most part uncompromisingly repressive.

Before 1796, internal order was maintained through an increased use of the military to aid the magistracy. The composition of the military had altered much since 1792, as militia regiments grew in size (to 25,000 by 1795) and considerably outnumbered regular forces. They were officered by Irish Protestant gentry, manned mostly by Catholics (except in the case of Ulster county militias), and quartered within the country but far from their own areas. Discipline was very uneven, and both Defenders and United Irish emissaries inducted many militiamen into their ranks. Yet for all the undoubted evidence of militia disaffection, the greatest limitations of the militia as a fighting force lay in the quality of their officers and in military administration.[18] 1798 would show that the militia were in general more remarkable for their loyalty than their lawlessness.

Early in 1796 the government had received confused warnings of the possibility of French invasion, and in the light of this and the evident politicisation of the Defenders, novel measures of control were introduced. Magistrates in the midlands who had dispensed summary justice and sent suspected Defenders to serve in the navy were given retrospective sanction by an Indemnity Act, the first of six measures which protected magistrates who went beyond the law. At the same period, parliament passed an Insurrection Act which gave magistrates much greater power to counter what was primarily seen as a Defender threat: a quorum of JPs could now get their county or barony 'proclaimed' on the grounds that it was gravely disturbed, and with that official status they could then enforce a curfew, try and sentence 'disorderly persons' to serve at sea (although there was still some appeals machinery), and could search any house for arms. Tendering an illegal oath now became a capital offence, with transportation for those convicted of merely taking such an oath.

With such draconian legislation, much rested on the quality and level-headedness of JPs. Some were intimidated and deterred from taking vigorous action, others concentrated on keeping their own tenants and estates out of trouble. But there were magistrates in every county who engaged in counter-terrorism and were happy so to do. They resented the inflexibility of the legal system which up to 1798 still protected the innocent albeit in a haphazard way: of the 475 persons brought before county assizes on political charges in 1797, three-quarters were found not guilty and only 7 per cent were executed.[19] The difficulties JPs experienced in securing quick and exemplary punishments, the problems in bringing forward prosecution witnesses, and the frequent intimidation of juries bred a new contempt for due process. Some of the younger and newer magistrates were the law's most bitter critics; they also seem to have been the ones who commanded least social respect.

In October 1796, following gentry pressure, Camden agreed to the formation of an auxiliary 'yeomanry' force. Unlike the militia these corps were to remain in their own localities, to be officered by government-appointed gentry and manned by volunteers, and to have police rather than military functions. Regular army commanders had a supervisory role, but the officers were to have wide discretionary powers. The gentry strongly supported the new institution: by June 1798 there were 540 corps and more than 40,000 men mustered, mostly Protestant and politically anti-radical, some extravagantly Orange in their symbols and regalia. With the yeomanry so widely dispersed, magistrates in proclaimed districts were now able to enforce their draconian powers more flexibly.

Until the autumn of 1797, the government regarded Ulster as the main domestic threat to peace. There the regular army and militia were used to break the United system; with orders from the Castle 'not to suffer the cause of justice to be frustrated by the delicacy which might possibly have actuated the magistracy',[20] General Lake spent much of 1797 in the province. Radical activists in Belfast were harassed and arrested (including many of the leaders), the *Northern Star* broken up, the houses of suspected persons burnt down and corporal punishment widely used. The United organisation survived, very shaken, but the search for arms across the north-east had produced by July 1797 10,000 guns. The rural network of cells was seriously weakened and many more volatile supporters foreswore their political engagement and publicly took an oath of allegiance to the crown. Similar tactics were used in the winter and spring of 1797–98 in the south, as evidence of United Irish organisation in Leinster and parts of Munster flowed into the Castle. In addition, the free-quartering of troops in suspect houses and parishes was sanctioned to flush out illegal arms in west Leinster, Tipperary and Cork (where General Moore noted how 'the better sort of people seem delighted with the operation … they were pleased that the people were humbled and would be civil').[21]

Irish troops, mainly militia regiments and the yeomanry, provided the manpower for these low-intensity operations, and magistrates no longer had to be present during routine searches. There was in effect creeping martial law, although this was not formally declared until March 1798. Brutal official action reflected the disposition of individual army officers and magistrates rather than shifts in government policy. In some counties severity worked (Tipperary and south Cork for instance), in others counter-terror, especially when carried out by the local yeomanry displaying Orange symbols, only inflamed matters. The lack of consistency and the discretionary powers of officers in the field frightened professional soldiers. When Dundas' friend and fellow Scot Abercromby, the commander-in-chief, publicly criticised the army in Ireland for its gross 'licentiousness' and the subordination of its strategic defence function to a less appropriate internal policing role, his sharpest critics were the government troika, fully supported by an outraged gentry, and they forced his resignation. Lord Camden, the last in a line of unassertive viceroys, made ineffective attempts to resist the prevailing mood for indiscriminate and quasi-legal repression.

The revolutionary strategy of the United Irishmen since 1795 had been simple: the organisation of a large, lightly-armed popular fighting force, recruited in part from the militia, which would assist a small French army in the rapid defeat of crown forces, leading to the establishment of an independent Irish government. The growth of the 'brotherhood' in Ulster, especially in the months after Bantry Bay, encouraged the Belfast leadership to advocate an independent rising, starting across the north of Leinster and culminating in an attack on Dublin. O'Connor and Fitzgerald were alone among the Dublin leaders in supporting this and similar high-risk plans: the majority there feared an uncontrollable chain reaction if the go-ahead for independent revolutionary action was given.

The militant Ulster leaders still at large abandoned their efforts and fled during the summer of 1797. The wait for fresh French assistance was an excruciating one: British blockade, French politics and Hoche's death destroyed the hopes for a 1797 expedition. 1798 promised better. However most of the southern leadership who had favoured prudent delay were arrested in Dublin in mid-March after a substitute member of the Leinster committee had turned informer. The Leinster leaders who escaped arrest, notably Lord Edward Fitzgerald, continued to advocate a rising independent of French help, but they had limited success in rebuilding an effective command structure in the wake of the arrests. Months of waiting had had a corrosive effect on their rural supporters, and the extended military repression during April and May 1798, more overtly Orange than ever, damaged revolutionary morale – and also heightened religious tensions. Chapel-burning by over-zealous yeomanry in south Ulster began an insidious fashion. Apparent irresolution on the part of the United Irish leadership in Dublin ended with disaster: Fitzgerald's arrest in mid-May. The decision to rise was sent out shortly afterwards to the Leinster county committees, even before the remaining Ulster leaders had agreed. In fact the military planning of Lord Edward in the two months prior to his arrest had in the circumstances been quite sophisticated, and the quality of the Castle's intelligence system far poorer than appeared in retrospect. The actual prospects for a vast popular *jacquerie* were still quite good past May Day 1798.

The great insurrection in Leinster of May/June 1798 was however a short and very nasty civil war. The great majority of combatants were Irish-born and as in any civil war the conventions of the battlefield were not observed. The official United Irish plan was for a series of co-ordinated county risings, with the insurgents converging on Dublin, where the suborned militia would act as a fifth column. County risings occurred only in Carlow, Kildare, Meath and Wexford, with isolated actions in neighbouring counties. Military organisation had suffered from the long wait and from official repression, and was fairly rudimentary. Equipment was light – but pikes in profusion and a pent-up anger compensated. However, the combined government forces (now about 76,000 including over 40,000 yeomen) outnumbered the Leinster rebels. They were also far better trained and armed. Militia defections to the rebels occurred, but were fewer than the United Irishmen leadership had counted on.

Most of the Leinster risings were unconcerted ambushes, attacks on magistrates' houses, and attempts to seize and hold smaller towns. There were bloody defeats for the Meath and Kildare forces in the first few days, and within a week the rebels were on the defensive everywhere except in Wexford where the numbers initially involved in the rising were larger than elsewhere; the rebels quickly coalesced at two points in the county. Crown forces there were dispersed and unprepared, for Wexford had not been overtly disturbed or disarmed in the recent past. Enniscorthy and Wexford town were captured and held for over three weeks. A number of minor county gentry and the sons of gentry, Catholic or Protestant, shared the leadership of the county rising with Wexford merchants, large tenant-farmers, and a handful of colourful priests; within rebel-held territory they maintained an order of sorts. But despite energetic efforts, the rebel army failed to break out into neighbouring counties and, after the United Irish failure to take the strategic town of New Ross, crown forces began to squeeze them during the second half of June. At this stage atrocities on both sides of the fighting line raised the spectre of religious war and sectarian revenge. The critical engagement took place around Vinegar Hill where perhaps 20,000 rebels were challenged by crown forces of half that size. The informal army was

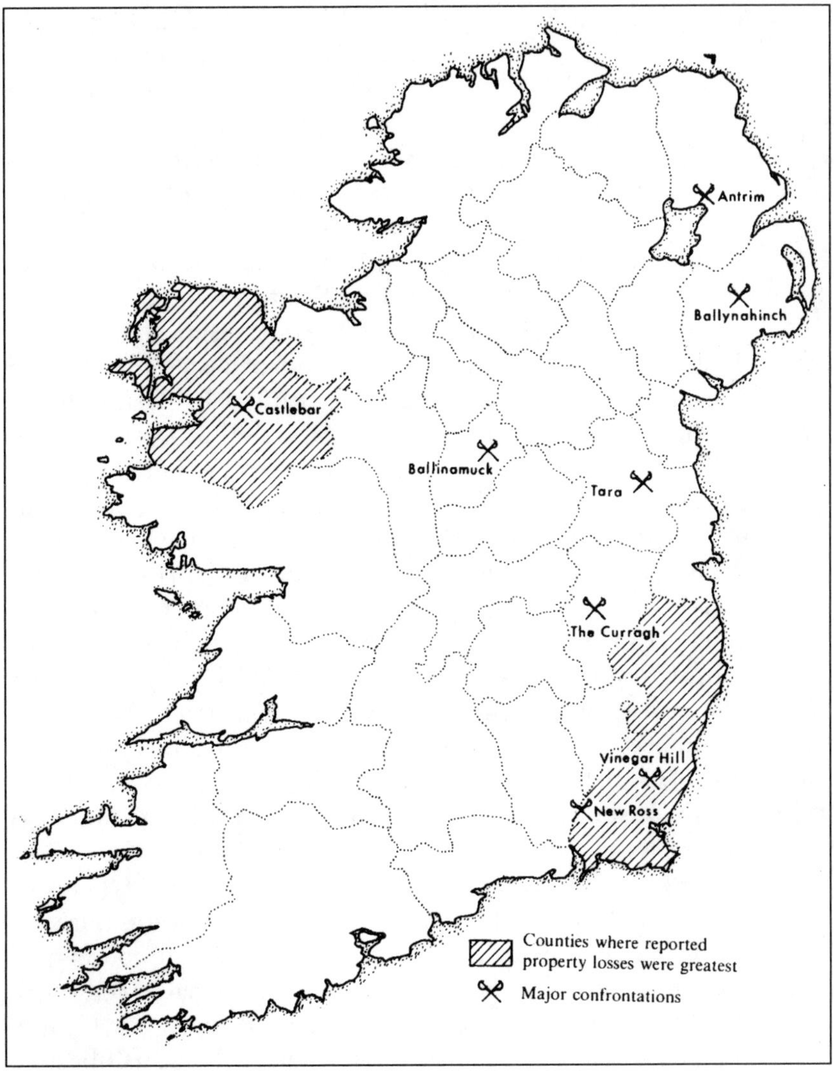

Ireland in 1798

routed with high casualties. It then faded into the hills and for weeks rebel fragments fought isolated engagements across five counties.

The risings in east Ulster began a fortnight after the first flames in Wexford. The decision to rise was taken independently by the Antrim and Down leaders, and only after several key figures had refused to become involved. Antrim town was briefly captured with the aid of an old Volunteer cannon, and fitful attacks were made on a handful of garrisons from Limavady to Carrickfergus. Government forces were on the offensive within five days, helped by Scottish reinforcements. In Down much of the Presbyterian north of the county came briefly under United Irish control, albeit under the command of a Church of Ireland linen draper, Henry Munro. But in a major battle at Ballynahinch, the United Irishmen were decimated before the arrival of Defender help from south Down. Indeed Catholics and dissenters failed to make common cause in any fighting field, but the ill-planned nature of the June risings was the main reason for this. East Ulster continued however to simmer before going off the boil. By the end of June tales of the massacres of Wexford Protestants were helping to cool revolutionary ardour.

The final act of the summer was in Connacht: two small French invasion forces, less than 4,000 men in all, were quickly organised after news of the Leinster insurrection reached Paris. The first of these under General Humbert landed at Killala in late August; and after one major engagement at Castlebar they controlled County Mayo for a week. There was no United Irishman network in the region, and although Humbert found no shortage of local volunteers, the province did not rise *en masse* in the way the émigrés had predicted. Humbert moved towards Leinster, where a sympathetic rising did occur in County Westmeath. But with no major rebellion in progress, the government was free to concentrate massive resources against Humbert's small if professional force. After a week-long chase the French were overwhelmed at Ballinamuck, County Longford, and surrendered after a short fight. The tardy and half-hearted support of the French continued through the autumn. A larger fleet destined for a Donegal landing was harried along the north-west coast in October; six ships were captured and one of the uniformed French soldiers arrested was Wolfe Tone.

Thirty to fifty thousand men had turned out during 1798 in a series of insurrections which affected in all about eighteen counties, but acutely convulsed seven at most. 'Loyalists' subsequently claimed damage to property in excess of a million pounds, 61 per cent of which was in Wexford, Wicklow and Kildare.[22] As many as 20,000 may have been killed during the long summer of rebellion and reprisal; casualties among crown forces and Protestant civilians were predictably a very small fraction of rebel and rebel-associated losses.

Some of the reasons why 1798 was such a failure for the radicals were self-evident: government-sanctioned counter-terror and the disarming campaigns over the previous year; the reorientation of French offensive plans from the Atlantic to the Mediterranean in 1798; the fortuitous arrests of key conspirators in March and May; the less than clearcut final preparations by Dublin and northern leaders after the arrests. But a more fundamental set of reasons were the divisions among the radical leadership, and the cumbersome and overly transparent hierarchical organisation which derived from the constitutional precedents of the early 1790s; it was a structure which made it possible for government eventually to penetrate. But, aside from these considerations, was the fundamental premise of the revolution – the possibility of a strategic alliance between urban and dissenter radicals, rural Defenders and disaffected members of the Catholic middling orders – a chimera? To answer this we must stand back and ask why such a social explosion happened where it happened.

Historians have supplied three types of general explanation: economic, political and social. The economic argument was first developed in 1799 by Whitley Stokes, an erstwhile radical himself: population growth and economic development over the previous generation had increased inequality in Irish society, devalued labour and made land the scarce resource, thus creating novel tensions and resentments.[23] Stokes' perception is broadly correct, for real wages were falling more sharply in the 1790s, and every county was now feeling the effects of four decades of high natural increase. Irish population had more than doubled since mid-century, and was now passing five million. Much of the Defenders' activities were devoted to restoring conacre rents, tithe payments, wages and milk prices to former levels, and they blamed the war for hurting the poor by inflating food and land prices. The problem was of course deeper, but the war did sharpen inequality; the runaway growth of the Irish military budget after 1793, while in large part financed by government borrowing, meant higher excise taxes of the kind which hit wage-earners disproportionately. A financial crisis in 1797 led to the sudden imposition of a new salt tax, the cancellation of the subsidy on the inland transport of grain to Dublin, and a major change in the licensing of maltings. The Castle was warned from the four provinces that such measures made men desperate and disaffected – and not just the very poor. Wexford, the great barley county, was particularly disturbed by the new malting arrangements, and their imposition was followed by a general fall in cereal prices. Thus in the winter of 1797–98 when the United system was spreading through the south, grain farmers who had grown prosperous after a decade of high prices faced financial crisis.[24] Indeed some contemporaries saw recent positive developments in the economy as having seeded the rebellion. The Rev. James Little, a Protestant witness of the French invasion at Killala, noted in 1798 that:

> it is not in the poorest but the richest parts of this kingdom that sedition and a revolutionary spirit prevail and first raised their heads: an extreme degree of poverty and distress will sink the mind of man, divest him of the courage even to complain, and bury in silence himself and his sufferings …

He went on to ask whether in Co. Mayo,

> where the lower orders of the people had never been drunk with prosperity … whether a certain alleviation of that poverty which took place for some time previous to the invasion had not upon them the same effect of invigorating their patriotism, as it had upon their country men of the capital and whether the frost which benumbed their faculties, being succeeded by a gentle thaw, they were not thereby rendered more alert in their civic functions, and enabled to exert … all the energies of *active citizens*: in a word, whether the amelioration of their circumstances, which ought to have produced a sentiment of benignity and affection for the government and order of things whence it was derived, had not the opposite effect, for Machiavel has too truly observed that man is ungrateful.[25]

Political interpretations of the failed revolution emphasise the crucial role of disaffected local elites, the men involved in barony and county organisation, the 'captains' in the shadowy military command structure. The mobilisation of Catholic middle-class support in the counties between 1792 and 1795 by the Dublin leadership had cultivated the political appetites of a previously timid and introverted segment of literate Irish society, and the bitterness of expectations dashed – the incomplete emancipation of 1793, the English veto on emancipation in 1795 – soured them against the Castle and, temporarily, against the British connection as well. The alienation was clearly much more strongly felt where local Protestants endorsed the new freemasonry of Orangeism and cast aspersions on the loyalty of their Catholic neighbours. The strength of the 'ultras' in such areas as Dublin city, Wicklow, Carlow, Wexford and Cork was soon counterbalanced by the success the United Irishmen emissaries in recruiting well-to-do Catholics.

The withering away of the Whig/independent interest in parliament, most noticeable in the subdued 1797 general election, put those gentry who championed the Catholic interest in an extreme dilemma: the bleak choice was between endorsing the state-directed machinery of magisterial and martial repression or opposing it, thereby becoming the object of suspicion and on occasion physical victimisation. The polarised politics of County Wexford between 1790 and 1798 are a striking example, and they alone can account for the extraordinary involvement of Protestant gentry among the rebel leaders.[26]

The social interpretation relates to the motivation of the masses who followed the rebel elites into battle with such enthusiasm, and of the many more who had sworn United oaths between 1795 and 1798. There is no evidence of subversive political motives underlying any agrarian agitation before 1790, even though the whole of Irish-speaking Ireland had come to share a taste for poetry and song obsessed by themes of slavery and deliverance, anglophobia and a celebration of a golden Irish past. This formerly upper-class genre was mediated and reproduced by the very schoolteacher/scribes who by the 1790s were at the centre of a revolution in *English*-language literacy. The growth of informal elementary education since the mid-century upswing in tenant farmers' incomes had owed little to landlord enterprise and nothing to the state (for the cumulative effect of the proselytising Protestant charter-schools over the previous sixty years had been marginal). The only partners of the itinerant schoolteachers had been the Catholic parish clergy, anxious to broaden popular knowledge of the catechism and works of devotion, but they almost without exception were still preaching a doctrine of submission, deference and political passivity. The new pool of anglophone literates now present throughout rural Ireland, educated and influenced by a potentially disaffected and usually poverty-stricken caste of teachers, were the willing readers of the output of radical presses. United Irish newspapers, with circulations of at most 6,000, were of limited importance in this context, but the spring tide of handbills 'incessantly inculcating on the multitude that they were the most wretched, abused, oppressed people ... that their misery was solely from a political cause ...',[27] the proliferation of ballad sheets, and the subsidised printings of, above all, Tom Paine's writings, had some broad political effect. Already a large rural chapbook market had existed, dominated by racy accounts of celebrated highwaymen and rapparees, leading 'youth ... to look upon robbers, incendiaries, murderers ... as objects of admiration'.[28] Was the sudden exposure to the propaganda of the radicals merely quick-germinating seed on well-watered soil?

In Presbyterian Ulster, the loam was different. Rural literacy levels were much higher, income inequality less, and both religious ideology and religious structures encouraged Presbyterians to question the anglican establishment and the prevailing structure of government. And although the 'New Light' wing of orthodox Presbyterianism, with its rational world view, was the most congenial theology for middle-class radicals, the other more Calvinistic strands of Presbyterianism could provide a religious context for revolutionary thoughts, with their abundant use of biblical prophecy and reference to a millenarian future. The Belfast radicals had no scruples about propagating the works of Presbyterian divines who predicted the imminent fall of a monarchical Antichrist. In that Ulster insurrection some thirty Presbyterian ministers were implicated, a strikingly large participation; but they were fairly evenly drawn from the 'New Light' and orthodox theological traditions.[29]

From these essentially complementary approaches to the phenomenon of 1798, the depth of alienation from the state and the governing coalition which ruled Ireland is apparent. Some counter-coalition was conceivable, some convergence of the disaffected. The radical/Defender, Presbyterian/Catholic alliances were for a time formidable and radiated a sense of potency, but they were destroyed by misunderstandings and indeed by bad luck. Nemesis in the form of the sectarian excesses in the south-east and of the contagious growth of the Orange system within Protestant Ulster was neither predictable nor inevitable.

EPILOGUE

The resignation of Abercromby was followed during the Leinster rebellion by the recall of Camden himself. In Pitt's eyes the Irish government by 1798 was, like the Irish treasury, on the edge of bankruptcy. The appointment of the older and wiser Lord Cornwallis to the viceroyalty marked a complete departure: known for his Catholic sympathies and his military efficiency, he distanced himself completely from the Castle troika and kept a much tighter rein over the military establishment. His willingness to treat leniently with the rebels – pardons for the rank and file, imprisonment or deportation for some of the United Irishmen leadership in return for full disclosures of the ramifications of the conspiracy – did much to pacify the country, and to enrage most of the 'ultras'.

The great matter of state as domestic peace returned in the autumn of 1798 was the question of an Anglo-Irish parliamentary union. Pitt now shared the long-held views of many Irish conservatives that only a union could restabilise the social and political *status quo*. In the long campaign of 1799 the Castle went to battle against what was at first a parliamentary majority against the idea of union, and sought to win over the uncommitted. Directed by the Ulster-born chief secretary Lord Castlereagh, the government mounted a remarkable offensive. The Irish gentry were completely split on the issue, probably a majority remaining against it in the belief that integration represented a diminution of their power. Opposition was hardened by rumours of covert negotiations between the Castle and the Catholic hierarchy, who were given informal undertakings that emancipation would be high on the post-union agenda if they lent their moral support to the union proposal. But the expenditure of the equivalent of a decade's patronage by the Castle in wooing the uncommitted, helped along by the anti-anglican sentiment of north-east Ulster and the anti-Dublin sentiment in the provincial cities, secured victory for the government and created a convincing majority in February 1800 in support of the liquidation of a separate Irish parliament.

The old Anglo-Irish coalition was not however dead; in the early post-union years the access of Protestant gentry to patronage and local power remained not only intact but was actually enhanced. However in the longer run they paid a high price for failing to adapt to the challenges of the late eighteenth century and for abusing their strength in the 1790s. After 1830 their power, political, economic and social, was diluted, subverted and finally destroyed, all within the framework of a united parliament and long before its dissolution.

Collective memory of the Irish parliament and of the patriots' struggle to affirm its status as the fountain head of an autonomous kingdom lived on in the nineteenth century, and was of course comprehensively appropriated by the new nationalism of Catholic Ireland. It became apparent that Protestant Ireland in the eighteenth century had – almost unintentionally – laid the constitutional foundations for an Irish polity and erected the shell, only to abandon the project in 1800 amid rancour and division. The precedent of a parliament-centred Irish political community was, for all its flaws and limitations, a potent legacy, and the restoration of that parliament became the holy grail for the children of those it had so effectively excluded.

Gillray's entirely irreverent treatment of Anglo-Irish parliamentary nuptials was not so much an attack on the government's methods of achieving majorities for the Union legislation in the two parliaments, more a cynical judgment on the disunited Whigs, drowning their sorrows after Pitt's victory. But there was unintended irony in the empty bottle-bespattered throne of the Prince of Wales. (James Gillray, 'The Union Club', 1801: N.G.I.)

Notes

CHAPTER 1 (pp. 1–29)

1. Sir William Petty, 'The political anatomy of Ireland, 1672', in *Tracts relating to Ireland* (Dublin, 1769), pp. 305, 312.
2. Ibid., p. 305.
3. Thomas Carte, *An history of the life of James, first duke of Ormonde* (Oxford, 1735–36), ii, 316.
4. See Sean Egan, 'Finance and the government of Ireland, 1660–85' (unpublished Ph.D. dissertation, University of Dublin, 1983), passim. I have drawn extensively on this work which transformed our understanding of Restoration government.
5. Carte, *Ormonde*, 409.
6. See Liam Irwin, 'The suppression of the Irish presidency system', in *IHS*, xxii (1980–81), 26–9.
7. Egan, 'Finance', i, 240–42.
8. Ibid., ii, 7.
9. Earl of Essex and Lord Chancellor Boyle to the earl of Arlington, 21 Sept. 1672, quoted in Richard Bagwell, *Ireland under the Stuarts* (London, 1909–16), iii, 111.
10. Essex to the earl of Danby, 26 June 1675, quoted in *Letters written by … Arthur Capel earl of Essex … in the year 1675* (Dublin, 1773), p. 320.
11. Cf. Ormond to the earl of Arran, 31 July 1683 in *Ormonde MSS* (HMC, 1895–1920), n.s. vii, 92–3.
12. L. M. Cullen, 'Economic trends, 1660–91' in T. W. Moody et al., *A new history of Ireland*, iii: *1534–1691* (Oxford, 1976), p. 403.
13. O. Airy, ed., *Burnet's history of my own time* (Oxford, 1900), ii, 292.
14. Ibid., p. 292n.
15. Egan, 'Finance', ii, 131.
16. Ibid., ii, 199, 204–7.
17. Quoted in ibid., ii, 168.
18. See Maurice Craig, *The architecture of Ireland …* (London, 1982), chapter 9; Rolf Loeber, *A biographical dictionary of architects in Ireland 1600–1720*

(London, 1981), p. 84.
19. MS tract, 'Of the Irish' [*c.*1680], Bodleian Library, Oxford, Locke MS *c.* 31, f.39.
20. The remark was made by the earl of Halifax, protesting at MacCarthy's appointment: J. A. Murphy, *Justin MacCarthy, Lord Mountcashel* (Cork, 1959), p. 11.
21. John Miller, *James II: A study in kingship* (Hove, 1977), p. 149.
22. Clarendon to the earl of Rochester, 12 Oct. 1686, in S. W. Singer, ed., *The correspondence of Henry Hyde, earl of Clarendon ...* (London, 1823), ii, 25.
23. See Miller, 'The earl of Tyrconnell and James II's Irish policy 1685–88', *Historical Journal*, xx, 4 (1977), 803–23.
24. Thomas Sheridan's judgement, quoted in ibid., 818.
25. Clarendon to the earl of Sunderland, 20 Nov. 1686, *Clarendon corr.* ii, 73.
26. William Hovell to John Houblon, 8 Sept. 1685, Hovell letter-book 1683–89, NLI Mic. P.4652.
27. Hovell to Houblon, 4 and 25 May 1686; Hovell to Thomas Putland, 10 June 1686.
28. Miller, 'Thomas Sheridan (1646–1712), and his "Narrative"', *IHS*, xx (1976–77), esp. 120–21.
29. Miller, 'Tyrconnell', 820–21.

CHAPTER 2 (pp. 31–65)

1. [?], Cork to Chidley Brooks, 1 March 1688–89, in David Dickson, ed., 'The account-book of a Kerry revenue official 1687–9', in *Jnl. Kerry Arch. Hist. Soc.*, vi (1973), 82.
2. Quoted in Richard Bagwell, *Ireland under the Stuarts* (London, 1909–16), iii, 191.
3. Quoted in J. G. Simms, *Jacobite Ireland 1685–91* (London, 1969), p. 82.
4. Dr R. Gorges, Lysnigarvey, to the earl of Clarendon, 4 Feb. 1689–90, in *Calendar of the Clarendon papers*, v (Oxford, 1970), p. 689.
5. Sir Richard Cox, Dublin, to Sir Robert Southwell, 11 Oct. 1691, in Southwell papers, Trinity College Dublin MS 1160, pp. 157–8.
6. Quoted in Simms, *Jacobite Ireland*, p. 244.
7. Quoted in ibid., p. 256.
8. See D. Dickson, C. Ó Gráda and S. Daultrey, 'Hearth tax, household size and Irish population change 1672–1821', in *Proc. RIA*, lxxxii, C (1982), 180.
9. J. G. Simms, *The Williamite confiscation in Ireland 1690–1703* (London 1956), pp. 108, 193; Kenneth Ferguson, 'The army in Ireland from the Restoration to the Act of Union' (unpublished Ph.D., University of Dublin, 1981), p. 48.
10. See J. I. McGuire, 'The Irish parliament of 1692', in Thomas Bartlett and

D. W. Hayton, eds., *Penal era and golden age* (Belfast, 1979), p. 22.

11. Quoted in F. G. James, *Ireland in the empire, 1668–1770* (Cambridge, Mass, 1973), p. 22.
12. Alan Brodrick to St John Brodrick, 17 Dec. 1695, quoted in Isolde Victory, 'Colonial nationalism in Ireland 1692–1725' (unpublished Ph.D. dissertation, University of Dublin, 1985), p. 17.
13. Lord Capel, Dublin to the duke of Shrewsbury, 7 Oct. 1695, in D. W. Hayton, ed., *Ireland after the glorious revolution* (Belfast, 1976), doc. no. 225.
14. See J. G. Simms, 'The Bishops' Banishment Act of 1697 (9 Will. III, c.1)', *IHS*, xvii (1970–71), 185–99.
15. Simms, *Williamite confiscation,* pp. 62–4; Victory, 'Colonial nationalism', p. 23.
16. Memorandum, 'The Scots in Ireland, 1697', University of London MS 30, ff. 11–12.
17. See L. M. Cullen, *An economic history of Ireland since 1660* (London, 1972), pp. 29–34.
18. William Molyneux, *The case of Ireland's being bound by acts of parliament in England, stated* (Dublin, 1977), p. 93.
19. Bishop Wetenhall of Cork, quoted in J. I. McGuire, 'The Church of Ireland and the "Glorious Revolution" of 1688', in Art Cosgrove and Donal McCartney, eds, *Studies in Irish history* ... (Dublin, 1979), p. 141. Cf. [Sir Richard Cox], *An essay for the conversion of the Irish* (Dublin, 1698), p. 35.
20. Christopher Crofts, Cork to [?], 2 June 1699, quoted in David Dickson, 'An economic history of the Cork region in the eighteenth century' (unpublished Ph.D. dissertation, University of Dublin, 1977), p. 549.
21. Thomas Southwell, Cork to Lord Coningsby, 6 Aug. 1699, in Hayton, *Ireland after the glorious revolution,* doc. no. 228.
22. Ferguson, 'Army in Ireland', p. 80.
23. Simms, *Williamite confiscation*, p. 193.
24. Archbishop King, Dublin, to Sir Robert Southwell, 28 March 1702, quoted in Joseph Johnston, *Bishop Berkeley's Querist in historical perspective* (Dundalk, 1970), p. 42.
25. See J. G. Simms, 'The making of a penal law (2 Anne, c.6) in 1703–4', *IHS,* xii (1960–61), 105–18.
26. D. W. Hayton, 'Ireland and the English ministers, 1707–16' (unpublished D.Phil. thesis, University of Oxford, 1975), p. 36.
27. Alan Brodrick to Thomas Brodrick, 15 Aug. 1710, quoted in Hayton, 'Ireland', p. 29.
28. Thomas Keightly to the duke of Ormond, 28 Oct. 1710, quoted in James, *Ireland in the empire.* p. 72.
29. Hayton, 'Ireland', p. 143.
30. See S. J. Connolly, *Religion, law, and power: The making of Protestant Ireland 1660–1760* (Oxford, 1992), pp. 294–306; Toby Barnard, 'Protestants and the Irish language, 1675–1725', in *Jnl. of Ecclesiastical Hist.*, xliv (1993), 243–72.

CHAPTER 3 (pp. 67–106)

1. Robert Molesworth, London to Archbishop King, 28 Sept. 1714, in Sir Charles S. King, ed., *A great archbishop of Dublin, William King D.D. 1650–1729* (London, 1906), p. 168.
2. Rev. William Percival to Rev. R. Charlet, 10 Aug. 1714, Bodleian Library, Ballard MS 36, f.85.
3. *Journal of the house of lords of Ireland*, ii, 27 July, 1719.
4. Ibid., ii, 17 Oct. 1719.
5. J. C. Simms, *Colonial nationalism, 1698–1776* (Cork, 1976), pp. 49–50. See also Patrick McNally, *Parties, patriots, and undertakers: Parliamentary politics in early Hanoverian Ireland* (Dublin, 1997), pp. 205–6.
6. Archbishop King to Edward Southwell, 9 June 1724, quoted in A. Goodwin, 'Wood's halfpence', in *Eng. Hist. Rev.*, li (1936), 674.
7. The best edition, which includes many other documents relating to the affair, is *The prose writings of Jonathan Swift*, x: *The Drapier's letters and other works 1724–1725*, ed. Herbert Davis (Oxford, 1941).
8. Quoted in Davis, *Drapier's letters*, p. xii.
9. Ibid., p. 62.
10. Ibid. See Victory, 'Colonial nationalism', esp. pp. 201–21.
11. Davis, *Drapier's letters*, p. 205.
12. Victory, 'Colonial nationalism', pp. 130–31. See also D. W. Hayton, 'The beginnings of the "Undertaker system"', in Bartlett and Hayton, *Penal era and golden age*, pp. 32–54.
13. The castration clause in the 1719 popery bill was inserted by the Irish privy council in place of one sanctioning the branding of unregistered priests – apparently it was Midleton's suggestion – but the former draft was reinserted by the British privy council; even George I was shocked at the castration proposal. The altered bill was then rejected on its return by the Irish lords; other clauses relating to property were deemed too severe. The 1723 popery bill was lost sight of at the London end because, it seems, of diplomatic pressure. See Patrick Fagan, *Catholics in a Protestant country …* (Dublin, 1998), pp. 53–73.
14. The estimate in Thomas Prior, *List of the absentees of Ireland* (Dublin, 1729) that four-fifths of pension-holders were absentee seems rather too high.
15. R. B. McDowell, *Ireland in the age of imperialism and revolution, 1760–1801* (Oxford, 1979), p. 62; McNally, *Parties, patriots and undertakers*, chaps 4 and 5.
16. This is calculated for the years ending 25 Dec. 1715–19, and the years ending 25 March 1751–55: George O'Brien, *An economic history of Ireland in the eighteenth century* (Dublin, 1918), pp. 322, 326.
17. J. C. Beckett, 'The Irish parliament in the eighteenth century', in *Belfast Natur. Hist. Soc. Proc.*, iv (1950–55), 33.
18. Patrick Fagan, *Divided loyalties: The question of an oath for Irish Catholics in the*

Eighteenth Century (Dublin, 1997), p. 64.
19. 'Draft letter, Henry Boyle to the marquis of Hartington', [early May, 1755], P.R.O.N.I. Shannon MSS, D2707/19/l/4/310.
20. Craig, *Irish architecture*, pp. 164–5.
21. 'Irish politics displayed', memorandum *c*.1737, Gilbert Library, Dublin, Robinson MS 38, p. 29.
22. William Cooley, Lohort to Lord Percival, 11 Oct. 1745, Brit. Lib., Egmont MSS, Add. MS 47005A, f.106; John Potter, Dublin Castle to Sir Robert Wilmot, 14 Sept. 1745, P.R.O.N.I. Wilmot MSS, T3019/681. See Connolly, *Religion, law and power*, pp. 245–8.
23. Owen Callanan, Cork to Dominick Sarsfield, 7 Oct. 1745, N.L.I. MS 2643/9.
24. Richard Purcell, Kanturk to Lord Percival, 7 Jan. 1746, Brit. Lib., Egmont MSS, Add. MS 47002A, f. 4.
25. Earl of Chesterfield to the bishop of Waterford, 23 May 1758, in John Bradshaw, ed., *The letters of Philip Dormer Stanhope, earl of Chesterfield* (London, 1893), iii, 1222–3.
26. Sean Murphy, 'The Lucas affair: a study of municipal and electoral politics in Dublin 1742–9' (M.A. dissertation N.U.I. [U.C.D.], 1981), p. 173.
27. Murphy, 'Lucas affair', pp. 171, 250–52.
28. Ibid., p. 190.
29. There was however only a 2:1 majority against La Touche in the final commons' vote.
30. Archbishop George Stone to Andrew Stone, 24 Dec. 1753, in C. L. Falkiner, ed., 'The correspondence of Archbishop Stone and the duke of Newcastle ...', in *Eng. Hist. Rev*., xx (1905), 538.
31. *Universal Advertiser*, 22 Dec. 1753.
32. Duke of Newcastle to the duke of Dorset, 28 Dec. 1753, Falkiner, 'Stone-Newcastle corr.', p. 540.
33. A. P. W. Malcomson, 'Introduction, iii: Lord Shannon', in Esther Hewitt, ed., *Lord Shannon's letters to his son* (Belfast, 1982), p. xxxi.
34. Archbishop Stone to Newcastle, 14 Jan. 1754, in Falkiner, 'Stone-Newcastle corr.', p. 737.
35. For a general survey of the crisis see Declan O'Donovan, 'The money bill dispute of 1753', in Bartlett and Hayton, *Penal era and golden age*, pp. 55–87.
36. Connolly, *Religion, law and power*, p. 220.
37. Gerard O'Brien, ed., *Catholic Ireland in the eighteenth century: Collected essays of Maureen Wall* (Dublin, 1989), pp. 104–5, 109–10. See also Thomas Bartlett, *The fall and rise of the Irish nation: The catholic question 1690–1830* (Dublin, 1992), pp. 60–64; Fagan, *Divided loyalties*, pp. 87–126.
38. R. E. Ward, J. F. Wrynn and C. C. Ward, eds., *Letters of Charles O'Conor of Belnagare: A Catholic voice in eighteenth-century Ireland* (Washington, 1988), pp. xxi–xxxiv.
39. Eamon O'Flaherty, 'Burke and the catholic question', in *Eighteenth-Century Ireland*, xii (1997), 12–13.

40. A. T. Q. Stewart, *A deeper silence: The hidden origins of the United Irishmen* (London, 1993), p. 99.

CHAPTER 4 (pp. 109–41)

1. This comparison of export volume is calculated using official prices of 1664–65 for both that year and for 1775–76 (or in a few minor commodities the official prices for 1698). This calculation makes no allowance for product improvement e.g. in linen cloth, over the period, and is therefore something of an under-estimate.
2. Compare the map showing principal roads *c.*1692 in J. H. Andrews 'Land and people, *c.*1685', in Moody *et al.* eds, *A new history of Ireland*, iii: p. 470, with that by Taylor and Skinner dated 1778, and reproduced in Constantia Maxwell, *Country and town in Ireland under the Georges*, 2nd edn (Dundalk, 1949), facing p. 368.
3. Patrick O'Flanagan, 'Settlement development and trading in Ireland, 1600–1800 …', in T. M. Devine and David Dickson, eds., *Ireland and Scotland 1600–1850 …* (Edinburgh, 1983), pp. 146–50.
4. The estimate for the 1660s is drawn from Table I of L M Cullen, 'Income, foreign trade and economic development: Ireland as a case study' (unpublished paper, 1975); that for the 1770s is a modification of Prof. Cullen's estimate, but is calculated using his assumptions as to the relationship between the national rental and GNP.
5. Andrews, 'Land and society, *c.*1685', p. 465.
6. Peter Mathias, *The first industrial nation …*, 2nd edn (London, 1984), table ii, p. 26.
7. David Dickson, 'Social stratification in Ireland 1750–1850' (unpublished paper, 1982), pp. 7–8. Following Cullen's procedure used in the paper cited in note 4, gross household income has been assumed (heroically) to have been six times that of the annual rental value of the family property; per capita income has been calculated simply by assuming a mean household size of six persons.
8. Dickson, 'Social stratification', pp. 9–11.
9. W. H. Crawford, 'Landlord-tenant relations in Ulster 1609–1820', in *Ir. Econ. Soc. Hist.*, ii (1975), 13.
10. Arthur Young, *A tour in Ireland … made in the years 1776, 1777, and 1788 …* (Dublin, 1780), ii, append. p. 199.
11. For this process in County Clare, see Ciaran Ó Murchadha, 'Land and society in seventeenth-century Clare' (unpublished Ph.D. dissertation, N.U.I. [U.C.G.], 1982), pp. 123–5.
12. Some of the grants under the Williamite settlement obliged the new proprietors to let to Protestant tenants of British extraction exclusively. There is no evidence that these covenants were extensively enforced.

13. A three-lives lease term was the lifespan of the longest surviving of three persons nominated at the time of the initial agreement; the persons named were at this period chosen by the tenant, and were usually children or young adults, heirs, family members or close kin.
14. Sir Robert Southwell to Sir John Perceval, Sept. 1702, in *Report on Egmont MSS*, ii (HMC, 1909), p. 209.
15. Edward Newenham, Roxborough, Loughrea, County Galway, to Benjamin Franklin, 25 Aug. 1787, Library of the American Philosophical Society, Philadelphia, Franklin Correspondence, MS 35/112.
16. L. M. Cullen, 'Problems in the interpretation and revision of eighteenth-century Irish economic history', in *Trans. Roy. Hist. Soc.*, 5th ser., xvii (1967), 19.
17. Dickson, 'Cork region', pp. 321, 373.
18. Ibid., pp. 378–9; Raymond Crotty, *Irish agricultural production* ... (Cork, 1966), p. 26.
19. Charles Varley, *The unfortunate husbandman* ..., ed. Desmond Clarke (London, 1964), p. 69.
20. At Slane (Meath) and Michelstown (Cork) for instance: Young, *Tour*, ii, append. pp. 38–9.
21. See Dickson, 'Cork region', p. 366.
22. Dean Henry noted of south-west Fermanagh in 1739 that 'the chief profit of this tract comes from black cattle of which there are large herds, mostly of a small kind. Yet there are several herds also of a very large breed which were first imported from the choicest herds in England by the late Sir Ralph Gore and Sir Gustavus Hume, which have now spread over the country' (Armagh Public Library, MS G.1.14, p. 35).
23. William Cooley, Lohort, County Cork to the earl of Egmont, 29 July 1748, N.L.I. Egmont papers, Mic. P. 4679.
24. Dickson, 'Cork region', p. 500.
25. L. M. Cullen, 'The Dublin merchant community in the eighteenth century', in Cullen, ed., *Cities and merchants* ... (Dublin, 1986), pp. 195–210.
26. L. M. Cullen, 'Landlords, bankers and merchants: The early Irish banking world, 1700–1820', in *Hermathena*, cxxxv (1983), 27–9.
27. Varley, *Unfortunate husbandman*, p. 65.
28. John Molyneux, Liverpool, to the lords commissioners of the council of trade, 19 Nov. 1697, P.R.O. (London), CO/389/40, f.86.
29. W. H. Crawford, 'Drapers and bleachers in the early Ulster linen industry', in L. M. Cullen and P. Butel, eds, *Négoce et industrie en France et en Irlande aux XVIIIe et XIXe siècles* (Paris, 1980), pp. 113–20.
30. W. H. Crawford and B. Trainor, eds, *Aspects of Irish social history 1750–1800* (Belfast, 1969), pp. 72–4 and map of linen markets *c*.1782 (pl. vii). This is still a very useful volume of documents, with accompanying commentaries.

CHAPTER 5 (pp. 143–86)

1. Introduction to P.R.O.N.I. calendar of the Wilmot papers, T.3019.
2. See Connolly, *Religion, law and power*, chap. 6.
3. J. S. Donnelly, Jr, 'The Whiteboy movement, 1761–5', in *IHS*, xxi (1978–79), 44–8.
4. Christopher Musgrave, Tourin, County Waterford, to Aland Mason, 6 April 1766, in Villiers Stuart MSS (Ballynaparka, Villierstown, County Waterford).
5. Eoin F. Magennis, 'A "presbyterian insurrection"? Reconsidering the Hearts of Oak disturbances of July 1763', in *IHS*, xxxi (1998–99), 175–8.
6. Thomas Bartlett, 'The Townshend viceroyalty, 1767–72', in Bartlett and Hayton, *Penal era and golden age*, pp. 88–96.
7. Journal of Jabez M. Fisher, 1 May 1776, Friends' Historical Library, Swarthmore, Pennsylvania, RG5 Wharton papers, ser. 1-B, box 9, no. 2.
8. D. N. Doyle, *Ireland, Irishmen and revolutionary America* (Dublin, 1981), p. 170. See also Vincent Morley, '"Tá an cruatan ar Sheoirse" – folklore or politics?', in *Eighteenth-Century Ireland*, xiii (1998), 112–20.
9. *59th report of deputy keeper of the public records of Ireland* (Dublin, 1962), pp. 50–51. See also Eamon O'Flaherty, 'The catholic question in Ireland 1774–93' (unpublished M.A. dissertation, N.U.I. [U.C.D.] 1981), pp. 5–8.
10. R. B. McDowell, 'Ireland in the eighteenth-century British empire', in *Historical Studies*, ix, ed. J. G. Barry (Cork, 1974), p. 61.
11. R. K. Donovan, 'The military origins of the roman catholic relief programme of 1778', *Historical Journal*, xxviii (1985), 79–102; O'Flaherty, 'Burke and the catholic question', 16.
12. See P. D. H. Smith, '"Our cloud-cap't grenadiers": The Volunteers as a military force', in *Irish Sword*, xiii (1977–78), 185–207.
13. John Beresford, Dublin to John Robinson, 2 Aug. 1779, quoted in Maurice R. O'Connell, *Irish politics and social conflict in the age of American revolution* (Philadelphia, 1965), p. 160.
14. Quoted in O'Connell, *Irish politics*, pp. 196–7.
15. Earl of Carlisle, Dublin to Lord Cower, 30 June 1781, quoted in O'Connell, *Irish politics*, p. 295.
16. Quoted in ibid., p. 320.
17. Quoted in Peter Jupp, 'Earl Temple's viceroyalty and the question of renunciation, 1782–3', in *IHS*, xvii (1970–71), 516.
18. A. P. W. Malcomson, *John Foster: the politics of the Anglo-Irish ascendancy* (Oxford, 1978), p. 430. For a key discussion of the political mentalities of the troika and of other leading protagonists in Irish politics during Foster's career, see ibid., chapter 8.
19. Ibid., p. 358.
20. For what was a major reassessment of the parliamentary reform movements of the 1780s, see J. J. Kelly, 'The Irish parliamentary reform movement: the administration and popular politics 1783–5' (unpublished M.A. dissertation,

N.U.I. [U.C.D.], 1981). See also Kelly's more magisterial biography, *Henry Flood: Patriots and politics in eighteenth-century Ireland* (Dublin, 1998).

21. James Kelly, 'William Burton Conyngham and the north-west fishery of the eighteenth century', in *Journal of the Royal Society of Antiquaries of Ireland*, cxv (1985), 64–85.
22. F. G. Hall, *A history of the Bank of Ireland 1783–1946* (Dublin, 1949), pp. 508–10.

CHAPTER 6 (pp. 189–219)

1. Peter Jupp, 'County Down elections 1783–1831', in *IHS*, xviii (1972–73), esp. p. 196.
2. Malcomson, *Foster*, pp. 378–9.
3. Malcomson, 'Lord Shannon', pp. lxxvii–lxxix.
4. David W. Miller, 'The Armagh troubles, 1784–95', in Samuel Clark and James S. Donnelly, Jr, *Irish peasants: violence and political unrest 1780–1914* (Manchester, 1983), pp. 168–9.
5. O'Flaherty, 'Catholic question', pp. 109–10.
6. R. Barry O'Brien, ed., *The autobiography of Theobald Wolfe Tone, 1763–1798* (London, 1893), p. 161.
7. Ibid., p. 166.
8. W. J. McCormack, *Ascendancy and tradition in Anglo-Irish literary history 1789–1939* (Oxford, 1985), pp. 72–5.
9. Earl Camden to the marquis of Downshire, April 1795, quoted in Malcomson, 'The gentle leviathan', in Peter Roebuck, ed., *Plantation to partition ...* (Belfast, 1981), p. 117.
10. *Northern Star*, i, 3.
11. R. B. McDowell, 'The personnel of the Dublin Society of United Irishmen', in *IHS*, ii (1940–41), 12–53; McDowell, 'United Irish plans of parliamentary reform, 1793', in *IHS*, iii (1942–43), 39–59.
12. *Tone autobiography*, pp. 70–71; Nancy J. Curtin, 'The transformation of the Society of United Irishmen into a mass-based revolutionary organization', in *IHS*, xxiv (1984–85), 469–70.
13. Marianne Elliott, 'The origins and transformation of early Irish republicanism', in *International review of social history*, xxiii (1978), 305–28; Elliott, *Partners in revolution: The United Irishmen and France* (New Haven, 1982), chap. 2; Bartlett, 'Defenders and defenderism in 1795', in *IHS*, xxiv (1984–85), 373–94.
14. Elliott, *Partners in revolution*, p. 43; Bartlett, 'The Irish militia disturbances of 1793', *Past & Present*, xcix (May 1983), 43.
15. Bartlett, 'Militia disturbances', 58.
16. Elliott, 'The United Irishman as diplomat', in P. J. Corish, ed., *Radicals, rebels, and establishments* (Belfast, 1985), p. 86n; McDowell, *Ireland in the age of*

imperialism, p. 475.

17. See Jim Smyth, *The men of no property: Irish radicals and popular politics in the late eighteenth century* (London,1992), chap. 6.
18. Bartlett, 'Indiscipline and disaffection in the armed forces in Ireland in the 1790s', in Corish, *Radicals*, pp. 115–34.
19. McDowell, *Ireland in the age of imperialism*, p. 542.
20. Thomas Pelham to General Lake, 3 March 1797, quoted in McDowell, *Ireland in the age of imperialism*, p. 574.
21. J. F. Maurice, ed., *The diary of Sir John Moore* (London, 1904), i, 290.
22. McDowell, *Ireland in the age of imperialism,* pp. 60–65.
23. Whitley Stokes, *Projects for re-establishing the internal peace and tranquillity of Ireland* (Dublin, 1799), pp. 2–4.
24. Thomas Powell, 'An economic factor in the Wexford rebellion of 1798', in *Studia Hibernica,* xvi (1976), 140–57; David Dickson, 'Taxation and disaffection in late eighteenth-century Ireland', in Clark and Donnelly, *Irish peasants*, pp. 37–63. For a development of these arguments, see Dickson, 'The state of Ireland before 1798', in Cathal Póirtéir, ed., *The great Irish rebellion of 1798* (Cork, 1998), pp. 15–25.
25. Nuala Costello, ed., 'Little's diary of the French landing in 1798', in *Analecta Hibernica*, xi (1941), 70.
26. L. M. Cullen, *The emergence of modern Ireland 1600–1900* (London, 1981), pp. 210–33; Cullen, 'The 1798 rebellion in its eighteenth-century context', in Corish, *Radicals*, pp. 91–114.
27. Quoted in J. S. Donnelly, Jr, 'Propagating the cause of the United Irishmen', in *Studies*, lxix (1980), 7. Cf. Cullen, *Emergence*, pp. 235–8.
28. Robert Bell, *Description of the conditions and manners ... of the peasantry of Ireland ...* (London, 1804), pp. 40–41; Stokes, *Projects*, p. 41. See Niall O Ciosáin, *Print and popular culture in Ireland, 1750–1850* (London, 1997), esp. chap. 5.
29. David W. Miller, 'Presbyterianism and "modernization" in Ulster', in *Past & Present*, lxxx (Aug. 1978), 78–9.

Bibliography

The relevant volumes of *A new history of Ireland*, ed. T. W. Moody et al., – iii, *1534–1691* (2nd ed., Oxford, 1991) and iv, *1691–1800* (Oxford, 1986) – remain the best starting points for an exploration both of the sources and the established secondary literature on this period. The first edition of the present work appeared almost concurrently with the latter volume, and in view of the comprehensive bibliography to be found there (by the present author) it seemed appropriate on that occasion to provide only a very spartan bibliographical note. Only half a dozen modern general surveys demanded mention:

P. J. Corish, *The Catholic Community in the Seventeenth and Eighteenth Centuries* (Dublin, 1981)

L. M. Cullen, *An Economic History of Ireland since 1660* (London, 1972)

F. G. James, *Ireland in the Empire, 1688–1770* (Cambridge, Mass., 1973)

E. M. Johnston, *Ireland in the Eighteenth Century* (Dublin, 1974)

R. B. McDowell, *Ireland in the Age of Imperialism and Revolution 1760–1801* (Oxford, 1979)

J. G. Simms, *Jacobite Ireland 1685–91* (London, 1969).

In addition four monographs were selected as intellectual landmarks in the historiography of the previous fifty years:

R. B. McDowell, *Irish Public Opinion 1750–1800* (London, 1944)

Maurice Craig, *Dublin 1660–1860: A Social and Architectural History* (London, 1952)

L. M. Cullen, *Anglo-Irish Trade 1660–1800* (Manchester, 1968)

A. P. W. Malcomson, *John Foster: The Politics of the Anglo-Irish Ascendancy* (Oxford, 1978).

But as noted in the Preface to this edition, a very great deal of new work has appeared since the mid-1980s. What follows is a rather more inclusive bibliography, but one restricted to items published since the first edition was written. No publication is mentioned more than once.

GENERAL SURVEYS AND REVIEW ESSAYS

T. C. Barnard, 'Farewell to Old Ireland', in *Hist. Jnl.*, xxxvi (1993), 909–28

Thomas Bartlett, *The Fall and Rise of the Irish Nation: The Catholic Question 1690–1830* (Dublin, 1992)

——, 'Ireland and the British Empire', in P. J. Marshall (ed.), *The Oxford History of the British Empire*, ii: *The Eighteenth Century* (Oxford, 1998)

Thomas Bartlett and Keith Jeffrey (eds), *A Military History of Ireland* (Cambridge, 1996)

S. J. Connolly, *Religion, Law and Power: The Making of Protestant Ireland 1660–1760* (Oxford, 1992)

——, 'Eighteenth-Century Ireland: Colony or *Ancien Régime*?', in D. G. Boyce and Alan O'Day (eds), *The Making of Modern Irish History* (London, 1997)

Roy Foster, *Modern Ireland 1600–1972* (London, 1988)

Jacqueline Hill, *From Patriots to Unionists: Dublin Civic Politics and Irish Protestant Patriotism 1660–1840* (Oxford, 1997)

F. G. James, *Lords of the Ascendancy: The Irish House of Lords and its Members, 1600–1800* (Dublin, 1995)

P. H. Kelly, 'Ireland and the Glorious Revolution: From Kingdom to Colony', in Robert Beddard (ed.), *The Revolutions of 1688* (Oxford, 1991)

N. L. York, *Neither Kingdom nor Nation: The Irish Quest for Constitutional Rights 1698–1800* (Washington, 1994)

COMPOSITE COLLECTIONS OF ESSAYS ON MAINLY POLITICAL TOPICS

Louis Bergeron and L. M. Cullen (eds), *Culture et pratiques politiques en France et en Irlande XVIe–XVIIIe siècles* (Paris, 1991)

D. G. Boyce, R. Eccleshall and V. Geoghegan (eds), *Political Theory in Ireland since the Seventeenth Century* (London, 1993)

S. J. Connolly (ed.), *Kingdoms United? Great Britain and Ireland since 1500* (Dublin, 1999)

David Dickson, Daire Keogh and Kevin Whelan (eds), *The United Irishmen: Republicanism, Radicalism and Rebellion* (Dublin, 1993)

Hugh Gough and David Dickson (eds), *Ireland and the French Revolution* (Dublin, 1990)

Kevin Herlihy (ed.), *The Politics of Irish Dissent* (Dublin, 1997)

W. A. Maguire (ed.), *Kings in Conflict: The Revolutionary War in Ireland and its Aftermath 1689–1750* (Belfast, 1990)

Gerard O'Brien (ed.), *Politics, Parliament and People: Essays in Eighteenth-Century Irish History* (Dublin, 1989)

POLITICS AND POLITICAL IDEOLOGY, 1660–1714

T. C. Barnard, 'Settling and Unsettling Ireland: The Cromwellian and Williamite Revolutions', in Jane Ohlmeyer (ed.), *Ireland from Independence to Occupation* (Cambridge, 1995)

Aidan Clarke, 'Colonial Constitutional Attitudes in Ireland 1640–60', in *Proc. RIA*, xc, (1990), C, 357–75

Thomas Doyle, 'Jacobitism, Catholicism and the Irish Protestant Elite, 1700–1710', in *ECI*, xii (1997), 28–59

David Hayton, 'The Williamite Revolution in Ireland, 1688–91', in J. I. Israel (ed.), *The Anglo-Dutch Moment: Essays on the Glorious Revolution and its World Impact* (Cambridge, 1991)

J. G. Simms, *War and Politics in Ireland 1649–1730*, eds. D. W. Hayton and Gerard O'Brien (London, 1986)

James Kelly, 'The Origins of the Act of Union: An Examination of Unionist Opinion in Britain and Ireland 1650–1800', in *IHS*, xxv (1984–5), 236–63

Jim Smyth, '"Like Amphibious Animals": Irish Protestants, Ancient Britons 1691–1707', in *Hist. Jnl.*, xxxvi (1993), 785–97

——, 'The Communities of Ireland and the British State, 1660–1707', in Brendan Bradshaw and John Morrill (eds), *The British Problem, c.1534–1707: State Formation in the Atlantic Archipelago* (London, 1996)

POLITICS AND POLITICAL IDEOLOGY AFTER 1714

Robert E. Burns, *Irish Parliamentary Politics in the Eighteenth Century*, 2 vols. (Washington, 1989–90)

P. H. Kelly, 'William Molyneux and the Spirit of Liberty in Eighteenth-Century Ireland', in *ECI*, iii (1988), 133–48

——, 'Perceptions of Locke in Eighteenth-Century Ireland' in *Proc. RIA*, lxxxix (1989), C, 2–35

——, '"Industry and Virtue versus Luxury and Corruption": Berkeley, Walpole, and the South Sea Bubble Crisis', in *ECI*, vii (1992), 57–74

C. D. A. Leighton, *Catholicism in a Protestant Kingdom: A Study of the Irish Ancien Regime* (Dublin, 1994)

Gerard McCoy, '"Patriots, Protestants and Papists": Religion and the Ascendancy, 1714–1760', in *Bullán*, i, 1 (1994), 105–18

Patrick McNally, *Patriots and Undertakers: Parliamentary Politics in Early Hanoverian Ireland* (Dublin, 1997)

Sean Murphy, 'Charles Lucas and the Dublin Election of 1748–49', in *Parliamentary History*, ii (1983), 93–111

M. J. Powell, 'The Reform of the Undertaker System: Anglo-Irish politics 1750–1767', in *IHS*, xxxi (1998–99), 19–36

Maureen Wall, *Catholic Ireland in the Eighteenth Century*, ed. Gerard O'Brien (Dublin, 1989)

POLITICS AND POLITICAL IDEOLOGY IN THE LATE EIGHTEENTH CENTURY

Ronald Asch, 'The Protestant Ascendancy in Ireland from the American Revolution to the Act of Union 1776–1801', in Ronald Asch (ed.), *Three Nations – A Common History? England, Scotland, Ireland and British History c.1600–1920* (Bochum, 1993), pp. 161–90

Nancy Curtin, *The United Irishmen: Popular Politics in Ulster and Dublin 1791–1798* (Oxford, 1994)

James Kelly, 'The Parliamentary Reform Movement of the 1780s and the Catholic Question', in *Archivium Hibernicum*, lxiii (1988), 95–117

——, *Prelude to Union: Anglo-Irish Politics in the 1780s* (Cork, 1992)

Daire Keogh, *'The French Disease': The Catholic Church and Irish Radicalism 1790–1800* (Dublin, 1993)

——, and Nicholas Furlong (eds), *The Mighty Wave: The 1798 Rebellion in Wexford* (Dublin, 1996)

Ian McBride, *Scripture Politics: Ulster Presbyterians and Irish Radicalism in the late Eighteenth Century* (Oxford, 1998)

W. J. McCormack, *The Dublin Paper War of 1786–87* (Dublin, 1993)

Gerard O'Brien, *Anglo-Irish Politics in the Age of Grattan and Pitt* (Blackrock, 1987)

Eamon O'Flaherty, 'Ecclesiastical Politics and the Dismantling of the Penal Laws in Ireland, 1774–82', in *IHS*, xxvi (1988–9), 33–50

——, 'Burke and the Catholic Question', in *ECI*, xii (1997), 7–27

James Quinn, 'The United Irishmen and Social Reform', in *IHS*, xxxi (1998–9), 188–201

Cathal Póirtéir (ed.), *The Great Irish Rebellion of 1798* (Cork, 1998)

Jim Smyth, *The Men of No Property: Irish Radicals and Popular Politics in the late Eighteenth Century* (Dublin, 1992)

A. T. Q. Stewart, *A Deeper Silence: The Hidden Origins of the United Irishmen* (London, 1993)

Kevin Whelan, *The Tree of Liberty: Radicalism, Catholicism and the Construction of Irish Identity* (Cork, 1996)

ADMINISTRATION, LAW AND ORDER

T. C. Barnard, 'Lawyers and the Law in later Seventeenth-Century Ireland', in *IHS*, xxviii (1992–3), 256–82

S. J. Connolly, 'The Houghers: Agrarian Protest in Early Eighteenth-Century Ireland', in C. H. Philpin (ed.), *Nationalism and Popular Protest in Ireland* (Cambridge, 1987)

Neal Garnham, *The Courts, Crime and Criminal Law in Ireland 1692–1760* (Dublin, 1996)

Brian Henry, *Dublin Hanged: Crime, Law Enforcement and Punishment in late*

Eighteenth-Century Dublin (Dublin, 1994)
Colm Kenny, 'The Exclusion of Catholics from the Legal Profession in Ireland, 1537–1828', in *IHS*, xxv (1986–7), 337–57
——, *King's Inns and the Kingdom of Ireland* (Dublin, 1992)
E. F. Magennis, 'A "Presbyterian Insurrection"? Reconsidering the Hearts of Oak Disturbances of July 1763', in *IHS*, xxxi (1998–9), 165–87
Stanley H. Palmer, *Police and Protest in England and Ireland 1780–1850* (Cambridge, 1988)

BIOGRAPHIES AND BIOGRAPHICAL ESSAYS

T. C. Barnard, 'Land and the Limits of Loyalty: The second Earl of Cork and first Earl of Burlington (1612–98)', in T. C. Barnard and J. Clark (eds), *Lord Burlington: Architecture, Art and Life* (London, 1995)
J. C. Beckett, *The Cavalier Duke: A Life of James Butler, first Duke of Ormond 1610–88* (Belfast, 1990)
Joseph Byrne, *War and Peace: The Survival of the Talbots of Malahide 1641–71* (Dublin, 1997)
Denis Carroll, *The Man from God knows where: Thomas Russell 1767–1803* (Dublin, 1995)
L. A. Clarkson and E. M. Crawford, *Ways to Wealth: The Cust Family of Eighteenth-Century Armagh* (Belfast, 1985)
Marianne Elliott, *Wolfe Tone: Prophet of Irish Independence* (New Haven and London, 1989)
Denis Cronin, *A Galway Gentleman in the Age of Improvement: Robert French of Monivea 1716–79* (Dublin, 1995)
Aileen Douglas and P. H. Kelly (eds), *Locating Swift ...* (Dublin, 1998)
Patrick Fagan, *Dublin's Turbulent Priest: Cornelius Nary 1658–1738* (Dublin, 1991)
——, *An Irish Bishop in Penal Times: ... Sylvester Lloyd OFM, 1680–1747* (Dublin, 1993)
Alan Harrison, *The Dean's Friend: Anthony Raymond 1675–1726, Jonathan Swift and the Irish Language* (Blackrock, 1999)
Karen Harvey, *The Bellews of Mount Bellew: A Catholic Gentry Family in Eighteenth-Century Ireland* (Dublin, 1998)
Anne Kavanaugh, *John Fitzgibbon, Earl of Clare* (Dublin, 1997)
James Kelly, *Henry Flood: Parties and Politics in Eighteenth Century Ireland* (Dublin, 1998)
——, *Henry Grattan* (Dundalk, 1993)
F. P. Lock, *Edmund Burke*, i: *1730–84* (Oxford, 1998)
Joseph McMinn, *Jonathan's Travels: Swift and Ireland* (Belfast, 1994)
A. P. W. Malcomson, 'A Lost Natural Leader ... the first Marquis of Abercorn (1756–1818)', in *Proc. RIA*, lxxxviii (1988), C, 64–86
Monica Nevin, 'General Charles Vallancey', in *JRSAI*, cxxiii (1993), 19–58

C. C. O'Brien, *The Great Melody: A Thematic Biography … of Edmund Burke* (London, 1992)
Jane Ohlmeyer, *Civil War and Restoration in the three Stuart Kingdoms: The Career of Randall MacDonnell, Marquis of Antrim 1609–83* (Cambridge, 1992)
Philip O'Regan, *Archbishop William King (1650–1729) and the Constitution in Church and State* (Dublin, 1999)
Patrick Wauchope, *Patrick Sarsfield and the Williamite War* (Dublin, 1992)

ECONOMY, DEMOGRAPHY AND SOCIETY

J. H. Andrews, *Plantation Acres: An Historical Study of the Irish Land Surveyor and his Maps* (Belfast, 1985)
——, *Shapes of Ireland: Maps and their Makers 1564–1839* (Dublin, 1997)
T. C. Barnard, *The Abduction of a Limerick Heiress* (Dublin, 1998)
——, 'Integration or Separation: Hospitality and Display in Protestant Ireland', in W. B. Brockliss and D. Eastwood (eds), *A Union of Multiple Identities: The British Isles, c.1750–1850* (Manchester, 1997)
——, 'Public and Private Uses of Wealth in Ireland, c. 1660–1760', in Jacqueline Hill and Colm Lennon (eds), *Luxury and Austerity* (Dublin, 1999)
C. E. J. Caldicott, Hugh Gough and J-P. Pittion (eds), *The Huguenots and Ireland: Anatomy of an Emigration* (Dun Laoghaire, 1987)
S. J. Connolly, R. A. Houston and R. J. Morris (eds), *Conflict, Identity and Economic Development: Ireland and Scotland 1600–1939* (Preston, 1995)
W. H. Crawford, 'The Evolution of the Linen Trade in Ulster before Industrialization', in *IESH*, xv (1988), 32–53
——, 'The Significance of Landed Estates in Ulster 1600–1820', in *IESH*, xvii (1990), 44–61
L. M. Cullen, 'Catholics under the Penal Laws', in *ECI*, i (1986), 23–36
——, 'The Irish Diaspora of the Seventeenth and Eighteenth Centuries', in Nicholas Canny (ed.), *Europeans on the Move: Studies on European Migration, 1500–1800* (Oxford, 1994)
David Dickson, *Arctic Ireland …* (Belfast, 1997)
J. S. Donnelly, Jr and K. A. Miller (eds), *Irish Popular Culture 1650–1850* (Dublin, 1998)
M. W. Dowling, *Tenant Right and Agrarian Society in Ulster 1600–1850* (Dublin, 1999)
Raymond Gillespie, *The Transformation of the Irish Economy, 1550–1700* (Dublin, 1991)
Brian Graham and L. J. Proudfoot (eds), *An Historical Geography of Ireland* (London, 1993)
——, (eds), *Urban Improvement in Provincial Ireland 1700–1840* (Athlone, 1994)
James Kelly, 'Harvests and Hardship: Famine and Scarcity in the late 1720s', in *Studia Hibernica*, xxvi (1991–2), 65–103

——, 'Infanticide in Eighteenth-Century Ireland', in *IESH*, xix (1992), 5–26
——, 'Scarcity and Poor Relief: The Subsistence Crisis of 1782–84', in *IHS*, xxviii (1992–3), 38–62
——, 'The Abduction of Women of Fortune in Eighteenth-Century Ireland', in *ECI*, ix (1994), 7–43
——, '"A most Inhuman and Barbarous Piece of Villainy": An Exploration of the Crime of Rape in Eighteenth-Century Ireland', in *ECI*, x (1995), 78–107
——, *'That Damn'd Thing called Honour': Duelling in Ireland 1570–1860* (Cork, 1995)
Liam Kennedy and M. W. Dowling, 'Prices and Wages in Ireland 1700–1850', in *IESH*, xxxiv (1997), 62–104
Gerard Long (ed.), *Books beyond the Pale: Aspects of the Provincial Book Trade in Ireland before 1850* (Dublin, 1996)
Margaret MacCurtain and Mary O'Dowd (eds), *Women in Early Modern Ireland* (Edinburgh, 1991)
Rosalind Mitchison and Peter Roebuck (eds), *Economy and Society in Scotland and Ireland 1500–1939* (Edinburgh, 1988)
Joel Mokyr and Cormac O Gráda, 'The Height of Irishmen and Englishmen in the 1770s: Some Evidence from the East India Army Records', in *ECI*, iv (1989), 83–92
M. Pollard, *Dublin's Trade in Books 1550–1880* (Oxford, 1989)
T. P. Power and Kevin Whelan (eds), *Endurance and Emergence: Catholics in Ireland in the Eighteenth Century* (Dublin, 1990)
W. J. Smyth, 'Society and Settlement in Seventeenth-Century Ireland: The Evidence of the "1659 Census"', in W. J. Smyth and Kevin Whelan (eds), *Common Ground: Essays on the Historical Geography of Ireland* (Cork, 1988)
C. C. Trench, *Grace's Card: Irish Catholic Landlords 1690–1800* (Cork, 1997)
Thomas Truxes, *Irish American Trade 1660–1783* (Cambridge, 1988)
M. S. Wokeck, 'Irish Immigration to the Delaware Valley before the American Revolution', in *Proc. RIA*, xcvii (1996), C, 103–35

CULTURE, RELIGION AND EDUCATION

T. C. Barnard, 'Crises of Identity among Irish Protestants 1641–1685', *Past and Present*, cxxvii, (1990), 39–83
——, 'The Uses of 23 October 1641 and Irish Protestant Celebrations', in *EHR*, cvi (1991), 889–920
——, 'Protestants and the Irish Language 1675–1725', in *Journal of Ecclesiastical History*, xliv (1993), 243–72
——, 'Learning, the learned, and literacy in Ireland, c.1660–1760', in T. C. Barnard, Daibhí O Cróinín and Katherine Simms (eds), *'A Miracle of Learning': Studies in Manuscripts and Irish Leaning* (Aldershot, 1998)
——, 'Protestantism, Ethnicity and Irish Identities, 1660–1760', in A. Clayton

and Ian McBride (eds), *Chosen Peoples: Protestantism and National Identity in Britain and Ireland* (Cambridge, 1998)

Brian Boydell, *A Dublin Musical Calendar 1700–60* (Dublin, 1988)

L. W. B. Brockliss and P. Ferté, 'Irish Clerics in France in the Seventeenth and Eighteenth Centuries', in *Proc. RIA*, lxxxvii (1987), C, 527–72

David Dickson and Mary Daly (eds), *The Origins of Popular Literacy in Ireland* (Dublin, 1990)

Patrick Fagan, *Divided Loyalties: The Question of the Oath for Catholics in the Eighteenth Century* (Dublin, 1997)

Hugh Fenning, *The Irish Dominican Province 1698–1797* (Dublin, 1990)

Alan Ford, James McGuire and Kenneth Milne (eds), *The Church of Ireland since the Reformation* (Dublin, 1995)

Graham Gargett and Geraldine Sheridan (eds), *Ireland and the French Enlightenment 1700–1800* (London, 1999)

Raymond Gillespie, *Devoted People: Belief and Religion in Early Modern Ireland* (Manchester, 1997)

R. C. Greaves, *God's Other Children: Protestant Nonconformists and the Emergence of Denominational Churches in Ireland, 1660–1700* (Stanford, 1997)

David Hayton, 'Anglo-Irish Attitudes: Changing Perspectives of National Identity among the Protestant Ascendancy in Ireland, ca.1690–1750', in *Studies in the Eighteenth Century*, xvii (1987), 145–67

David Hempton and Myrtle Hill, *Evangelical Protestantism in Ulster Society 1740–1890* (London, 1992)

Kevin Herlihy (ed.), *The Irish Dissenting Tradition 1650–1750* (Dublin, 1995)

——, (ed.), *The Religion of Irish Dissent 1650–1800* (Dublin, 1996)

——, (ed.), *Propagating the Word of Irish Dissent* (Dublin, 1999)

Jacqueline Hill, 'Popery and Protestantism, Civil and Religious Liberty: The Disputed Lessons of Irish History, 1690–1812', in *Past and Present*, cxviii (1988), 96–129

James Kelly, 'Inter-denominational Relations and Religious Toleration in the late Eighteenth-Century Ireland: The Paper War of 1786–88', in *ECI*, iii (1988), 39–68

——, '"The Glorious and Immortal Memory": Commemoration and Protestant Identity 1660–1800', in *Proc. RIA*, xciv (1994), C, 25–52

Phil Kilroy, *Protestant Dissent and Controversy in Ireland 1660–1714* (Cork, 1994)

J. T. Leerssen, *Mere Irish and Fior-Ghael: Studies in the Idea of Irish Nationality* (Cork, 1996)

M. P. Magray, *The Transforming Power of the Nuns: Women, Religion and Cultural Change in Ireland, 1750–1900* (New York, 1998)

Kenneth Milne, *The Irish Charter Schools 1730–1830* (Dublin, 1997)

Breandan O Buachalla, *Aisling Ghéar: Na Stíobhartaigh agus an t-Aos Léinn, 1603–1788* (Dublin, 1996)

——, 'Irish Jacobism and Irish Nationalism: The Literary Evidence',

in Michael O'Dea and Kevin Whelan (eds), *Nations and Nationalisms: France, Britain and Ireland in the Eighteenth-Century Context* (Oxford, 1995)
Niall O Ciosáin, *Print and Popular Culture in Ireland, 1750–1800* (London, 1997)
Kevin Whelan, 'The Regional Impact of Irish Catholicism 1700–1850', in Smyth and Whelan, *Common Ground*

REGIONAL STUDIES

Geography Publications' series of multi-authored histories of Irish counties (general editor, William Nolan) now covers nearly half the thirty-two counties and includes some of the most important recent writing on the regional history of the period. Apart from this series, there have appeared:

Jean Agnew, *Belfast Merchant Families in the Seventeenth Century* (Dublin, 1996)
Liam Chambers, *Rebellion in Kildare 1790–1803* (Dublin, 1998)
L. A. Clarkson, 'The Demography of Carrick-on-Suir in 1799', in *Proc. RIA*, lxxxvii (1987), C, 2–36
——, 'The Carrick-on-Suir Woollen Industry in the Eighteenth Century', in *IESH*, xvi (1989), 23–41
Marilyn Cohen, *Linen, Family and Community in Tullylish, Co. Down, 1690–1914* (Dublin, 1997)
David Dickson (ed.), *The Gorgeous Mask: Dublin 1700–1850* (Dublin, 1987)
Tom Dunne, '"A Gentleman's Seat should be a Moral School": Edgeworthstown in Fact and Fiction 1760–1840', in Raymond Gillespie and Gerard Moran (eds), *Longford: Essays in County History* (Dublin, 1991)
Patrick Fagan, *Catholics in a Protestant Country: The Papist Constituency in Eighteenth-Century Dublin* (Dublin, 1998)
Daniel Gahan, *The People's Rising: Wexford 1798* (Dublin, 1995)
Raymond Gillespie (ed.), *The Brownlow Leasebook 1667–1711* (Belfast, 1988)
James Kelly, 'The Formation of the Modern Catholic Church in the Diocese of Kilmore, 1580–1880', in Raymond Gillespie (ed.), *Cavan: Essays on the History of an Irish County* (Dublin, 1995)
John Mannion, 'The Maritime Trade of Waterford in the Eighteenth Century', in Smyth and Whelan, *Common Ground*
Ignatius Murphy, *The Diocese of Killaloe in the Eighteenth Century* (Dublin, 1991)
W. J. Neely, *Kilkenny: An Urban History 1391–1843* (Belfast, 1989)
Brian O Dalaigh, *Ennis in the Eighteenth Century: Portrait of an Urban Community* (Dublin, 1995)
Ruan O'Donnell, *The Rebellion in Wicklow 1798* (Dublin, 1998)
Mary O'Dowd, *Power, Politics and Land: Early Modern Sligo 1568–1688* (Belfast, 1991)
Eamon O'Flaherty, 'Urban Politics and Municipal Reform in Limerick, 1723–62', in *ECI*, vi (1991), 105–20

T. P. Power, *Land, Politics and Society in Eighteenth-Century Tipperary* (Oxford, 1993)

L. J. Proudfoot, *Urban Patronage and Social Authority: The Management of the Duke of Devonshire's Towns in Ireland, 1764–1891* (Washington, 1995)

Liam Swords, *A Hidden Church: The Diocese of Achonry 1689–1818* (Dublin, 1997)

NEW EDITIONS OF PRIMARY SOURCES, SOURCE COLLECTIONS AND PUBLISHED CALENDARS

Jean Agnew, *The Drennan-McTier Letters*, 3 vols. (Dublin, 1999)

Andrew Carpenter (ed.), *Verse in English from Eighteenth-Century Ireland* (Cork, 1998)

Angelique Day (ed.), *Letters from Georgian Ireland: The Correspondence of Mary Delaney 1731–68* (Belfast, 1991)

Patrick Fagan, *Ireland in the Stuart Papers 1719–65* (Dublin, 1995)

James Kelly (ed.), *The Letters of Lord Chief Baron Edward Willes to the Earl of Warwick 1757–1762* (Aberystwyth, 1990)

Patrick Kelly, '"A Light to the Blind": The Voice of the Dispossessed Elite in the Generation after the Defeat at Limerick', in *IHS*, xxiv (1984–5), 431–62

Mary-Louise Legg (ed.), *The Synge Letters 1746–52* (Dublin, 1996)

Mary Lyons (ed.), *The Memoirs of Mrs Leeson, Madam, 1727–1797* (Dublin, 1995)

John McVeagh (ed.), *Richard Pococke's Irish Tours* (Dublin, 1995)

W. J. McCormack, *The Pamphlet Debate on the Union … 1797–1800* (Dublin, 1996)

A. P. W. Malcomson (ed.), *Eighteenth Century Irish Official Papers in Great Britain: Private Collections*, 2 vols. (Belfast, 1973–90)

T. W. Moody, R. B. McDowell and C. J. Woods (eds), *The Writings of Theobald Wolfe Tone*, 3 vols. (1999–)

C. J. Woods (ed.), *Journals and Memoirs of Thomas Russell, 1791–95* (Dublin, 1991)

ABBREVIATIONS

ECI = Eighteenth-Century Ireland: Iris an Dá Chultúr; *EHR* = English Historical Review; *IESH* = Irish Economic and Social History; *IHS* = Irish Historical Studies; *Hist. Jnl.* = Historical Journal; *JRSAI* = Journal of the Royal Society of Antiquaries of Ireland; *Proc. RIA* = Proceedings of the Royal Irish Academy

Index